ENDORSEM_...

Magnificent Jesus is a resource combining solid theology, a plethora of quotes and illustrations, and valuable historical facts you are unlikely to find anywhere else. Tony Cooke is a meticulous scholar who has provided a riveting volume on the most important life ever lived—that of Jesus Christ. In my opinion, this is the strongest one-volume "Christology" published in decades. It is with great enthusiasm that I recommend this unique and powerful work, *Magnificent Jesus.*

Alex McFarland, MA

Christian Apologist, Author, Evangelist, and
Broadcaster Greensboro, North Carolina

Amidst a plethora of Christian interests, there are those rare souls whose hearts have been distilled to One thing. Tony Cooke has set our minds upon the excellencies of Christ. Let us grip this work with our hearts and feast our souls upon the unfading beauty of the King of kings.

Eric Gilmour

Sonship International Orlando, Florida

I was deeply moved as I read this new book by church historian and author Tony Cooke. The magnificence of the Son of God, who became the Son of man that he might endure unutterable suffering to redeem us, induces reverential fear leading to joy unspeakable and full of glory. This book is proof that sound theology leads to profound doxology, something of which God's people in the 21st century are in dire need.

I want to encourage you to read this book straight through and then take time to ponder it, page by page. As you absorb it little by little, I believe your faith and love will abound more and more. Preachers and lay people alike may profitably use it as a study guide, as a devotional, and as fuel for your faith.

The truth recorded on these pages will ignite your love for Jesus!

Joseph Purcell, DMin, JD
Missionary to Asia, Church and Bible School Planter
Singapore

As I read Tony Cooke's book *Magnificent Jesus,* I kept thinking, *Every page of this book drips with the anointing.* Indeed, I have found it to be one of the richest books I have ever read on the Person of Jesus Christ. I have read many of Tony's books and count him a dear friend, but as I read this one, I had the profound awareness that I was holding a classic in my hands. I was so impacted that I kept cutting and pasting key phrases to use in my own future teachings. From beginning to end, every word in these pages conveys deep, powerful, and rich insights on the Person of Jesus Christ that will make you feel overwhelmed with a sense of awe about Jesus and all that he has done and has made available to you. I not only recommend this book to you, but I plan to do my part to make this book available to as many people as possible because it so powerfully describes the unmatched, unrivaled, unparalleled magnificence of Jesus Christ.

Rick Renner, PhD
Minister, Author, and Broadcaster
Moscow, Russia

Tony Cooke has written a masterpiece on the Messiah, clearly laying out an accurate and delightful description of Jesus. This book will serve as a reference for me for the facts about Jesus because, as always, Tony's material is accurate and well researched. He gathers in one edition many Scriptures and historical quotes that cause you to think deeply about who Jesus was and what he did. In addition to being true, it is refreshing and encouraging to read because it presents Jesus well.

Terry Roberts, DMin
Pastor, Bible Teacher, Author
Warrenton, Missouri

In the New Testament Book of Matthew chapter 16, Jesus asks his disciples, "Who do men say that I, the Son of man, am?" Verse 14 records their responses, which Jesus follows up with the question of the ages, "But who do *you* say that I am?" How we answer that single question makes a profound difference in our lives in the here and now and actually determines our state for the rest of eternity! Tony Cooke's book *Magnificent Jesus* will help open your eyes, your heart, and your mind to the reality of the awesome majesty of the Lord Jesus Christ and will forever benefit your accepted perception of who, and how *magnificent,* Jesus really is! I highly recommend this book!

Mark D. Clements, BMin
Pastor, Law Enforcement Chaplain, Broadcaster, Author
La Crosse, Wisconsin

Tony Cooke's new book *Magnificent Jesus* is a soaring work that is both a brilliant survey of biblical Christology and a song of worship to the King of kings. This book is a godsend to believers and unbelievers alike—presenting the fullness of Christ at a critical time when false teaching about Jesus abounds. The sheer comprehensiveness of this work makes it an instant Christian classic. It is filled with lists of biblical teachings on the Son of God, including the prophecies of Jesus, the purposes of Jesus, the names of Jesus, the pre-existence of Jesus, the humanity of Jesus, the deity of Jesus, the blood of Jesus, and the present-day ministry of Jesus. I found myself stopping several times as I read to spontaneously worship the Lord. Far more than a scholastic textbook, *Magnificent Jesus* is a living celebration of the second person of the Trinity, inviting the reader to know Him intimately and love Him deeply.

John Carter, MA
Pastor, Author of *The Transformed Life*
Host of *The Shepherd's Network* Podcast
Syracuse, New York

As expected, Tony Cooke has once again produced a work thoroughly rooted in Scripture, seasoned with the Spirit, and immensely practical for new believers, long-time church leaders, and everyone in between. *Magnificent Jesus* proves at once both simply profound in its weight of truth and profoundly simple in its readability. Its content does not stand on the shaky foundations of salacious, self-serving assertions or fallacious, trendy "new revelations." Instead, readers will come to know the heart of the Father as Tony uncovers several key facets reflecting the mediative manifestation of his heart in the person of the Son. Therefore, I express my heartfelt thanks for a book that provides a massive measure of life-giving, "magnificent," brilliant, and transformative light to individual believers, church leaders, and those currently in death-dealing darkness.

Keith Trump, MDiv

Pastor, Biblical Languages Instructor, and Author

Carmel, Indiana

MAGNIFICENT
JESUS

MAGNIFICENT
JESUS

UNMATCHED,

UNRIVALED,

UNPARALLELED

TONY COOKE

Published by Harrison House Publishers
Shippensburg, PA 17257

ISBN 13 TP: 978-1-6675-0465-0
ISBN 13 eBook: 978-1-6675-0466-7

For Worldwide Distribution, Printed in the U.S.A.
1 2 3 4 5 6 7 8 / 28 27 26 25 24

"Make Christ magnificent in the eyes of man."

—Henrietta Mears (1890–1963)

DEDICATION

Before marrying Lisa in 1979, I was profoundly impressed with her love for and devotion toward Jesus. During our engagement period, I purchased a framed picture for her that showed a Raggedy Ann-type of doll sitting on a porch swing in a garden. The caption beneath the picture read, "I would rather be alone with Jesus than in a crowd without him." For four and a half decades, I have seen her adoration of him only increase. It is with loving appreciation that I dedicate this work, Magnificent Jesus, to my wife, Lisa.

CONTENTS

INTRODUCTION

Jesus is absolutely magnificent, and dozens of other superlatives fit him perfectly as well. I couldn't seem to write this introduction until I had finished the rest of the manuscript and now I know why. I began writing as a devoted follower, disciple, lover, and worshiper of Jesus, but throughout the process of researching and putting the chapters together, my sense of awe and amazement toward him progressively grew and substantially multiplied.

Time and again as I meditated on how to best describe Jesus, I found myself saying, "Lord, you are too awesome for words," and "You are far more amazing than what I can convey in writing." I found myself saying, "Lord, no one should be content to have a superficial knowledge of you. People need to know just how awesome and wonderful you really are. People don't need to simply know about you; they need to know you!"

The apostle John made a remarkable comment about Jesus at the conclusion of the fourth Gospel. He wrote that *"Jesus also did many other things. If they were all written down, I suppose the whole world could not contain the books that would be written"* (John 21:25). That is quite a statement, but it is important to remember that the apostle did not just know Jesus in the context of his earthly life, but he had an overall perspective of his eternal existence.

John's remark about "book capacity" stirred my curiosity, so I checked out the website of the United States Library of Congress. A search for "Jesus Christ" yields 79,357 results in their records, and 85 percent of those are in English.[1] It's hard to imagine how many titles have been produced about Jesus over the past two millennia if we could somehow ascertain how many works have been produced in all the other languages of the world. Surely it would be hundreds of thousands, if not a million or more.

In terms of people who identify as Christians, the Global Center for Christianity estimates that there were 2.6 billion adherents in 2023,[2] and this number is expected to reach more than 3.4 billion by 2050.[3] How can one who lived such a simple life continue to have so much influence—that much impact—2,000 years after he walked upon the earth? This is what this book will seek to present. How could someone be so magnificent that his life is literally unmatched, unrivaled, and unparalleled.

I make no apologies for writing this as one who believes that the Bible is true and that it is the inspired word of God. Therefore, I will be writing from a biblical perspective and sharing what Scripture itself teaches about Jesus. I realize that there are countless and divergent opinions about Jesus—that he is merely a great spiritual figure, some type of guru, or some type of glorified life coach. But this book will be presenting Jesus as far more.

If someone critiques this book and states that I basically told people what the Bible says, I will consider that a great honor. In addition, I have included a large number of quotes reflecting the insights of godly men and women throughout many centuries. Their brilliance has impacted me greatly, and I concur with Spurgeon, who wisely said, "He who will not use the thoughts of other men's brains proves that he has no brains of his own."

While I diligently sought to present Jesus in a God-honoring way, I often found myself recognizing the inadequacy of my best efforts. There were so many truths that need to be understood about the Savior, and they are not all covered in this book. I pray this volume can be a helpful supplement in your studies, but no book about Jesus—mine or anyone else's—will ever rival or take the place of reading the accounts of Matthew, Mark, Luke, and John. Scripture itself is the ultimate guide, and if anything I say or imply contradicts or violates the Gospels or any other Scripture (which I trust it doesn't), I pray that you will have the good sense to completely disregard what I have written and stay with the Bible.

So that you know up front, let me share about what this does not cover. This not a "life of Christ" book that traces his earthly life from one location to another, describing comprehensively all the places he went, all the teachings that he gave, and all the healings and miracles he performed. Such books certainly have their place and are important, but that is not what this book is. Instead, this book is focused specifically on the Person of Christ—identifying the magnitude of who he is and painting the big picture of what he accomplished.

I have sought to depict the seamless flow of Jesus moving from one role to another across the ages, revealing himself and carrying out the Father's will—from his eternal existence with the Father, to his incarnation (becoming a man) through the virgin birth, to his sinless life, his miraculous ministry, his sacrificial death, his glorious resurrection, his mighty ascension, his present-day ministry, and his future return, all the way through to the eternal state.

One of the things I have endeavored to convey is the cohesiveness and consistency of Jesus as he strides through the scriptural account, from Genesis to Revelation. His person and his works are woven masterfully and harmoniously throughout the entirety of Scripture and across eternity itself. There is nothing contradictory about the Person of Christ, neither is there anything erratic regarding his activities. *"Jesus Christ is the same yesterday, today, and forever"* (Hebrews 13:8).

After celebrating the Last Supper, Jesus and his disciples *"sang a hymn and went out to the Mount of Olives"* (Matthew 26:30). Traditionally, the Hallel Psalms (Psalm 113–118) were sung at Passover. With that being the case, one of the last phrases Jesus and his disciples would have vocalized before he went to the Garden of Gethsemane would have been:

> *The stone that the builders rejected*
> *has become the cornerstone.*
> *This is the Lord's doing;*
> *it is marvelous in our eyes.*
> *This is the day that the Lord has made;*
> *let us rejoice and be glad in it*

(Psalm 118:22-24 ESV).

From the time the disciples sang that with Jesus for the next 24 hours and more, what happened with Jesus was anything but marvelous in their eyes. He agonized in prayer in the garden, was arrested, unfairly tried, beaten beyond recognition, and savagely crucified. But then Sunday came—the resurrection came—and Jesus, along with all that had happened, became marvelous in all of our eyes. It launched a new era—the day the Lord made—and now believers everywhere can rejoice forever.

In closing, I pray that the contents of this book will result in a significant increase of your adoration and worship of the Father, the Son, and the Holy Spirit. If that is the result of your reading these pages, this book will have accomplished its intended purpose.

Chapter One

LIFE'S MOST IMPORTANT QUESTION: WHY THIS BOOK MATTERS

"Jesus Christ has no peers; there is no one to be compared with Him."
—D.L. Moody (1837–1899)

The most important question anyone will ever answer pertains to the identity and nature of Jesus Christ. Who is he? Jesus asked his disciples about what various people thought about him, and they conveyed some of the diverse opinions people had. Then Jesus made it more personal and pointedly asked, *"But who do you say I am?"* Peter ventured far beyond the guesses and speculations of others and said, *"You are the Messiah, the Son of the living God"* (Matthew 16:15-16).

If Jesus is a mere mortal, then his life and teaching, while they have some historic and moral value, are not of eternal significance. But if he really is the promised Son of the living God, then who he is and what he did matters more than any other issue in life and will absolutely have eternal ramifications for every person on earth.

Billy Graham once referenced Matthew 27:22 (NKJV) where Pontius Pilate asked the question, *"What shall I do, then, with Jesus who is called Christ?"* Graham then said, "This is the most important question that has ever been asked. It is also the question you must ask yourself."[4] When we combine these two issues—"Who is Jesus and what will we do with him?"—we have encountered something of eternal and infinite value. We can't afford to get this wrong.

We will touch on some profound truths in this book, but we must not overlook the simplicity of divine truth. A world-renowned European theologian was visiting the United States many decades ago. As he lectured at an American university, he was asked for a one sentence summation of his acclaimed theological attainments. He responded by referencing "the words of a song I learned at my mother's knee: 'Jesus loves me, this I know, for the Bible tells me so.'"

Maybe you sang that exact song as a child, "Jesus loves me, this I know, for the Bible tells me so. Little ones to him belong; they are weak, but he is strong. Yes, Jesus loves me! Yes, Jesus loves me! Yes, Jesus loves me! The Bible tells me so." I pray that we never stray from the simplicity and beauty of that heartfelt sentiment. If you are facing what seem to be insurmountable challenges and if doubts are assailing you, may you revisit the simplicity and the fundamental truth expressed in that song.

The apostle Paul spoke to believers about *"pure and undivided devotion to Christ"* (2 Corinthians 11:3). All wholesome studies of Christ will lead us in that direction and establish us in childlike faith. Never allow studies *about* Christ to lead you away from *loving* Christ. We should always explore his wondrous Person with a sense of awe and worship. Intellectual pride and haughtiness have no place in learning about the Savior.

Remember what Jesus taught:

I tell you the truth, unless you turn from your sins and become like little children, you will never get into the Kingdom of Heaven. So anyone who becomes as humble as this little child is the greatest in the Kingdom of Heaven

(Matthew 18:3-4).

Pastor and author Alistair Begg shares a delightful and impacting story regarding what it may have been like for the penitent thief on the cross beside Jesus when he showed up at Heaven's gates. In his message "The Power and Message of the Cross," Begg imaginatively suggests an angel may have posed various questions pertaining to what the man had believed about various doctrines, such as justification by faith and the doctrine of Scripture.

The man clearly doesn't understand any of the doctrines he is being asked about, so the angel inquires directly, "On what basis are you here?" The man replies, "The man on the middle cross said I can come." What a beautiful glimpse into the simplicity of childlike faith in Christ. Don't make salvation more complicated than it should be. Christ died for us and extends the free gift of forgiveness to us. We trust him and receive his free gift of eternal life.

MOVING BEYOND SPIRITUAL INFANCY

So, why do we need to deeply study the Person of Christ? We should never move beyond simple, childlike faith, but we must build upon that faith. Growing in faith means, among other things, that we develop a profound appreciation for the person and work of the Lord Jesus Christ. Staying humble and pure in our love for Jesus is different than remaining ignorant and unaware of his greatness.

Peter made it clear that we are not to remain perpetually in a state of spiritual infancy. He admonished believers, *"Like newborn babies, you must crave pure spiritual milk so that you will grow into a full experience of salvation"* (1 Peter 2:2). Paul recognized that believers in one church had remained in a state of spiritual infancy. He writes, *"when I was with you I couldn't talk to you as I would to spiritual people. I had to talk as though you belonged to this world or as though you were infants in Christ"* (1 Corinthians 3:1). The same sentiment is expressed in Hebrews 5:12-13: *"You are like babies who need milk and cannot eat solid food. For someone who lives on milk is still an infant."*

One trait of immaturity is gullibility, or a lack of discernment. Think of a baby who has just begun to crawl or walk. One of the things he might do is to pick up an item—any item—off the floor and immediately put it in his mouth. It may be a part of a cookie, or it might be a dead spider. At that age, a child has little or no discernment.

Similarly, a spiritual baby does not necessarily have a strong sense of discernment and could likely to fall into deceptive traps regarding who Jesus is and what he accomplished. Having an accurate understanding of Jesus (followed by faith and obedience) is the most important aspect of our lives. Therefore, it is no surprise that countless false beliefs are propagated to lead people away from the truth.

Philosophers and proponents of other belief systems all have their views about who Jesus is, but I am interested in who the Bible says he is. Jesus and New Testament writers made it abundantly clear that there would be numerous distortions pertaining to his identity, and such views have abounded over the centuries. Consider the warnings given in Scripture:

JESUS

Then if anyone tells you, "Look, here is the Messiah," or "There he is," don't believe it. For false messiahs and false prophets will rise up and perform great signs and wonders so as to deceive, if possible, even God's chosen ones. See, I have warned you about this ahead of time

(Matthew 24:23-25).

PAUL

You happily put up with whatever anyone tells you, even if they preach a different Jesus than the one we preach, or a different kind of Spirit than the one you received, or a different kind of gospel than the one you believed

(2 Corinthians 11:4).

JOHN

And who is a liar? Anyone who says that Jesus is not the Christ. Anyone who denies the Father and the Son is an antichrist. Anyone who denies the Son doesn't have the Father, either. But anyone who acknowledges the Son has the Father also

(1 John 2:22-23).

A person who loves and reveres the Lord can easily forget how many people disliked and even despised Jesus when he was living and ministering on this earth. The confusion and controversy over Jesus' identity and the derision he experienced were most notable.

• He was accused of blasphemy (Matthew 9:3; 26:65; Mark 2:6-7; 14:63-64; Luke 5:21). Because of these charges his enemies said, *"He deserves to die!"* (Mark 14:64).

- He was laughed at (Matthew 9:24), scoffed at (Matthew 13:55), mocked (Matthew 27:41), and ridiculed (Luke 16:14 NASB).

- He was accused of being demon possessed and getting his power from Satan (Matthew 9:34; 12:24; Mark 3:22; Luke 11:15; John 7:20; 8:48, 52; 10:20).

- He was called *"a glutton and a drunkard, and a friend of tax collectors and other sinners"* (Matthew 11:19). He was accused of eating and drinking with *"scum"* (Luke 5:30) *"and associating with such sinful people—even eating with them!"* (Luke 15:1-2).

- Herod thought Jesus was John the Baptist raised from the dead (Matthew 14:1-2).

- Early in his ministry, Jesus' own family thought he was out of his mind (Mark 3:21), and his brothers did not believe in him (John 7:5).

- His authority was called into question (Mark 11:27-28; Luke 20:2).

- In his hometown, people *"were deeply offended and refused to believe in him."* They said *"He's just the carpenter's son, and we know Mary, his mother, and his brothers—James, Joseph, Simon, and Judas. All his sisters live right here among us"* (Matthew 13:55-57).

- He was called a lawbreaker (Luke 6:2; John 5:16).

- He was accused of leading people astray by telling them not to pay taxes and of causing riots wherever he went (Luke 23:2,5).

- Regarding the Roman government, he was accused of *"inciting the people to rebellion"* (Luke 23:14 NIV).

- Some said of Jesus, *"He's nothing but a fraud who deceives the people"* (John 7:12).

- He was called a criminal (John 18:30) and a *"rebel against Caesar"* (John 19:12).

Yet others, with adoring hearts and childlike faith said things like:

What kind of a man is this, that even the winds and the sea obey Him?
(Matthew 8:27 NASB)

You are the Messiah, the Son of the living God
(Matthew 16:16).

Come and see a man who told me everything I ever did! Could he possibly be the Messiah?
(John 4:29)

We have never heard anyone speak like this!
(John 7:46)

Even upon his death, the Roman centurion and the others who crucified Jesus exclaimed, *"This man truly was the Son of God!"* (Matthew 27:54).

During his lifetime on earth, some cursed Jesus and others worshiped him. There has never been an individual in human history who has sparked so many different views, opinions, and perspectives. To all who receive him, Jesus not only brings peace, but he is *"the Prince of Peace"* (Isaiah 9:6). Yet in another sense, Jesus is a highly divisive figure. *"Don't imagine that I came to bring peace to the earth! I came not to bring peace, but a sword"* (Matthew 10:34).

Worshiped, adored, and followed by billions. Cursed and reviled by some. Dismissively ignored by others. He is arguably the most controversial figure in history. The divisiveness that resulted from his words and actions was no surprise; actually, it was prophesied. When

Joseph and Mary brought the infant Jesus to the Temple for dedication, a godly man named Simeon met them and said, *"This child is destined to cause many in Israel to fall, and many others to rise. He has been sent as a sign from God, but many will oppose him"* (Luke 2:34).

Still today, Jesus is Savior to some and stumbling block to others. Who is he to you, and what will you do with him? Perhaps you are reading this book as one who is already fully persuaded that Jesus is exactly who he claimed to be. If so, this book will reinforce your faith in the Son of God who came from the Father as the Redeemer of mankind. Perhaps you are uncertain and are seeking for truth. Either way, continue reading and ask God to show you the truth. I know he will.

QUOTES

"I have read in Plato and Cicero sayings that are very wise and very beautiful; but I never read in either of them: 'Come unto me all ye that labor and are heavy laden.'"

—Augustine (353–430)

"I must know Jesus, not as the visionary dreams of him, but as the Word reveals him."

—Charles H. Spurgeon (1834–1892)

"Grieve not the Christ of God, who redeems us; and remember that we grieve Him most when we will not let Him pour His love upon us."

—Alexander MacLaren (1826–1910)

"A man who was merely a man and said the sort of things Jesus said wouldn't be a great moral teacher. He would either be a lunatic—on a level with a man who says he is a poached egg—or else he'd be the Devil of Hell. You must make your choice. Either this man was and is the son of God, or else a madman or something worse."[5]

—C.S. Lewis (1898–1963)

QUESTIONS FOR REFLECTION AND DISCUSSION

1. Did you learn something new about Jesus in this chapter? Describe what you learned.

2. Did something you already knew about Jesus become strengthened or reinforced? Describe it.

3. If Jesus asked you who he is, how would you respond?

4. Have you ever lost simple, childlike faith in Jesus? If so, what did you do to regain it?

5. Have you ever believed something about Jesus that you later discovered was not true? How did that discovery come about, and what did you to do align your faith with the truth?

6. How do you deal with the idea of Jesus being "worshiped, adored, and followed by billions" and yet he is "cursed and reviled by some"? Do the negative opinions of some shake or undermine your faith in Jesus?

7. Did anything you read in this chapter change the way you will relate to Jesus? If so, how?

Chapter Two

WHY JESUS CAME: THE MISSION DEFINES THE MAN

"Jesus did not come merely to disclose God's character. He came to make it possible to be remade in the likeness of that character. He came to redeem us from what we are and to remake us in the likeness of what he is. He is not merely a teacher, a doer—he is a redeemer."

—E. Stanley Jones (1884–1972)

Before we begin addressing the identity and character of Jesus Christ, let's look at a vital question: "Why did he come to begin with? What were his goals, and what did he seek to accomplish?" In the case of Jesus, "the mission defines the man." We will look later at specific statements about Jesus' identity, but here we will examine his purpose, and as we do, ask yourself if any ordinary person, like you or I, could do what is stated of Christ's clearly defined and articulated purpose.

Many people want to make a positive difference with their lives, make the world a better place, and leave the world better off than how they found it. These are all noble goals, and many people throughout history have made great contributions. But the purpose Jesus came to fulfill is light years beyond ordinary, positive achievements. For someone to accomplish his articulated goals, that person would have to be extraordinary beyond comprehension, a person like no other who has walked the face of the planet.

No ordinary person would state the things Jesus did about their reason for being on earth. Either the person would have to be truly unique, like no one else who had ever lived, or people would rightly accuse them of being grandiose beyond imagination. Many Bible characters had a divine calling, but no one came remotely close to making the kinds of extravagant claims that Jesus made about his assignment and mission.

PURPOSE 1: JESUS CAME TO REVEAL THE FATHER

Anyone who has seen me has seen the Father!

(John 14:9)

More than four decades ago, I heard someone say, "If you want to know what God is like—if you want to know what the Father is like—look at Jesus." Similarly, a statement made in Hebrews 1:3 in various translations is most revealing:

The Son radiates God's own glory and expresses the very character of God (NLT).
He is the radiance of His glory and the exact representation of His nature (NASB).

Who, being the outshining of his glory, the true image of his substance
(BBE).
This Son perfectly mirrors God, and is stamped with God's nature
(MSG).

Paul writes that *"Christ is the visible image of the invisible God"* (Colossians 1:15). This is not simply a matter of Jesus trying to act like the Father. Because they are of the same substance and nature, when Jesus speaks or acts, he speaks the word of God and acts from the very nature of God.

PURPOSE 2: JESUS CAME TO CARRY OUT THE WILL OF THE FATHER

For I have come down from heaven to do the will of God who sent me,
not to do my own will

(John 6:38).

Then I said, "Look, I have come to do your will, O God—as is written
about me in the Scriptures"

(Hebrews 10:7).

It is human nature to be self-focused and self-seeking (see Philippians 1:21), but Jesus was 100 percent submitted to doing and carrying out the will of God. He frequently referred to his commitment to pleasing the Heavenly Father, and even as he was facing death by crucifixion, he prayed *"not my will, but yours be done"* (Luke 22:42 NIV).

Jesus was so submitted to the will of God that he said, *"The words I speak are not my own, but my Father who lives in me does his work through me"* (John 14:10). All of Jesus' actions reflected the Father's will. He stated, *"My nourishment comes from doing the will of God, who sent me, and from finishing his work"* (John 4:34). There was nothing self-willed or rebellious about Jesus; he was completely in sync with the will of his Father in attitudes, words, and actions.

PURPOSE 3: JESUS CAME TO TESTIFY TO THE TRUTH

I was born and came into the world to testify to the truth

(John 18:37).

Even in Jesus' day there was skepticism and cynicism about the meaning of truth. When Jesus made the above statement, Pilate dismissively asked, *"What is truth?"* (John 18:38). For a person without biblical grounding, there can be a thick "fog" about what truth even is. For many, truth is no longer objectively related to reality. Rather, it is a floating individualistic concept based on personal preferences and perspectives. It is common for people to refer to *my* truth and *your* truth.

When Jesus came into the earth, he boldly declared, *"I am the way, the truth, and the life. No one can come to the Father except through me"* (John 14:6). Unlike human theories, philosophies, and speculations that are always changing, actual truth does not change. The psalmist wrote, *"All your words are true; all your righteous laws are eternal"* (Psalm 119:160 NIV). Shortly after this, we read, *"Your eternal word, O Lord, stands firm in heaven."* (Psalm 119:89).

PURPOSE 4: JESUS CAME TO SHINE AS A LIGHT

I am the light of the world. If you follow me, you won't have to walk in darkness, because you will have the light that leads to life

(John 8:12).

The themes of light and darkness were among the first introduced in Scripture. God's first recorded utterance was *"Let there be light"* and then he *"separated the light from the darkness"* (Genesis 1:3-4). After this, light and darkness are contrasted frequently throughout all of Scripture.

In our modern world, it seems like light is always available to us, so we may fail to appreciate it as we should. But imagine how meaningful and valued light would be to you if you had been lost deep within a cave for days, and had felt the hopelessness of complete, overwhelming darkness. At the very onset of Jesus' ministry, he cited the prophecy of Isaiah 9:2 and personalized it to the work that he was beginning:

The people who sat in darkness have seen a great light. And for those who lived in the land where death casts its shadow, a light has shined

(Matthew 4:16).

Writing from a transcendent perspective of Jesus and his ministry, John wrote, *"his life brought light to everyone. The light shines in the darkness, and the darkness can never extinguish it"* (John 1:4-5). Then, in the Revelation, we learn that Jesus will be that light throughout eternity. Speaking of the heavenly Jerusalem, John writes, *"The city had no need of the sun or of the moon to shine in it, for the glory of God illuminated it. The Lamb is its light"* (Revelation 21:23).

PURPOSE 5: JESUS CAME TO FULFILL THE LAW AND THE PROPHETS

Don't misunderstand why I have come. I did not come to abolish the law of Moses or the writings of the prophets. No, I came to accomplish their purpose

(Matthew 5:17).

I enjoy the way *The Message* renders Matthew 5:17–18:

Don't suppose for a minute that I have come to demolish the Scrip-tures—either God's Law or the Prophets. I'm not here to demolish but to complete. I am going to put it all together, pull it all together in a vast panorama. God's Law is more real and lasting than the stars in the sky and the ground at your feet. Long after stars burn out and earth wears out, God's Law will be alive and working.

Jesus came to fulfill, accomplish, and complete all that was ini-tiated and proclaimed under the Old Testament. What does it mean when something is fulfilled? A dream can be fulfilled, a mission can be fulfilled, or requirements can be fulfilled. Jesus did this relative to the entirety of the redemptive history that preceded him.

The assertion that Jesus fulfilled the writings of the prophets is straightforward and easily understood. The prophets spoke exten-sively about the coming Messiah and what he would accomplish. Jesus fulfilled what the prophets said he would do. His conception by a virgin (see Isaiah 7:14), his humble birth in Bethlehem (see Micah

5:2), his miracles and his message (see Isaiah 61:1) were all foretold by the Old Testament prophets.

But what about Jesus fulfilling the law of Moses? First, Jesus fulfilled the law through his sinless life; the law always required a spotless sacrifice. Second, Jesus fulfilled the law by then offering himself as the final sacrifice for human sin. He fulfilled the promises made in the Old Testament that God would someday send a redeemer (see Genesis 3:15) who would bear the iniquities of the people as a substitute (see Isaiah 53:4-6).

The law of Moses was unable to save us because of the weakness of our sinful nature. So God did what the law could not do. He sent his own Son in a body like the bodies we sinners have. And in that body God declared an end to sin's control over us by giving his Son as a sacrifice for our sins

(Romans 8:3).

There was nothing wrong with the Law, but there was something wrong with us. The Law of Moses revealed our sinfulness, but Jesus fulfilled the Law perfectly and offered a solution for our sinfulness. Paul was correct when he said that *"the law itself is holy, and its commands are holy and right and good"* (Romans 7:12). However, we couldn't measure up to the requirements of the Law (even though Jesus did), and therefore, it became an unbearable burden for us relative to acquiring salvation—no one was going to be saved by perfectly keeping the Law.

The Law was not given to make us holy, but to reveal how utterly incapable we are to become holy on our own. Paul teaches this in his letter to the Galatians.

Why, then, was the law given? It was given alongside the promise to show people their sins. But the law was designed to last only until the coming of the child who was promised. ...Is there a conflict, then, between God's law and God's promises? Absolutely not! If the law could give us new life, we could be made right with God by obeying it. But the Scriptures declare that we are all prisoners of sin, so we receive God's promise of freedom only by believing in Jesus Christ

(Galatians 3:19, 21-22).

Jesus kept the Law perfectly and offered a solution for our sinfulness. He lived the life we could not live and then went to the cross to pay the price we could not pay on our own. Paul said, *"He did this so that the just requirement of the law would be fully satisfied for us"* (Romans 8:4).

At the first great church council in Jerusalem, the issue of Gentiles and the Law was addressed. Some legalists were saying that non-Jews needed to be circumcised and keep the Law to become a true follower of Jesus, but the apostolic leaders resoundingly rejected this notion. Peter declared, *"Why are you now challenging God by burdening the Gentile believers with a yoke that neither we nor our ancestors were able to bear? We believe that we are all saved the same way, by the undeserved grace of the Lord Jesus"* (Acts 15:10-11).

Jesus fulfilled and completed the Law by living a life of perfect obedience and becoming its ultimate sacrifice. He was the crescendo, the apex, and the culmination of the Old Testament; he was its ultimate sacrificial offering. He was the champion who fulfilled all that the Old Testament predicted, promised, and required. Having accomplished all of this, he then became the pioneer and the very foundation of the New Covenant.

PURPOSE 6: JESUS CAME TO BRING LIBERTY AND FREEDOM

The Spirit of the Lord is upon me, for he has anointed me to bring Good News to the poor. He has sent me to proclaim that captives will be released, that the blind will see, that the oppressed will be set free, and that the time of the Lord's favor has come

(Luke 4:18-19).

When Jesus preached that in the synagogue in his hometown of Nazareth, he was quoting from Isaiah 61, just one of many prophetic declarations about what Jesus would accomplish during his life on earth. As you study Jesus' earthly life in the gospels, his compassion for the hurting and suffering is demonstrated over and over. Peter declared that *"you know that God anointed Jesus of Nazareth with the Holy Spirit and with power. Then Jesus went around doing good and healing all who were oppressed by the devil, for God was with him"* (Acts 10:38).

PURPOSE 7: JESUS CAME TO SEEK AND TO SAVE THE LOST—TO SAVE THE WORLD

For the Son of Man came to seek and save those who are lost

(Luke 19:10).

For God so loved the world that He gave His only begotten Son, that whoever believes in Him should not perish but have everlasting life. For God did not send His Son into the world to condemn the world, but that the world through Him might be saved

(John 3:16-17 NKJV).

I have come to save the world and not to judge it

(John 12:47).

Christ Jesus came into the world to save sinners

(1 Timothy 1:15).

When Jesus came, he was truly on a rescue mission. He did not wait for us to seek for him; he came seeking us. Before we were even born or had ever sinned, Jesus had already worked powerfully and effectively on our behalf. Paul writes that *"God showed his great love for us by sending Christ to die for us while we were still sinners"* (Romans 5:8).

When it comes to our salvation, we should acknowledge that God is the Initiator. We did not seek him, but he sought us. We did not love him, but he loved us. Before we had ever committed a sin, Jesus had already come and died for our forgiveness, acceptance, and salvation. He illustrated his saving mission by talking about a lost sheep that was found (see Luke 15:4-7), a lost coin that was recovered (see Luke 15:8-10), and a wayward son who was restored to his father's love (see Luke 15:11-32).

PURPOSE 8: JESUS CAME TO CALL SINNERS TO REPENTANCE

Healthy people don't need a doctor—sick people do. I have come to call not those who think they are righteous, but those who know they are sinners

(Mark 2:17).

In Luke 18:9, Jesus began telling a parable, referring to *"some who had great confidence in their own righteousness and scorned everyone else."*

The Bible makes it clear that none of us are righteous in ourselves. Isaiah said, *"all our righteous acts are like filthy rags"* (Isaiah 64:6 NIV), and Paul, quoting from the Psalms, asserts that *"No one is righteous— not even one"* (Romans 3:10). Those who falsely believe that they are righteous—in right standing with God—based on their own performance in life will see no need to submit themselves to the righteousness that God offers us freely.

However, when we acknowledge that we have all sinned and that we all need God's mercy and forgiveness, we are in position to humbly receive the gift of God. This is why Paul, who had worked incessantly to be righteous (before he met Christ), said, *"I no longer count on my own righteousness through obeying the law; rather, I become righteous through faith in Christ. For God's way of making us right with himself depends on faith"* (Philippians 3:9).

Simply put, until you acknowledge that you have a problem, you aren't even aware that you need a solution. If you think you are right with God because you've been a pretty good person, you don't think you need a Savior. It's only when you recognize your lost condition—that you are separated from God—that you will open your heart to Jesus to receive him and all that he has done for you.

PURPOSE 9: JESUS CAME TO SERVE AND TO GIVE HIS LIFE AS A RANSOM FOR MANY

For even the Son of Man came not to be served but to serve others and to give his life as a ransom for many

(Mark 10:45).

Jesus did not come to subjugate others, but to serve others sacrificially, even to the point of surrendering his own life for the welfare of others. He could have used his power to dominate us, but he didn't. Instead, he gave his life to deliver us. In short, Jesus didn't come to earth to see how much he could get, but to see how much he could give. When Jesus washed the feet of the disciples (see John 13:6-15), he was demonstrating the servant's heart that was at the core of his being.

The word *ransom* (*lutron* in the Greek) refers to the price that was paid to purchase total freedom for prisoners of war or slaves, or the payment to bail someone out of jail. Ransom speaks of Jesus becoming our substitute on the cross and giving his very life as a payment to deliver us from the guilt and penalty of sin.

Peter powerfully describes the means by which Jesus redeemed us back to God.

> *For you know that God paid a ransom to save you from the empty life you inherited from your ancestors. And it was not paid with mere gold or silver, which lose their value. It was the precious blood of Christ, the sinless, spotless Lamb of God. God chose him as your ransom long before the world began, but now in these last days he has been revealed for your sake*
>
> (1 Peter 1:18-20).

What motivated Jesus to become our ransom? Love. He said, *"There is no greater love than to lay down one's life for one's friends"* (John 15:13).

PURPOSE 10: JESUS CAME TO TAKE AWAY OUR SINS

And you know that Jesus came to take away our sins, and there is no sin
in him. ... This is real love—not that we loved God, but that he loved
us and sent his Son as a sacrifice to take away our sins

(1 John 3:5; 4:10).

He has once for all at the consummation and close of the ages appeared
to put away and abolish sin by His sacrifice [of Himself]

(Hebrews 9:26 AMPC).

When John the Baptist saw Jesus approaching, he declared, *"Look! The Lamb of God who takes away the sin of the world!"* (John 1:29). Both the apostles Peter and Paul describe how Jesus did this, and we should never take his marvelous work of removing our sins for granted.

Peter explained that Jesus *"bore our sins in His own body on the tree, that we, having died to sins, might live for righteousness"* and then proceeded to say that it was the stripes of Jesus that brought healing to us (1 Peter 2:24 NKJV). Paul powerfully states that *"God made him who had no sin to be sin for us, so that in him we might become the righteousness of God"* (2 Corinthians 5:21 NIV).

Jesus carried and bore away our sins on the cross so we would never have to bear them. By taking our sins away, he destroyed both the power and penalty of sin over our lives. None of this was accidental or an afterthought; it was pre-planned and foreordained. Hundreds

of years before Jesus came, the prophet Isaiah wrote about a Suffering
Servant and described what he would accomplish:

The Lord laid on him the sins of us all

(Isaiah 53:6).

His life is made an offering for sin

(Isaiah 53:10).

*He will bear all their sins…. He bore the sins of many and interceded
for rebels*

(Isaiah 53:11-12).

Why did Jesus do this? It is one of the simplest and yet most profound truths of the universe. Jesus bore our sins so we would not have
to. He took the punishment and the penalty that our sins deserved so
we could be forever free from the dominion of sin.

PURPOSE II: JESUS CAME TO BREAK THE POWER OF THE DEVIL AND DESTROY HIS WORKS

*Because God's children are human beings—made of flesh and blood—
the Son also became flesh and blood. For only as a human being could
he die, and only by dying could he break the power of the devil, who had
the power of death*

(Hebrews 2:14).

The Son of God came to destroy the works of the devil

(1 John 3:8).

In Hebrews 2:14 above, the word *destroy* means "to render powerless or ineffective, to make of no effect, to nullify, or to take away the power of a thing." The statement does not mean that Jesus annihilated the devil or that he no longer exists. Rather, he rendered Satan's power inoperative toward us. In 1 John 3:8, when John writes that Jesus was manifested to *destroy* the works of the devil, a different Greek word is used. John's word means to "loosen, break up, do away with, to undo, release, or melt."

The triumph of Jesus over the devil and his works was promised immediately after sin came into the world. God wasted no time and spoke directly to the serpent about the Seed of woman: *"He shall bruise your head, and you shall bruise His heel"* (Genesis 3:15 NKJV). This vanquishing of darkness and its works was later articulated by Paul when he wrote that Jesus *"disarmed the spiritual rulers and authorities. He shamed them publicly by his victory over them on the cross"* (Colossians 2:15).

PURPOSE 12: JESUS CAME TO LIBERATE THOSE WHO WERE SLAVES TO FEAR

And free those who through fear of death were subject to slavery all their lives

(Hebrews 2:15 NASB).

The above verse is a continuation from what is stated in Purpose 11. In addition to Jesus destroying him who had the power of death, he also came to free people from the fear of death and its bondage. In that great chapter on the resurrection, the apostle Paul is exulting in Christ's resurrection and the eventual resurrection of all believers. After declaring that "*Death is swallowed up in victory,*" he asks, "*O death, where is your victory? O death, where is your sting?*" (1 Corinthians 15:54-55).

Jesus has indeed taken the sting out of death—a truth the following story so beautifully illustrates:

> A boy and his father were driving down a country road on a beautiful spring afternoon, when a bumblebee flew in the car window. The little boy, who was allergic to bee stings, was petrified. The father quickly reached out, grabbed the bee, squeezed it in his hand, and then released it. The boy grew frantic as it buzzed by him. Once again the father reached out his hand, but this time he pointed to his palm. There stuck in his skin was the stinger of the bee. "Do you see this?" he asked. "You don't need to be afraid anymore. I've taken the sting for you." We do not need to fear death anymore. Christ has died and risen again. He has taken the sting from death.[6]

PURPOSE 13: JESUS CAME TO DIE

As he faced imminent death by crucifixion, Jesus said,

> *Now my soul is deeply troubled. Should I pray, "Father, save me from this hour"? But this is the very reason I came!*

(John 12:27)

Jesus' death was neither accidental nor an afterthought. Rather, it was part of a master plan that existed before time began. Revelation 13:8 describes Jesus as "*the Lamb who was slaughtered before the world was made.*" Preaching on the Day of Pentecost, Peter referred to the role that men played in the death of the Savior, but then revealed that

"God knew what would happen, and his prearranged plan was carried out when Jesus was betrayed" (Acts 2:23).

Not only was Jesus' death prefigured and predicted throughout the Old Testament (see Chapter Five in this book), but he was acutely aware that his ultimate purpose would be fulfilled through his death and resurrection. Matthew describes how Jesus acknowledged and affirmed this.

> *From then on Jesus began to tell his disciples plainly that it was necessary for him to go to Jerusalem, and that he would suffer many terrible things at the hands of the elders, the leading priests, and the teachers of religious law. He would be killed, but on the third day he would be raised from the dead*
>
> (Matthew 16:21).

Though he knew that suffering and death awaited him, Jesus did not try to run away or hide. Luke stated that as the time approached, *"Jesus resolutely set out for Jerusalem"* (Luke 9:51). He knew exactly what he would face and demonstrated his mastery when he said:

> *The Father loves me because I sacrifice my life so I may take it back again. No one can take my life from me. I sacrifice it voluntarily. For I have the authority to lay it down when I want to and also to take it up again. For this is what my Father has commanded*
>
> (John 10:17-18).

We should never look at Jesus as a helpless victim who was carried away by the violence of a hostile mob. Though human elements were involved, Jesus deliberately surrendered his life and intentionally sacrificed himself for our benefit and for our salvation. Jesus did not come just to die in general, but he came to die for us. For us! Paul writes that *"Christ died for the ungodly"* and that *"while we were still sinners, Christ died for us"* (Romans 5:6,8 NKJV). Jesus was born so that he could die and rise again, and that's exactly what he did.

PURPOSE 14: JESUS CAME TO GIVE ABUNDANT LIFE

I have come that they may have life, and that they may have it more abundantly

(John 10:10 NKJV).

Jesus here is not referring to biological life—to mere earthly existence. People with or without Christ have that. Even animals have biological life. Rather, he is referring to something far more significant. To appreciate the life that Jesus brings, we need to understand that before he entered our lives, we were spiritually dead—disconnected and separated from God.

Perissos, translated "more abundantly" in John 10:10, carries various shades of meaning that communicate just how wonderful the life that Jesus gives us really is. *Perissos* implies having a surplus, having more than enough or necessary, or going beyond the expected limit. It carries ideas of superabundant, excessive, superior, extraordinary, surpassing, and beyond measure.

What the Lord brings has sometimes been called "the God-kind of life." Referring to their lives before Christ, Paul told believers, *"Once you were dead because of your disobedience and your many sins"* (Ephesians 2:1). John told believers, *"Whoever has the Son has life; whoever does not have God's Son does not have life"* (1 John 5:12).

We gain more insight into this overall theme by looking at John 10:10 in various translations.

My purpose is to give them a rich and satisfying life (NLT).

I have come that they may have life, and have it to the full (NIV).

I came so that they could have life—indeed, so that they could live life to the fullest (CEB).

I have come so that they may have life and have it in greater measure (BBE).

I came so they can have real and eternal life, more and better life than they ever dreamed of (MSG).

I came that they may have and enjoy life, and have it in abundance (to the full, till it overflows) (AMPC).

We first understand that Jesus giving us life means that he gives us the gift of eternal life. That is not merely a state of eternal existence, although we will live eternally with him. Eternal life is not merely quantitative, but it is qualitative. Eternal life is the very life of God living inside of us, making us new creatures, and enabling us to live in eternal union with him. Second, it is life more abundant, a rich and satisfying life, a full life, a better life, an overflowing life, and life in greater measure.

Countless believers can testify to the profound difference that Jesus has made in the quality of their lives, the enormous enrichment he has brought to them. Jesus is the *"friend who sticks closer than a brother"* (Proverbs 18:24 NKJV). He promised that he would always be with us (see Matthew 28:20). Jesus also enriches our lives with peace. He said, *"I am leaving you with a gift—peace of mind and heart. And the peace I give is a gift the world cannot give. So don't be troubled or afraid"* (John 14:27). In addition to all of this, he also gives joy to his followers (see John 15:11).

GREAT QUOTES

"He won me over entirely by giving himself entirely to me."
—Bernard of Clairvaux (1090–1153)

"Cling, therefore, to Jesus in life and death; trust yourself to the glory of Him who alone can help you when all others fail."
—Thomas à Kempis (1380–1471)

"Learn to know Christ and him crucified. Learn to sing to him, and say, 'Lord Jesus, you are my righteousness, I am your sin. You have taken upon yourself what is mine and given me what is yours. You have become what you were not so that I might become what I was not.'"
—Martin Luther (1483–1546)

"Without Christ, God will not be found, known, or comprehended."
—Martin Luther (1483–1546)

"We could never recognize the Father's grace and mercy except for our Lord Jesus Christ, who is a mirror of his Father's heart."
—Martin Luther (1483–1546)

"I want to know one thing—the way to Heaven. God himself has shown the way. For this purpose Jesus came from Heaven."
—John Wesley (1703–1791)

"The end for which Christ lives, and for which he has left his church in the world, is the salvation of sinners."

—Charles Finney (1792–1875)

"I have a great need for Christ; I have a great Christ for my need."

—Charles H. Spurgeon (1834–1892)

"You have trusted Christ as your dying savior; now trust Him as your living savior. Just as much as he came to deliver you from future punishment, did he also come to deliver you from present bondage."

—Hannah Whitall Smith (1832–1911)

"God Himself became a Man to give us a concrete, definite, tangible idea of what to think of when we think of God."

—Henry H. Halley (1874–1965)

"The Son of God became the Son of Man so that sons of men may become sons of God."

—C.S. Lewis (1898–1963)

"One of Jesus' specialties is to make somebodies out of nobodies."

—Henrietta Mears (1890–1963)

"Christ came to earth for one reason: to give his life as a ransom for you, for me, for all of us. He sacrificed himself to give us a second chance. He would have gone to any lengths to do so. And he did. He went to the cross, where man's utter despair collided with God's unbending grace."[7]

—Max Lucado (1955–)

QUESTIONS FOR REFLECTION AND DISCUSSION

1. Did you learn something new about Jesus in this chapter? Describe what you learned.

2. Did something you already knew about Jesus become strengthened or reinforced? Describe it.

3. Of the fourteen different purposes stated for Jesus' coming, which ones spoke most strongly to you? Why?

4. What do you think is the least understood reason why Jesus came? Why do you think people misunderstand that particular aspect regarding Jesus' purpose in coming to earth?

5. Think about your own purpose in life and the life purpose of other believers you know. Jesus said to his disciples, *"As the Father has sent me, so I am sending you"* (John 20:21). In what ways can we be sent as the Father sent Jesus?

6. In the Quotes section, we saw where Martin Luther said, "Without Christ, God will not be found, known, or comprehended." What do you think of that statement, and what are its ramifications?

7. Did anything you read in this chapter change the way you will relate to Jesus? If so, how?

Chapter Three

TITLES AND DESCRIPTIONS OF JESUS: A ROSE BY ANY OTHER NAME

"He is all in all: Patriarch among the Patriarchs; Law in the Laws; Chief Priest among the Priests; Ruler among Kings; the Prophet among the Prophets; the Angel among Angels; the Man among Men; Son in the Father; God in God; King to All Eternity."

—Irenaeus of Lyon (125–202)

In Shakespeare's famous play, Juliet says to Romeo, "What's in a name? That which we call a rose by any other name would smell as sweet." The name of Jesus is adored and revered by believers around the world, and it certainly should be. Of Jesus, we read that *"God elevated him to the place of highest honor and gave him the name above all other names"* (Philippians 2:9). Perhaps one of the reasons, among many, of why Jesus has been given the name that is above every other name is because *"there is no other name under heaven given to mankind by which we must be saved"* (Acts 4:12 NIV).

A person often has a legal name as well as a name they go by with their friends, and perhaps even another nickname or two. The legendary baseball player Babe Ruth (his legal name was George Herman Ruth) had several nicknames. Many have heard him described as the Sultan of Swat, but others referred to him as the Bambino, the Colossus of Clout, the Caliph of Clout, the Wazir of Wham, the Mammoth of Maul, the Mauling Mastodon, and other titles as well.

While Babe Ruth went by various descriptive titles, everyone understood he was one and the same person no matter what he was called at a certain time. Also, his various nicknames tended to reflect a single aspect of his life—his ability to hit the baseball. Likewise, just as Jesus wears many crowns (see Revelation 19:12), he is also described in a myriad of ways in Scripture, but his titles reflect the broad spectrum of his character and his works. I would suggest that Jesus' magnificence and grandeur is so vast that it takes a multitude of terms to begin to capture and express the magnitude of who he is.

However, before we get into the vast array of titles and descriptions, let's look at the two most common terms describing the Savior: *Jesus* and *Christ*. To the Christian who speaks English, there is no more wonderful name than that of Jesus. That is our English rendering of the Greek word *Iēsous*. To the Hebrew speaking, he is Yeshua. To those who speak Arabic, his name is Isa. To those whose mother tongue is Spanish, he is Jesús. The Bible speaks of the gospel spreading *"to every nation, tribe, language, and people"* (Revelation 14:6), so this is significant. Whatever our background, God speaks our language!

We might think that the name of Jesus was a unique name for a unique person, but it really was not. Certainly, Jesus Christ was and is the most unique person in the universe, but the actual name of Jesus was quite common in his day. I was surprised as a youngster to discover that a certain Jesús was playing Major League Baseball (from the baseball cards I collected).

When Paul and Barnabas reached Paphos on the island of Cyprus as part of their first missionary journey, they encountered *"a Jewish sorcerer, a false prophet named Bar-Jesus"* (Acts 13:6). Bar-Jesus simply means "Son of Jesus," but he certainly had no connection to Jesus of Nazareth. In Colossians 4:11, Paul refers to another individual he calls *"Jesus (the one we call Justus)."* Some ancient New Testament manuscripts even refer to Barabbas (the notorious criminal who appears at Jesus' trial) as *Jesus Barabbas* (see Matthew 27:16-17 in the NIV or NET).

Jesus was simply the Greek form of the Hebrew word *Joshua* (*Yeshua*), and many babies were given that name in biblical times; it meant "YHWH is Salvation" or "God Saves." Not only did the angel Gabriel tell Mary that she would conceive supernaturally and name her son Jesus (see Luke 1:31), but he told Joseph on a separate occasion that Mary *"will have a son, and you are to name him Jesus, for he will save his people from their sins"* (Matthew 1:21).

But what about the term *Christ*? Was that Jesus' last name? No, the term *Christ* means "the anointed one" and is derived from the Greek word *Christos*. The equivalent word in Hebrew is *Mashiach*, from which we get the English word *Messiah*. In the Old Testament, certain ones, such as prophets, priests, and kings, were anointed with oil to represent the empowerment of the Holy Spirit coming into their lives to enable them to carry out their tasks.

But Jesus wasn't just anointed in that common sense; he was *the* Anointed One, the promised Messiah. That's why Psalm 45:7 speaks prophetically of Jesus, *"God, your God, has anointed you, pouring out the oil of joy on you more than on anyone else."* Jesus was not anointed to simply stand in one of those temporary offices; he was anointed to be the Savior of the world.

When you and I speak of Jesus, we know exactly who we are talking about, but for overall clarity, we are not just speaking of anyone in the world with that name; we are speaking of Jesus Christ of Nazareth, the Son of the Living God. The apostle Paul tells us the name of Jesus is *"the name above all other names"* and that *"at the name of Jesus every knee should bow, in heaven and on earth and under the earth, and every tongue declare that Jesus Christ is Lord, to the glory of God the Father"* (Philippians 2:9–11).

THE POWER OF JESUS' NAME

The earliest disciples learned that they were not designed to operate by their own authority but by that conferred upon them by Jesus, and that his name represented all of his power and virtue. Jesus once sent them out on what we might call a short-term ministry practicum, and this is what resulted: *"When the seventy-two disciples returned, they joyfully reported to him, 'Lord, even the demons obey us when we use your name!'"* (Luke 10:17). They saw powerful results when they used Jesus' name.

While Jesus was with them, he gave them insight about using his name, both in prayer and in exercising authority over demonic powers (see Mark 16:17–18; John 14:13–14; 15:16; 16:23–24,26).

The apostles took Jesus' injunction to use his name very seriously, and the results were remarkable. Consider these examples:

- Peter said to the lame man at the Gate Beautiful, *"**In the name of Jesus Christ the Nazarene**, get up and walk!"* (Acts 3:6) and the miraculous happened. Peter later explained that *"Through **faith in the name of Jesus**, this man was healed—and you know how crippled he was before. **Faith in Jesus' name** has healed him before your very eyes"* (Acts 3:16).

- Paul spoke to the demon possessing the slave girl in Philippi, *"I command you **in the name of Jesus Christ** to come out of her"* (Acts 16:18). As a result, she was gloriously delivered.

- James, Jesus' half-brother, gave the church these instructions: *"Are any of you sick? You should call for the elders of the church to come and pray over you, anointing you with oil **in the name of the Lord**. Such a prayer offered in faith will heal the sick, and the Lord will make you well"* (James 5:14-15).

Of course, Jesus' name was not simply some kind of good luck charm or magic wand that someone could use indiscriminately. Hoping to emulate Paul's effectiveness, a group of men who were hoping to exorcise a demon *"tried to use the name of the Lord Jesus in their incantation, saying, 'I command you in the name of Jesus, whom Paul preaches, to come out!'"* (Acts 19:13). It did not go well for them as they had no personal relationship with God nor genuine faith in Jesus as Savior and Lord.

If Jesus had no other names or descriptions ascribed to him, he would still be absolutely wonderful. But the Bible provides a myriad of other windows into his remarkable character. Consider the following titles and consider what they represent (corresponding Scriptures will follow).

Advocate

Alpha and Omega

Amen

Ancient of Days

Apostle and High Priest of Our Confession

Atoning Sacrifice

Author and Finisher

Author of Life

Beginning

Beginning and the End

Beginning of the Creation of God

Beloved

Branch of Righteousness

Bread of Life

Bridegroom

Bright Morning Star

Brightness of God's Glory

Carpenter

Cornerstone

Chief Shepherd

Chosen One of God

Christ

Consolation of Israel

Creator

Dayspring from on High

Dearly Loved Son

Deliverer

Desire of All Nations

Door

Elect One

Eternal High Priest

Everlasting Father

Exact Likeness of God

Faithful and True

Faithful and True Witness

Faithful Witness

First and Last

Firstborn from the Dead

Forerunner

Friend

God

Good Shepherd

Great God and Savior

Great High Priest

Great Shepherd of the Sheep

Guarantor

Head of the Body

Head of the Church

Heavenly Man

Heir of All Things

High Priest

High Priest in the Order of Melchizedek

Holy and Righteous One

Holy Servant

Hope of Glory

Husband

I AM

Immanuel

Jesus

Jesus Christ

Jesus of Nazareth

Judge of the Living and Dead

King

King of Israel

King of the Jews

King of Kings and Lord of Lords

Lamb of God

The Last Adam

Life

Light of the World

Lion of the Tribe of Judah

Living One

Living Stone

Lord

Lord of All

Lord of the Living and the Dead

Lord of Glory

Lord from Heaven

The Lord our Righteousness

Lord of the Sabbath

The Man Christ Jesus

Man of Sorrows

Master

Mediator

Messenger of the Covenant

Messiah

Messiah the Prince

Mighty God

Mighty Savior

Nazarene

Only Begotten Son

Our Hope

Passover

Perfect Leader

Physician

Power and Wisdom of God

Prince of Peace

Prophet from Nazareth

Prophet Like Moses

Rabbi

Ransom

Redeemer

Resurrection and Life

Righteous One

Rock

Rock of Offense

Root of Jesse

Ruler in Israel

Ruler over the Kings of the Earth

Savior

The Second Man

Seed of Woman

Servant

Shepherd and Guardian of Our Souls

Shiloh

Son of Abraham

Son of the Blessed One

Son of David

Son of God

Son of the Most High

Son of Man

Source of David and the Heir to His Throne

Source of Eternal Salvation

Stone of Stumbling

Sun of Righteousness

Supreme over All Creation

Teacher from God

True Light

True Vine

Truth

The Visible Image of the Invisible God

The Way

Wonderful Counselor

Word

Word of God

Word of Life

In the following sections, we'll identify the section of the Bible in which these various titles appear, as well as a Scripture reference. Some titles appear multiple times in Scripture, but I often provide only a single reference. Likewise, some titles appear in more than one section, but I will only list them in one. In that sense, the following sections are not comprehensive or exhaustive. For a few of these, I will provide a brief definition, but in most cases, I just allow the Scripture to speak for itself.

DESCRIPTIONS AND TITLES OF JESUS FROM THE OLD TESTAMENT

ANCIENT OF DAYS

I watched till thrones were put in place, and the Ancient of Days was seated; His garment was white as snow. ...I was watching; and the same horn was making war against the saints, and prevailing against them, until the Ancient of Days came, and a judgment was made in favor of the saints of the Most High, and the time came for the saints to possess the kingdom

(Daniel 7:9, 21-22 NKJV).

BRANCH OF RIGHTEOUSNESS

"Behold, the days are coming," says the Lord, "that I will raise to David a Branch of righteousness"

(Jeremiah 23:5 NKJV).

CORNERSTONE

The stone that the builders rejected has now become the cornerstone

(Psalm 118:22; see also Matthew 21:42; Acts 4:11; Ephesians 2:20; 1 Peter 2:6-7, etc.).

DESIRE OF ALL NATIONS

"And I will shake all nations, and they shall come to the Desire of All Nations, and I will fill this temple with glory," says the Lord of hosts

(Haggai 2:7 NKJV).

ELECT ONE

Behold! My Servant whom I uphold, My Elect One in whom My soul delights! I have put My Spirit upon Him; He will bring forth justice to the Gentiles

(Isaiah 42:1 NKJV).

IMMANUEL

Therefore the Lord Himself will give you a sign: Behold, the virgin shall conceive and bear a Son, and shall call His name Immanuel

(Isaiah 7:14 NKJV).

In the first gospel, we are told exactly what *Immanuel* means. Matthew writes:

"Immanuel," which is translated, "God with us"

(Matthew 1:23 NKJV).

KING

Look, your king is coming to you. He is righteous and victorious, yet he is humble, riding on a donkey—riding on a donkey's colt

(Zechariah 9:9).

LEADER AND COMMANDER

Indeed I have given him as a witness to the people, a leader and commander for the people

(Isaiah 55:4 NKJV).

THE LORD OUR RIGHTEOUSNESS

In His days Judah will be saved, and Israel will dwell safely; now this is His name by which He will be called: THE LORD OUR RIGHTEOUSNESS

(Jeremiah 23:6 NKJV).

MAN OF SORROWS

He was despised and rejected—a man of sorrows, acquainted with deepest grief. We turned our backs on him and looked the other way. He was despised, and we did not care

(Isaiah 53:3).

MESSENGER OF THE COVENANT

Then the Lord you are seeking will suddenly come to his Temple. The messenger of the covenant, whom you look for so eagerly, is surely coming

(Malachi 3:1).

MESSIAH THE PRINCE

Know therefore and understand, that from the going forth of the command to restore and build Jerusalem until Messiah the Prince, there shall be seven weeks and sixty-two weeks

(Daniel 9:25 NKJV).

REDEEMER

But as for me, I know that my Redeemer lives, and he will stand upon the earth at last

(Job 19:25).

When Scripture calls Jesus a redeemer, it refers to the fact that he purchased us with his own blood, rescuing and delivering us from the hand of the enemy.

ROOT OF JESSE

And in that day there shall be a Root of Jesse, who shall stand as a banner to the people; for the Gentiles shall seek Him, and His resting place shall be glorious

(Isaiah 11:10 NKJV).

RULER IN ISRAEL

But you, Bethlehem Ephrathah, though you are little among the thousands of Judah, yet out of you shall come forth to Me the One to be Ruler in Israel, whose goings forth are from of old, from everlasting

(Micah 5:2 NKJV).

SEED OF WOMAN

And I will put enmity between you and the woman, and between your seed and her Seed; He shall bruise your head, and you shall bruise His heel

(Genesis 3:15 NKJV).

This verse is rich in meaning and has often been called the *protevangelion* (meaning "the first gospel"). Because it predicts the Seed of a woman crushing the head of the serpent, it is a prophetic reference—the very first one given in Scripture—to Jesus destroying Satan and his kingdom.

SERVANT

Look at my servant, whom I strengthen

(Isaiah 42:1).

SHILOH

The scepter shall not depart from Judah, nor a lawgiver from between his feet, until Shiloh comes; and to Him shall be the obedience of the people

(Genesis 49:10 NKJV).

Of this passage, Warren Wiersbe shared:

The name "Shiloh" in verse 10 has given rise to many interpretations and speculations, but the most reasonable is that it refers to the Messiah (Num. 24:17). The phrase could be translated "until he comes whose right it is [the scepter, i.e., the rule]," because the word Shiloh means "whose it is." The ancient rabbinical scholars took Shiloh to be a name of the promised Messiah, who alone had the right to claim rule over God's people Israel.[8]

SUN OF RIGHTEOUSNESS

But for you who fear my name, the Sun of Righteousness will rise with healing in his wings

(Malachi 4:2).

WONDERFUL COUNSELOR, MIGHTY GOD, EVERLASTING FATHER, PRINCE OF PEACE

For a child is born to us, a son is given to us. The government will rest on his shoulders. And he will be called: Wonderful Counselor, Mighty God, Everlasting Father, Prince of Peace

(Isaiah 9:6).

What about this reference to the Father? Let me share an insight from Henry Gariepy:

We usually associate the name of the Father with the first Person of the Godhead, but here the title belongs to Christ. However, the original text does not denote *father* in the usual association we have with that word. It means in this verse *author* or *possessor*. A more exact rendering of this verse would be "the Father of Eternity" as it is rendered in the *Amplified Old Testament*. Thus, the verse speaks of Christ as the Eternal One and as the One who holds eternity in His possession. Vast unfathomable eternity is His.[9]

DESCRIPTIONS AND TITLES JESUS GAVE HIMSELF

ALPHA AND OMEGA, FIRST AND THE LAST, BEGINNING AND THE END

I am the Alpha and the Omega, the First and the Last, the Beginning and the End

(Revelation 22:13).

Jesus begins his self-description by using the first and last letters of the Greek alphabet. He is not only the source and origin, but also the culmination of all things. He is the sum and substance of the entirety of God's redemptive plan. The comprehensiveness and completeness of Christ in these verses echoes Paul's statement, *"For of Him and through Him and to Him are all things"* (Romans 11:36 NKJV).

AMEN, FAITHFUL AND TRUE WITNESS, BEGINNING OF GOD'S NEW CREATION

These things says the Amen, the Faithful and True Witness, the Beginning of the creation of God

(Revelation 3:14 NKJV).

Bible scholar William Barclay sheds great light on this verse. He wrote:

In Isaiah 65:16 God is called the God of truth; but in the Hebrew he is called the *God of Amen*. Amen is the word which is often put at the end of a solemn statement in order to guarantee its truth. If God is the God of Amen, he is utterly to be relied upon. This would mean that Jesus Christ is the One whose promises are true beyond all doubt.[10]

Paul declares that Jesus Christ is:

God's ultimate "Yes," he always does what he says. For all of God's promises have been fulfilled in Christ with a resounding "Yes!" And through Christ, our "Amen" (which means "Yes") ascends to God for his glory
(2 Corinthians 1:19-20).

Jesus is both the fulfiller and the fulfillment of all that God's Word says.

"The Beginning of the creation of God" (Revelation 3:14 NKJV) is translated *the originator of God's creation* in the New English Translation. This correlates to the many verses in Scripture indicating that Jesus was an agent in all of creation along with the Father and the Spirit; Jesus was not a created being.

BREAD OF LIFE

The true bread of God is the one who comes down from heaven and gives life to the world. ...I am the bread of life. Whoever comes to me will never be hungry again. Whoever believes in me will never be thirsty
(John 6:33,35; see also John 6:48-58).

BRIDEGROOM

And Jesus said to them, "Can the friends of the bridegroom mourn as long as the bridegroom is with them? But the days will come when the bridegroom will be taken away from them, and then they will fast"

(Matthew 9:15 NKJV; see also John 3:29).

BRIGHT MORNING STAR

I am the bright morning star

(Revelation 22:16).

Sometimes we hear a person say, "A new day is dawning." Such a statement refers to transition and change. The night has gone and a new day is beginning. The past is past and something brand-new is emerging. That is what Jesus brought to a world that was permeated with hopelessness, despair, and death. Because of whom Christ is, what he did, and what he brings, everyone who puts their faith in him is empowered to leave yesterday behind and step into a new future that is full of hope and opportunities.

DOOR

I am the door. If anyone enters by Me, he will be saved, and will go in and out and find pasture

(John 10:9 NKJV).

FRIEND

I no longer call you slaves, because a master doesn't confide in his slaves. Now you are my friends, since I have told you everything the Father told me

(John 15:15; see also Matthew 11:19; John 11:11).

Surely no one has ever been a friend to us like Jesus. Solomon told us that *"there is a friend who sticks closer than a brother"* (Proverbs

18:24 NKJV). Some may see Jesus as being too austere to be a friend, or even to be friendly, but that is to not understand Jesus well. Though Jesus never engaged in sinful behavior, his critics called him a *"friend of tax collectors and sinners"* (Matthew 11:19 NKJV). Jesus referred to *"our friend Lazarus"* (John 11:11 NKJV) and spoke of his imminent sacrifice for us when he said, *"There is no greater love than to lay down one's life for one's friends"* (John 15:13).

GOOD SHEPHERD

I am the good shepherd. The good shepherd sacrifices his life for the sheep. …I am the good shepherd; I know my own sheep, and they know me

(John 10:11,14).

I AM

Jesus answered, "I tell you the truth, before Abraham was even born, I AM!"

(John 8:58; see also Exodus 3:14)

Jesus' hearers understood that he was claiming to be the eternal God who was never created but, rather, had existed from all eternity. The religious people considered this claim blasphemous and immediately sought to kill him.

LIGHT OF THE WORLD

I am the light of the world. If you follow me, you won't have to walk in darkness, because you will have the light that leads to life

(John 8:12).

LORD OF THE SABBATH

The Son of Man is Lord, even over the Sabbath

(Luke 6:5).

Jesus was sometimes accused of breaking the Sabbath, but he never violated God's law. Perhaps, though, he had transgressed some of the countless man-made regulations that they had attached to the law, which brought people under bondage. Jesus is saying that it was he, not the religious bureaucrats, who had the authority to define what the Sabbath was and what it was not.

MESSIAH

The woman said, "I know the Messiah is coming—the one who is called Christ. When he comes, he will explain everything to us." Then Jesus told her, "I AM the Messiah!"

(John 4:25-26; see also John 1:41).

RANSOM

For even the Son of Man came not to be served but to serve others and to give his life as a ransom for many

(Matthew 20:28).

THE RESURRECTION AND THE LIFE

I am the resurrection and the life. Anyone who believes in me will live, even after dying

(John 11:25).

SON OF MAN

For the Son of Man has come to seek and to save that which was lost

(Luke 19:10 NKJV; see also Matthew 8:20).

THE SOURCE OF DAVID AND THE HEIR TO HIS THRONE

I am both the source of David and the heir to his throne

(Revelation 22:16).

THE WAY, THE TRUTH, AND THE LIFE

I am the way, the truth, and the life. No one can come to the Father except through me

(John 14:6).

TRUE VINE

I am the true vine, and my Father is the gardener

(John 15:1 NIV).

DESCRIPTIONS AND TITLES OF JESUS THROUGHOUT THE REST OF THE NEW TESTAMENT

ADVOCATE

If anyone does sin, we have an advocate who pleads our case before the Father. He is Jesus Christ, the one who is truly righteous

(1 John 2:1).

APOSTLE AND HIGH PRIEST OF OUR CONFESSION

Therefore, holy brethren, partakers of the heavenly calling, consider the Apostle and High Priest of our confession, Christ Jesus

(Hebrews 3:1 NKJV).

ATONING SACRIFICE

He is the atoning sacrifice for our sins, and not only for ours but also for the sins of the whole world

(1 John 2:2 NIV).

AUTHOR AND FINISHER

Looking unto Jesus the author and finisher of our faith

(Hebrews 12:2 KJV).

AUTHOR OF LIFE

You killed the author of life, but God raised him from the dead

(Acts 3:15).

BELOVED

To the praise of the glory of His grace, by which He made us accepted in the Beloved

(Ephesians 1:6 NKJV).

BRIGHTNESS OF GOD'S GLORY

Who being the brightness of His glory and the express image of His person

(Hebrews 1:3 NKJV).

The phrase "express image" is the Greek word *charakter*. Kenneth Wuest writes, "This word was used in classical Greek of an engraver, one who mints coins, a graving tool, a die, a stamp, a branding iron, a mark engraved, an impress, a stamp on coins and seals."[11] When a coin comes out of the die, it carries the exact representation of the die itself. This is why Jesus could say with complete accuracy, *"Anyone who has seen me has seen the Father!"* (John 14:9).

CARPENTER

Then they scoffed, "He's just a carpenter, the son of Mary and the brother of James, Joseph, Judas, and Simon. And his sisters live right here among us"

(Mark 6:3).

CHIEF SHEPHERD

And when the Chief Shepherd appears, you will receive the crown of glory that does not fade away

(1 Peter 5:4 NKJV).

CHOSEN ONE OF GOD

I testify that he is the Chosen One of God

(John 1:34).

CHRIST

Simon Peter answered and said, "You are the Christ, the Son of the living God"

(Matthew 16:16 NKJV; see also Luke 2:26).

CONSOLATION OF ISRAEL

And behold, there was a man in Jerusalem whose name was Simeon, and this man was just and devout, waiting for the Consolation of Israel, and the Holy Spirit was upon him

(Luke 2:25 NKJV).

CREATOR

All things were made through Him, and without Him nothing was made that was made

(John 1:3 NKJV; see also Colossians 1:16; Hebrews 1:2).

DAYSPRING FROM ON HIGH

Through the tender mercy of our God, with which the Dayspring from on high has visited us

(Luke 1:78 NKJV).

DEARLY LOVED SON

And a voice from heaven said, "This is my dearly loved Son, who brings me great joy"

(Matthew 3:17).

DELIVERER

And so all Israel will be saved, as it is written: "The Deliverer will come out of Zion, and He will turn away ungodliness from Jacob"

(Romans 11:26 NKJV).

ETERNAL HIGH PRIEST

He has become our eternal High Priest in the order of Melchizedek

(Hebrews 6:20).

EXACT LIKENESS OF GOD

They are unable to see the glorious light of the Good News. They don't understand this message about the glory of Christ, who is the exact likeness of God

(2 Corinthians 4:4; see also Colossians 1:15; Hebrews 1:3).

FAITHFUL AND TRUE

Then I saw heaven opened, and a white horse was standing there. Its rider was named Faithful and True, for he judges fairly and wages a righteous war

(Revelation 19:11).

FAITHFUL WITNESS, FIRSTBORN FROM THE DEAD, AND RULER OVER THE KINGS OF THE EARTH

And from Jesus Christ, the faithful witness, the firstborn from the dead, and the ruler over the kings of the earth

(Revelation 1:5 NKJV).

FORERUNNER

Our forerunner, Jesus, has entered on our behalf

(Hebrews 6:20 NIV).

GOD

"My Lord and my God!" Thomas exclaimed

(John 20:28; see also Hebrews 1:8; Romans 9:5; Titus 2:13; 2 Peter 1:1; 1 John 5:20).

GREAT GOD AND SAVIOR

We look forward with hope to that wonderful day when the glory of our great God and Savior, Jesus Christ, will be revealed

(Titus 2:13).

GREAT HIGH PRIEST

So then, since we have a great High Priest who has entered heaven, Jesus the Son of God, let us hold firmly to what we believe

(Hebrews 4:14; see also Hebrews 2:17).

GREAT SHEPHERD OF THE SHEEP

The God of peace—who brought up from the dead our Lord Jesus, the great Shepherd of the sheep

(Hebrews 13:20).

GUARANTOR

Jesus has become the guarantor of a better covenant

(Hebrews 7:22 NIV).

Jesus himself is the one who guarantees this better covenant that we have with God. In the Latin Vulgate, Jerome translated this word *sponsor*. Outside of the New Testament, it "was a legal term within the Graeco-Roman world, referring to someone who assumed an obligation in place of another."[12] Think, perhaps, of a bail bondsman or a co-signer on a debt. Though we lacked the spiritual capital to secure our end of the "deal," Jesus stepped in and we have a secure covenant with God based on who he is and on all that he has accomplished. A friend of mine who specializes in the Greek language says that "guarantor has a root word meaning 'an extended limb (arm)' with a prefixed preposition signifying 'to remain in place.' Thus, it means 'to extend an arm of support that one can confidently count on.'"[13]

HEAD OF THE BODY, THE BEGINNING, FIRSTBORN FROM THE DEAD

And He is the head of the body, the church, who is the beginning, the firstborn from the dead, that in all things He may have the preeminence

(Colossians 1:18 NKJV).

HEAD OF THE CHURCH

Christ is the head of the church

(Ephesians 5:23 NIV; see also Ephesians 1:22; 4:15).

HEAVENLY MAN

As was the man of dust, so also are those who are made of dust; and as is the heavenly Man, so also are those who are heavenly. And as we have borne the image of the man of dust, we shall also bear the image of the heavenly Man

(1 Corinthians 15:48-49 NKJV).

HEIR OF ALL THINGS

Has in these last days spoken to us by His Son, whom He has appointed heir of all things

(Hebrews 1:2 NKJV).

HIGH PRIEST

Here is the main point: We have a High Priest who sat down in the place of honor beside the throne of the majestic God in heaven

(Hebrews 8:1).

HIGH PRIEST IN THE ORDER OF MELCHIZEDEK

And God designated him to be a High Priest in the order of Melchizedek

(Hebrews 5:10).

HOLY AND RIGHTEOUS ONE

But you disowned the Holy and Righteous One, and asked for a murderer to be granted to you

(Acts 3:14 NASB).

HOLY SERVANT

Stretch out your hand with healing power; may miraculous signs and wonders be done through the name of your holy servant Jesus

(Acts 4:30).

HOPE OF GLORY

Which is Christ in you, the hope of glory

(Colossians 1:27 NKJV).

HUSBAND

I promised you as a pure bride to one husband—Christ

(2 Corinthians 11:2).

JESUS

And she will have a son, and you are to name him Jesus, for he will save his people from their sins

(Matthew 1:21).

JESUS CHRIST, SON OF DAVID, SON OF ABRAHAM

The book of the genealogy of Jesus Christ, the Son of David, the Son of Abraham

(Matthew 1:1 NKJV).

JESUS OF NAZARETH

You are looking for Jesus of Nazareth, who was crucified. He isn't here! He is risen from the dead!

(Mark 16:6)

JUDGE OF THE LIVING AND THE DEAD

And he ordered us to preach everywhere and to testify that Jesus is the one appointed by God to be the judge of all—the living and the dead

(Acts 10:42; see also 2 Timothy 4:8).

KING OF ISRAEL

Then Nathanael exclaimed, "Rabbi, you are the Son of God—the King of Israel!"

(John 1:49)

KING OF KINGS AND LORD OF LORDS

On his robe and on his thigh he has a name written, King of kings and Lord of lords

(Revelation 19:16 ESV; see also Revelation 17:14).

KING OF THE JEWS

Where is the newborn king of the Jews? We saw his star as it rose, and we have come to worship him

(Matthew 2:2; see also Matthew 27:37).

LAMB OF GOD

The next day John saw Jesus coming toward him and said, "Look! The Lamb of God who takes away the sin of the world!"

(John 1:29; see also Revelation 13:8; 1 Peter 1:19)

LAST ADAM

The Scriptures tell us, "The first man, Adam, became a living person." But the last Adam—that is, Christ—is a life-giving Spirit

(1 Corinthians 15:45).

LION OF THE TRIBE OF JUDAH

But one of the twenty-four elders said to me, "Stop weeping! Look, the Lion of the tribe of Judah, the heir to David's throne, has won the victory. He is worthy to open the scroll and its seven seals"

(Revelation 5:5).

LIVING ONE

I am the living one. I died, but look—I am alive forever and ever!

(Revelation 1:18)

LIVING STONE

Coming to Him as to a living stone, rejected indeed by men, but chosen by God and precious

(1 Peter 2:4 NKJV).

LORD

If you openly declare that Jesus is Lord and believe in your heart that God raised him from the dead, you will be saved

(Romans 10:9).

LORD OF ALL

There is peace with God through Jesus Christ, who is Lord of all

(Acts 10:36).

LORD OF THE DEAD AND THE LIVING

Christ died and rose again for this very purpose—to be Lord both of the living and of the dead

(Romans 14:9).

LORD OF GLORY

Which none of the rulers of this age knew; for had they known, they would not have crucified the Lord of glory

(1 Corinthians 2:8 NKJV; see also James 2:1).

THE MAN CHRIST JESUS

There is one God and one Mediator who can reconcile God and humanity—the man Christ Jesus

(1 Timothy 2:5).

MASTER

Ten men with leprosy stood at a distance, crying out, "Jesus, Master, have mercy on us!"

(Luke 17:12-13)

MEDIATOR

There is one God and one Mediator who can reconcile God and humanity—the man Christ Jesus

(1 Timothy 2:5; see also Hebrews 9:15).

MIGHTY SAVIOR

He has sent us a mighty Savior from the royal line of his servant David
(Luke 1:69).

NAZARENE

So the family went and lived in a town called Nazareth. This fulfilled what the prophets had said: "He will be called a Nazarene"
(Matthew 2:23).

ONLY BEGOTTEN SON

For God so loved the world that He gave His only begotten Son, that whoever believes in Him should not perish but have everlasting life
(John 3:16 NKJV; see also John 1:18; 1 John 4:9).

OUR HOPE

Paul, an apostle of Jesus Christ, by the commandment of God our Savior and the Lord Jesus Christ, our hope

(1 Timothy 1:1 NKJV).

PASSOVER LAMB

Christ, our Passover Lamb, has been sacrificed for us

(1 Corinthians 5:7).

PERFECT LEADER

And it was only right that he should make Jesus, through his suffering, a perfect leader, fit to bring them into their salvation

(Hebrews 2:10).

PHYSICIAN

You will undoubtedly quote me this proverb: "Physician, heal yourself"

(Luke 4:23).

THE POWER AND WISDOM OF GOD

But to those called by God to salvation, both Jews and Gentiles, Christ is the power of God and the wisdom of God

(1 Corinthians 1:24).

PROPHET FROM NAZARETH

And the crowds replied, "It's Jesus, the prophet from Nazareth in Galilee"

(Matthew 21:11).

A PROPHET LIKE MOSES

Moses said, "The Lord your God will raise up for you a Prophet like me from among your own people. Listen carefully to everything he tells you"

(Acts 3:22).

RABBI

They replied, "Rabbi" (which means "Teacher"), "where are you staying?"

(John 1:38)

RIGHTEOUS ONE

Jesus Christ, the Righteous One

(1 John 2:1 NIV; see also Acts 7:52).

ROCK

And all of them drank the same spiritual water. For they drank from the spiritual rock that traveled with them, and that rock was Christ

(1 Corinthians 10:4).

SAVIOR

The Savior—yes, the Messiah, the Lord—has been born today in Bethlehem, the city of David!

(Luke 2:11; see also Ephesians 5:23; Titus 1:4, 3:6; 2 Peter 2:20)

THE SECOND MAN; THE LORD FROM HEAVEN

The first man was of the earth, made of dust; the second Man is the Lord from heaven

(1 Corinthians 15:47 NKJV).

SHEPHERD AND GUARDIAN OF OUR SOULS

But now you have turned to your Shepherd, the Guardian of your souls
(1 Peter 2:25).

SON OF THE BLESSED ONE

Then the high priest asked him, "Are you the Messiah, the Son of the Blessed One?"

(Mark 14:61)

SON OF GOD

Then the disciples worshiped him. "You really are the Son of God!"
(Matthew 14:33; see also John 1:49)

SON OF THE MOST HIGH

He will be very great and will be called the Son of the Most High
(Luke 1:32).

SOURCE OF ETERNAL SALVATION

God qualified him as a perfect High Priest, and he became the source of eternal salvation for all those who obey him

(Hebrews 5:9).

STONE OF STUMBLING; ROCK OF OFFENSE

"A stone of stumbling and a rock of offense." They stumble, being disobedient to the word

(1 Peter 2:8 NKJV).

SUPREME OVER ALL CREATION

He existed before anything was created and is supreme over all creation
(Colossians 1:15).

The English word *supreme* in this verse is from the Greek word *prōtotokos*. In many translations, this word is rendered "firstborn," but that does not mean that Jesus was the first created being. Rather, it refers to Jesus' preeminence over all created things. Noted scholar Kenneth Wuest translates this to read that Christ is *"the One who has priority to and sovereignty over all creation."*[14] Other translations render this verse, *"He is the image of the invisible God; his is the primacy over all created things"* (Colossians 1:15 NEB). Another version reads, *"He in his own person shows us what the unseen God is like. He takes precedence over all the created universe"* (Colossians 1:15 TNT).

TEACHER FROM GOD

This man came to Jesus by night and said to Him, "Rabbi, we know that You are a teacher come from God; for no one can do these signs that You do unless God is with him"

(John 3:2 NKJV).

TRUE LIGHT

The one who is the true light, who gives light to everyone, was coming into the world

(John 1:9).

THE VISIBLE IMAGE OF THE INVISIBLE GOD

Christ is the visible image of the invisible God

(Colossians 1:15).

WORD

In the beginning the Word already existed. The Word was with God, and the Word was God

(John 1:1).

WORD OF GOD

He wore a robe dipped in blood, and his title was the Word of God

(Revelation 19:13).

WORD OF LIFE

We proclaim to you the one who existed from the beginning, whom we have heard and seen. We saw him with our own eyes and touched him with our own hands. He is the Word of life

(1 John 1:1).

WHAT DOES ALL THIS MEAN TO US?

The immenseness of Jesus' titles can seem overwhelming. How could any one person be qualified to fulfill so many roles? People sometimes crave titles for themselves to fulfill their own ego, even if they lack the needed abilities. But Jesus' titles perfectly reflect his perfect character and competencies. Likewise, earthly titles are often temporary, but Jesus will carry all of his names and descriptions throughout eternity.

As you ponder his many names and titles, let me encourage you to draw from the meaning and the significance each of them carries. For example, when you read that Jesus is *"the author and finisher of our faith"* (Hebrews 12:2 KJV), pray into that. In other words, as you commune with him, say, "Jesus, thank you that you are the one who has started a good work in my life, and I know that you will continue to perfect my faith as I walk with you." When you read that Jesus is the Good Shepherd (see John 10:11,14 NKJV), thank him that he leads and guides you, that he cares for you as a shepherd does his sheep.

Let his names remind you of everything he has done for you, everything that he is and wants to be to you, and all that he will be for you throughout all eternity. Draw from his nature, his character, and his mighty works.

QUOTES

"For Christ is King, Priest, God, Lord, Angel, and Man."

—Justin Martyr (100–165)

"I have shown from the Scriptures that none of the sons of Adam are…called God, or named Lord. But Jesus is Himself in His own right, beyond all men who ever lived, God, Lord, King Eternal, and the Incarnate Word…He is the Holy Lord, the Wonderful, the Counselor, the Beautiful in appearance, and the Mighty God."

—Irenaeus of Lyon (125–202)

"When we speak about wisdom, we are speaking about Christ. When we speak about virtue, we are speaking about Christ. When we speak about justice, we are speaking about Christ. When we speak about peace, we are speaking about Christ. When we speak about truth and life and redemption, we are speaking about Christ."

—Ambrose of Milan (340–397)

"By a Carpenter mankind was made, and only by that Carpenter can mankind be remade."

—Desiderius Erasmus (1466–1536)

"Hail, great Immanuel, all divine! In thee thy Father's glories shine."

—Isaac Watts (1674–1748)

"You may study, look, and meditate, but Jesus is a greater Savior than you think Him to be, even when your thoughts are at their highest."

—Charles H. Spurgeon (1834–1892)

"The name Emmanuel takes in the whole mystery. Jesus is 'God with us.' He had a nature like our own in all things, sin only excepted. But though Jesus was 'with us' in human flesh and blood, He was at the same time very God."

—J.C. Ryle (1816–1900)

QUESTIONS FOR REFLECTION AND DISCUSSION

1. Did you learn something new about Jesus in this chapter? Describe what you learned.

2. Did something you already knew about Jesus become strengthened or reinforced? Describe it.

3. If someone asked you how could one individual possibly have so many descriptive titles, how would you respond?

4. Review the "Descriptions and Titles of Jesus from the Old Testament." Which of these is most meaningful to you, and why?

5. Review the "Descriptions and Titles Jesus Gave Himself." Which of these is most meaningful to you, and why?

6. Review the "Descriptions and Titles of Jesus Throughout the Rest of the New Testament." Which of these is most meaningful to you, and why?

7. Did anything you read in this chapter change the way you will relate to Jesus? If so, how?

Chapter Four

IN A CLASS BY HIMSELF: THE CENTRALITY AND SUPREMACY OF JESUS

"Christ is the great central fact in the world's history. To Him everything looks forward or backward. All the lines of history converge upon Him."

—Charles H. Spurgeon

Some people, especially those who are first exploring or are newer to the faith, find it daunting to read the Bible. One key to maximizing your benefit of reading Scripture is to understand its overall theme from a bird's-eye perspective. Simply put, the Bible is the story of Jesus redeeming and restoring fallen man back to God.

In his commentary on the Bible, C.I. Scofield writes:

> From beginning to end the Bible has one great theme—
> the person and work of the Christ.
> The books of the Bible fall into groups. Speaking broadly
> there are five great divisions in the Scriptures, and these

may be conveniently fixed in the memory by five key words, Christ being the one theme (Luke 24:25-27).

Preparation: The Old Testament

Manifestation: The Gospels

Propagation: The Acts

Explanation: The Epistles

Consummation: The Apocalypse

In other words, the Old Testament is the preparation for Christ; in the Gospels he is manifested to the world; in the Acts he is preached and his Gospel is propagated in the world; in the Epistles his Gospel is explained; and in the Revelation all the purposes of God in and through Christ are consummated.[15]

Not recognizing the centrality of Jesus is to have missed the entire focal point of all Scripture. The Bible contains historical information, but it is not about history. The Bible contains geographical information, but it is not about geography. The Bible contains information about kings, prophets, and preachers, but it is not primarily about them. The Bible is about God revealing himself and reconciling the world to himself through the Person and work of the Lord Jesus Christ.

INSIGHT FROM THE APOSTLE PAUL

Consider Paul's remarkable description of the centrality and supremacy of the Lord Jesus as given in Colossians 1:15-20:

- *Christ is the visible image of the invisible God.*
- *He existed before anything was created and is supreme over all creation,*
- *for through him God created everything in the heavenly realms and on earth.*

- *He made the things we can see and the things we can't see—such as thrones, kingdoms, rulers, and authorities in the unseen world.*
- *Everything was created through him and for him.*
- *He existed before anything else,*
- *and he holds all creation together.*
- *Christ is also the head of the church, which is his body.*
- *He is the beginning,*
- *supreme over all who rise from the dead.*
- *So he is first in everything.*
- *For God in all his fullness was pleased to live in Christ,*
- *and through him God reconciled everything to himself.*
- *He made peace with everything in heaven and on earth by means of Christ's blood on the cross.*

Clearly, Christ is in a class all by himself. There is no human, angel, or any created being who can remotely begin to rival his purpose, accomplishments, or magnificence. These verses show him not merely in the context of his earthly existence, but from a transcendent and eternal perspective.

WHAT DID JESUS SAY ABOUT HIMSELF?

Because of his uniqueness, Jesus said and did things unlike anyone else. John's Gospel records some astonishing statements Jesus made about himself.

I am the Messiah (John 4:26; 13:19).
I am the bread of life (John 6:35, 41, 48, 51).
I am the light of the world (John 8:12; 9:5).

I am the gate for the sheep (John 10:7, 9).

I am the Son of God (John 10:36).

I am the resurrection and the life (John 11:25).

I am the good shepherd (John 10:11, 14).

I am the way, the truth, and the life (John 14:6).

I am the true vine (John 15:1, 5 NKJV).

In addition to all of these statements, Jesus explained that he personally was the focus of many of the writings of the Old Testament, and that he was the fulfillment of them. Can you imagine if a preacher today made all of the same "I am" statements about himself, and claimed that he was uniquely the fulfillment of numerous Old Testament prophecies? Most people would consider that preacher to be highly arrogant, extremely narcissistic, strongly deceived, or all of the above.

But Jesus did exactly that—claimed that the Scriptures were written about him—and millions of people believe and follow him. He told the religious leaders of his day, *"You search the Scriptures because you think they give you eternal life. But the Scriptures point to me!"* (John 5:39). After his resurrection, Jesus spoke with two of his disciples on the road to Emmaus and said:

> *"You foolish people! You find it so hard to believe all that the prophets wrote in the Scriptures. Wasn't it clearly predicted that the Messiah would have to suffer all these things before entering his glory?" Then Jesus took them through the writings of Moses and all the prophets, explaining from all the Scriptures the things concerning himself*
>
> (Luke 24:25-27).

Shortly after this, he met with a larger group of disciples and said, *"When I was with you before, I told you that everything written about me in the law of Moses and the prophets and in the Psalms must be fulfilled"* (Luke 24:44).

BACK TO PAUL

The apostle Paul used this exact same approach—revealing Jesus from the pages of the Old Testament—when he met with leading Jews in Rome.

> *So a time was set, and on that day a large number of people came to Paul's lodging. He explained and testified about the Kingdom of God and tried to persuade them about Jesus from the Scriptures. Using the law of Moses and the books of the prophets, he spoke to them from morning until evening. Some were persuaded by the things he said, but others did not believe*
>
> (Acts 28:23-24).

Did you note that Paul did this from morning until evening? The fact that Paul spent an entire day attempting to persuade them from Scripture indicates that there must be massive amounts of information about Jesus in the Old Testament (though he did not actually assume that human name until Bethlehem). This illuminates Scofield's proposition that the Old Testament was preparation for the coming of Christ.

Not only did Jesus say that he alone was the way to the Father (see John 14:6), but Peter also acknowledged Jesus' uniqueness when he proclaimed, *"There is salvation in no one else! God has given no other name under heaven by which we must be saved"* (Acts 4:12).

Natural, pluralistically minded people are often offended at such an exclusive approach. "Surely," they think, "there must be many ways to God, many ways to Heaven." But that is simply not what the Bible teaches.

Later, in Chapter Nine in this book, we will examine how the pre-existent Son of God poured his deity into humanity, how God took on flesh in the person of the Lord Jesus Christ. In Philippians, Paul describes Jesus' humility, obedience, and suffering, and then remarks that:

> *Therefore, God elevated him to the place of highest honor and gave him the name above all other names, that at the name of Jesus every knee should bow, in heaven and on earth and under the earth, and every tongue declare that Jesus Christ is Lord, to the glory of God the Father*
> (Philippians 2:9-11).

We will not bow our knees to Peter, John, Mary, or any other biblical characters. Nor will we prostrate ourselves before angels, but every knee will bow before the Lord Jesus Christ.

"GREATER THAN" COMPARISONS AND CONTRASTS

Jesus' supremacy is also revealed through several comparisons and contrasts that are presented throughout the New Testament.

JESUS—GREATER THAN ABRAHAM

> *"Are you greater than our father Abraham? He died, and so did the prophets. Who do you think you are?" … "Your father Abraham rejoiced as he looked forward to my coming. He saw it and was glad." The people*

said, "You aren't even fifty years old. How can you say you have seen
Abraham?" Jesus answered, "I tell you the truth, before Abraham was
even born, I AM!" At that point they picked up stones to throw at him.
But Jesus was hidden from them and left the Temple

(John 8:53, 56-59).

A simple "Yes, I am greater than Abraham" would have been sufficient to outrage the religious leaders in Jesus' day. Abraham was their foremost patriarch, their most esteemed and revered ancestor. But Jesus took it a huge step further in claiming deity for himself. We'll look in depth at the deity of Christ in Chapter Seven in this book, but for now, let's simply explore why Jesus was greater than Abraham.

The Message renders John 8:56 this way: *"Abraham—your 'father'— with jubilant faith looked down the corridors of history and saw my day coming. He saw it and cheered."* Abraham certainly was a pioneer of faith and his significance in the overarching purpose of God is huge. Abraham is listed in the great "Hall of Faith" of Hebrews 11—part of the remarkable company who *"did not receive what was promised, but they saw it all from a distance and welcomed it"* (Hebrews 11:13).

What was his role? *"It was by faith that Abraham offered Isaac as a sacrifice when God was testing him"* (Hebrews 11:17). God would one day offer his own Son, the Lord Jesus Christ, as the ultimate sacrifice for the sins of mankind, and Abraham pre-enacted this epic event when he was willing to offer his own son on Mount Moriah (see Genesis 22:1-18). In this "prophetic rehearsal," Abraham told Isaac, *"My son, God will provide for Himself the lamb for a burnt offering"* (Genesis 22:8 NKJV), and that's exactly what God did when he sent his own Son, Jesus, to the cross.

Of course, God stopped Abraham before he carried out the sacrifice of Isaac, but Abraham's faith and willingness to obey completely was noted by God. Paul summarized the promise that was articulated in response to Abraham's obedience; *"Now to Abraham and his Seed were the promises made. He does not say, 'And to seeds,' as of many, but as of one, 'And to your Seed,' who is Christ"* (Galatians 3:16 NKJV). There is no argument against Abraham being a great man and demonstrating great faith, but the Savior who came, died, and rose again—the one who fulfilled Abraham's prophetic exercise—is greater still.[16]

JESUS—GREATER THAN JACOB

The woman at the well asked Jesus if he was **greater than Jacob**, who had dug that well (see John 4:12). Jesus expressed his superiority to Jacob in his response: *"whoever drinks the water I give them will never thirst. Indeed, the water I give them will become in them a spring of water welling up to eternal life"* (John 4:14 NIV).

The people of this area were very proud of their heritage and felt a certain amount of pride that Jacob, one of the great patriarchs, was credited with digging this well. No doubt it provided life-sustaining water for them. Jesus, however, offered something even greater—the water of everlasting life.

As Jesus spoke to her, he may have been thinking of the words of Isaiah, *"With joy you will drink deeply from the fountain of salvation!"* (Isaiah 12:3). This same theme appears later when Jesus cried out, *"Anyone who believes in me may come and drink! For the Scriptures declare, 'Rivers of living water will flow from his heart'"* (John 7:38). Jacob had provided the people of that area with a natural water source. Jesus himself is the source of eternal life for all mankind.

JESUS—GREATER THAN SOLOMON

The queen of Sheba will also stand up against this generation on judgment day and condemn it, for she came from a distant land to hear the wisdom of Solomon. Now **someone greater than Solomon is here—** *but you refuse to listen*

(Matthew 12:42).

Solomon's reputation was off the charts. He was primarily known for two things: wisdom and wealth. Let's look at his wisdom first.

His wisdom exceeded that of all the wise men of the East and the wise men of Egypt. He was wiser than anyone else.... His fame spread throughout all the surrounding nations. He composed some 3,000 proverbs and wrote 1,005 songs. He could speak with authority about all kinds of plants, from the great cedar of Lebanon to the tiny hyssop that grows from cracks in a wall. He could also speak about animals, birds, small creatures, and fish. And kings from every nation sent their ambassadors to listen to the wisdom of Solomon

(1 Kings 4:30-34).

In addition to his great wisdom, Solomon also had a staggering amount of wealth.

Each year Solomon received about 25 tons of gold. This did not include the additional revenue he received from merchants and traders, all the kings of Arabia, and the governors of the land. King Solomon made 200 large shields of hammered gold, each weighing more than fifteen pounds. He also made 300 smaller shields of hammered gold, each weighing nearly four pounds. The king placed these shields in the Palace of the

Forest of Lebanon. Then the king made a huge throne, decorated with ivory and overlaid with fine gold

(1 Kings 10:14-18).

A few verses later we discover that no other throne in the world could be compared to Solomon's (see 1 Kings 10:20). His was a life of unrestrained opulence. We also read:

All of King Solomon's drinking cups were solid gold, as were all the utensils in the Palace of the Forest of Lebanon. They were not made of silver, for silver was considered worthless in Solomon's day! The king had a fleet of trading ships of Tarshish that sailed with Hiram's fleet. Once every three years the ships returned, loaded with gold, silver, ivory, apes, and peacocks. So King Solomon became richer and wiser than any other king on earth. People from every nation came to consult him and to hear the wisdom God had given him. Year after year everyone who visited brought him gifts of silver and gold, clothing, weapons, spices, horses, and mules

(1 Kings 10:21-25).

By all appearances, Solomon was the man who had everything. But the stark reality is that he blew it. Though he was a success by every human standard, in his latter days we discover that he walked in blatant areas of disobedience and that his heart was turned away after other gods. Scripture states that he did evil in the sight of God, and that God was angry with him (see 1 Kings 11:1-10).

Though Solomon possessed and articulated wisdom, he did not allow that wisdom to govern his own life. Solomon may be considered one of Israel's great kings, but he had serious flaws in his life. Jesus alone is sinless and spotless, and he reigns eternally as the perfect king.

JESUS—GREATER THAN THE TEMPLE

Referring to himself, Jesus states, *"I tell you,* **there is one here who is even greater than the Temple!***"* (Matthew 12:6). Another time, Jesus was challenged by the religious leaders. He responded, *"Destroy this temple, and in three days I will raise it up"* (John 2:19). Of course, people misunderstood what Jesus was saying, but John clarified that he was not speaking about the great edifice in Jerusalem, but rather his own physical body (see John 2:21-22).

In the Revelation, John describes the new Jerusalem that descends from Heaven. After describing its glory and splendor, John writes:

> *I saw no temple in the city, for the Lord God Almighty and the Lamb are its temple. And the city has no need of sun or moon, for the glory of God illuminates the city, and the Lamb is its light*
>
> (Revelation 21:22-23).

In the Old Testament, people went to Jerusalem to worship at a physical structure, but today and throughout eternity, we come to and through Jesus to worship. The Old Testament temple was full of types and shadows, but in Jesus we find all the substance and reality.

JESUS—GREATER THAN THE SABBATH

For the Son of Man is Lord, even over the Sabbath!

(Matthew 12:8)

It was in the immediate context of Jesus' remarks about him being greater than the Temple that he claimed to be Lord even of the Sabbath. The Sabbath was originally given as a mercy to mankind—to provide a day of rest. However, dozens of man-made regulations had been added to what God originally said, and it had become something God never intended it to be.

Right after Jesus made this statement, he healed a man on the Sabbath (see Matthew 12:9-14) and it infuriated the Pharisees to the point that they began discussing a plan to kill Jesus. They loved their rules and regulations more than they loved a man with a deformed hand being healed. It never even dawned on them to rejoice over a person receiving mercy from God. It was contrary to their religious nature to accept Jesus' words: *"Yes, the law permits a person to do good on the Sabbath"* (Matthew 12:12). Jesus delighted in mercy more than legalistic compliance to man-made rules.

Jesus understood the heart of God like no one else and, therefore, was able to accurately interpret the law. Five different times in the fifth chapter of Matthew, Jesus said, *"You have heard that it was said.... But I say to you."*[17] He took statements that perhaps had been misunderstood or misapplied, and expressed God's true intentions. In many cases, he took statements that had only been applied externally and applied them instead to hearts of men.

JESUS—GREATER THAN JONAH

When Jesus was asked to provide a miraculous sign to validate himself, he replied:

> *Only an evil, adulterous generation would demand a miraculous sign; but the only sign I will give them is the sign of the prophet Jonah. For as Jonah*

was in the belly of the great fish for three days and three nights, so will the Son of Man be in the heart of the earth for three days and three nights. The people of Nineveh will stand up against this generation on judgment day and condemn it, for they repented of their sins at the preaching of Jonah. **Now someone greater than Jonah is here**—*but you refuse to repent*
(Matthew 12:39-41).

The comparison Jesus emphasized was the "three days and three nights" that Jonah spent in the belly of the great fish and that Messiah would spend in the belly of the earth. The time Jonah spent in the belly of the fish was because of his own disobedience. The time Jesus spent in the belly of the earth following his time on the cross was for our disobedience.

Jesus' superiority to Jonah is revealed in other ways. For example, Jonah initially disobeyed God's call to Nineveh and later went with reluctance. Jesus, however, did the Father's will with absolute willingness. When the Jonah's audience repented, he was angry and upset (see Jonah 4:1-3). When Jesus' listeners refused to repent, he wept with compassion (see Matthew 23:27; Luke 19:41).

JESUS—GREATER THAN JOHN THE BAPTIST

John the Baptist recognized the superiority of Jesus. John said, "**someone is coming soon who is greater than I am**—*so much greater that I'm not worthy even to be his slave and carry his sandals*" (Matthew 3:11).

To borrow some entertainment lingo, John the Baptist was the "opening act," while Jesus was the "main event." That is not to say that John the Baptist was unimportant; he was a vital part of God's plan. John simply understood that his role was preparatory and supportive to that of Jesus. Though John's ministry preceded Jesus' chronologically, John boldly affirmed the primacy of Jesus and his ministry. When John learned that the number of Jesus' followers had surpassed his own, he responded:

You yourselves know how plainly I told you, 'I am not the Messiah. I am only here to prepare the way for him.' It is the bridegroom who marries the bride, and the bridegroom's friend is simply glad to stand with him and hear his vows. Therefore, I am filled with joy at his success. He must become greater and greater, and I must become less and less

(John 3:28-30).

The apostle John said that John the Baptist *"was not the light; he was simply a witness to tell about the light"* (John 1:8). Because of his own dynamic impact, John the Baptist was questioned regarding his identity. He put to rest any speculation about him being the Messiah with a direct denial (see John 1:20). He proceeded to emphasize his preparatory role as a forerunner to the Messiah by quoting from the book of Isaiah: *"I am a voice shouting in the wilderness, 'Clear the way for the Lord's coming!'"* (John 1:23).

JESUS IN THE BOOK OF HEBREWS

Jesus' supremacy is taught in so many places throughout the New Testament, but the book of Hebrews has an especially high concentration of contrasts between Jesus and other great spiritual figures.

JESUS—GREATER THAN THE ANGELS

Hebrews 1:4 tells us, "***The Son is far greater than the angels****, just as the name God gave him is greater than their names."* Though Jesus intrinsically was *"far greater than the angels"* (Hebrews 1:4), we discover that he was *"made a little lower than the angels, for the suffering of death"* (Hebrews 2:9 NKJV). This will make more sense as we study the incarnation—his taking upon himself human nature.

While Jesus lived and functioned as a man during his time on earth, angels came and ministered to him when he was in need (see Matthew 4:11 and Luke 22:43). And yet Jesus is the one who had created the angels (see Colossians 1:15-16). Angels are servants, but Christ is the exalted Son. Christ was and is worshiped, but true angels refuse to be worshiped (see Revelation 22:8-9).

JESUS—GREATER THAN HIS COMPANIONS

Speaking of the Son, we discover that God anointed Jesus *"with the oil of exultant joy and gladness **above and beyond Your companions**"* (Hebrews 1:9 AMPC).

Who were Jesus' companions? In John 15:15 he said to his disciples, *"Now you are my friends, since I have told you everything the Father told me."* Jesus deeply loved and appreciated his disciples and at their last meal together before his crucifixion, he told them, *"You have stayed with me in my time of trial"* (Luke 22:28).

Some of those who companied with Jesus were called as preachers and were given a measure of the Holy Spirit's anointing for their work, but Jesus alone had *"the Spirit without limit"* (John 3:34). Peter, Mary, John, and many others were great followers of Jesus, but Jesus is the one who will receive our worship in Heaven. Those wonderful children of God and countless others will humbly bow with us before the Throne of God and of the Lamb.

JESUS—GREATER THAN MOSES

Jesus has been found worthy of greater honor than Moses

(Hebrews 3:3 NIV).

For the law was given through Moses; grace and truth came through Jesus Christ

(John 1:17 NIV).

Unfortunately, some people see Moses and Jesus as being in opposition to one another, as though they were somehow adversaries. As we discussed earlier in the second chapter, Jesus did not come to abolish the law, but to fulfill it. Consider what happened in Jesus' experience referred to as his transfiguration.

Jesus took Peter, John, and James up on a mountain to pray. And as he was praying, the appearance of his face was transformed, and his clothes became dazzling white. Suddenly, two men, Moses and Elijah, appeared and began talking with Jesus. They were glorious to see. And they were speaking about his exodus from this world, which was about to be fulfilled in Jerusalem

(Luke 9:28-31).

What is described here is certainly an exceptional, way-out-of-the-ordinary kind of happening.

Moses and Elijah, who had died centuries before, appeared to Jesus and they spoke about his impending death. Jesus had come to fulfill the law and the prophets (see Matthew 5:17). Moses represented the law, and Elijah represented the prophets. Wouldn't you love to have overheard that conversation? Moses and Elijah were certainly great men, but like John the Baptist, they were forerunners. They had paved the way for Jesus. Hebrews 3:5-6 proceeds to explain, *"Moses was certainly faithful in God's house as a servant. His work was an illustration of the truths God would reveal later. But Christ, as the Son, is in charge of God's entire house."*

Even though Jesus was greater, we never want to minimize the greatness of these other men. Not only did Jesus visit with these two men on the Mount of Transfiguration, but the collaborative nature of Moses and Jesus is referred together in the final book of Scripture. As you read the following, remember that this is what John saw happening in Heaven!

> *And they were singing the song of Moses, the servant of God, and the song of the Lamb: "Great and marvelous are your works, O Lord God, the Almighty. Just and true are your ways, O King of the nations"*
>
> (Revelation 15:3).

Moses and Elijah were great men, but they will be worshiping God and the Lamb together alongside of us in Heaven.

JESUS—BROUGHT A BETTER HOPE

The coming of Jesus involved *"the bringing in of **a better hope**"* (Hebrews 7:19 NKJV). Let's look at this in more detail.

> *Yes, the old requirement about the priesthood was set aside because it was weak and useless. For the law never made anything perfect. But now we have confidence in a better hope, through which we draw near to God*
>
> (Hebrews 7:18-19).

The law of Moses had a certain hope in that it pointed toward a future Savior. All the sacrifices of the Old Testament, the untold thousands of animals whose blood was shed, never provided the ultimate solution to the sin problem. They only prefigured the one who would come—the true Lamb of God who would, in fact and in substance, take away the sins of the world. Those living under the Old Covenant had "hope prophesied," but because Jesus has already come and accomplished the great work of redemption, we have "hope materialized."

JESUS—THE GUARANTEE OF A BETTER COVENANT

Jesus is the one who guarantees this better covenant with God

(Hebrews 7:22).

He personally stands behind and ensures that the covenant God has established with us will stand.

JESUS—A SUPERIOR MINISTRY, A FAR BETTER COVENANT, BETTER PROMISES

From Hebrews 8:6 we learn that Jesus "*has been given **a ministry that is far superior** to the old priesthood*" and that he "*mediates for us **a far better covenant** with God, based on **better promises**.*"

Centuries before, the prophet Jeremiah spoke of the day when God would establish a new and better covenant.

"But this is the new covenant I will make with the people of Israel after those days," says the Lord. "I will put my instructions deep within them, and I will write them on their hearts. I will be their God, and they will be my people"

(Jeremiah 31:33).

JESUS—ENTERED A GREATER, MORE PERFECT TABERNACLE

Unlike the Old Testament priests who entered a structure made by men, Jesus *"has entered that **greater, more perfect Tabernacle** in heaven"* (Hebrews 9:11).

The Tabernacle and Temple of the Old Testament were prophetic pictures, symbolic of the coming Messiah and his work. Whereas the high priests of the Old Testament would enter the holy of holies annually on earth, Jesus entered into Heaven itself. The very next verse reads:

> *With his own blood—not the blood of goats and calves—he entered the Most Holy Place once for all time and secured our redemption forever*
>
> (Hebrews 9:12).

JESUS—THE FAR BETTER SACRIFICE

The Old Covenant required animal sacrifices, but Jesus gave himself as the ultimate sacrifice.

> *But the real things in heaven had to be purified with **far better sacrifices** than the blood of animals*
>
> (Hebrews 9:23).

The Old Testament sacrifices did not have ultimate power to redeem us. That is why they had to be offered repeatedly, year after year.

*The sacrifices under that system were repeated **again and again**, year after year, but they were never able to provide perfect cleansing for those who came to worship*

(Hebrews 10:1).

*Under the old covenant, the priest stands and ministers before the altar day after day, offering the same sacrifices **again and again**, which can never take away sins*

(Hebrews 10:11).

But when Jesus presented himself as the perfect sacrifice, he did not have to do it repeatedly. Because it was efficacious, his single sacrifice took care of all of our sins.

*Unlike those other high priests, he does not need to offer sacrifices every day... But Jesus did this **once for all** when he offered himself as the sacrifice for the people's sins*

(Hebrews 7:27).

*With his own blood—not the blood of goats and calves—he entered the Most Holy Place **once for all** time and secured our redemption forever*

(Hebrews 9:12).

*And he [Jesus] did not enter heaven to offer himself **again and again**, like the high priest here on earth who enters the Most Holy Place **year after year** with the blood of an animal. If that had been necessary, Christ would have had to die **again and again**, ever since the world began. But now, **once for all time**, he has appeared at the end of the age*

*to remove sin by his own death as a sacrifice. ...Christ was offered **once
for all** time as a sacrifice to take away the sins of many people*

(Hebrews 9:25-26, 28).

*Christ suffered for our sins **once for all time***

(1 Peter 3:18).

When Solomon dedicated the Temple, 22,000 cattle and 120,000 sheep and goats were sacrificed (see 1 Kings 8:63). Countless sacrifices were offered in the years to come. When God redeemed fallen humanity, his only Son was offered up.

The summation of these many comparisons and contrasts is clear and consistent. The Old Testament sacrifices provided a temporary benefit—not an ultimate benefit. Jesus' sacrificial work on Calvary was absolutely sufficient, and because he is the "far better sacrifice," his redemptive provision on our behalf was done "once and for all."

JESUS—HIS BLOOD SPEAKS A BETTER WORD

Whereas Abel's blood cried out for vengeance, Christ's blood cries out for mercy. Hebrews 12:24 (NIV) refers to:

*Jesus the mediator of a new covenant, and to the sprinkled blood that **speaks a better word** than the blood of Abel.*

Another translation states:

To Jesus, the Mediator (Go-between, Agent) of a new covenant, and to the sprinkled blood which speaks [of mercy], a better and nobler and more gracious message than the blood of Abel [which cried out for vengeance]

(Hebrews 12:24 AMPC).

JESUS—EXALTED IN HEAVEN

Finally, we see Jesus' centrality, uniqueness, and supremacy in the Bible's final book. John is supernaturally enabled to witness a dramatic and moving scene in Heaven itself. The apostle sees a sealed scroll in Heaven and hears a loud voice asking who is worthy to open that scroll and to read its contents. John notes that *"no one in heaven or on earth or under the earth was able to open the scroll and read it"* (Revelation 5:3).

John proceeds to weep loudly because no one was worthy, but his mourning is interrupted. *"But one of the twenty-four elders said to me, 'Stop weeping! Look, the Lion of the tribe of Judah, the heir to David's throne, has won the victory. He is worthy to open the scroll and its seven seals'"* (Revelation 5:5). When no one else was worthy, Jesus was. Yesterday, today, and throughout eternity, Jesus remains the unique Person in the universe. He alone is worthy, and he reigns supreme!

SO, WHAT DO WE MAKE OF THIS?

The Bible makes no provision whatsoever for Jesus being *just* a great man, *just* a great teacher, or *just* a great prophet. Scripture portrays Jesus as entirely unique, matchless, and without equal. He is exalted above all others. He is supreme and superior. He is greater, "better than," and in a class by himself.

Will we accept the testimony of Scripture, or will we reject it? Was Jesus lying about who he was? Was he deceived and a deceiver? Was John the Baptist mistaken? Were the apostles Paul and John deluded? What about the countless others who gave their lives as martyrs because they believed that Jesus was unique, and that he had done something no one else had ever done? Were they also deceived?

In later chapters, we will learn more about the exact nature of Jesus' centrality, supremacy, and uniqueness, but the Bible makes it entirely and indisputably clear: Jesus was and remains in a class by himself.

QUOTES

"Christ is not something added to the world as an extra, he is not an embellishment, a king as we now crown kings, the owner of a great estate… He is the alpha and the omega, the principle and the end, the foundation stone and the keystone, the plenitude and the plenifier. He is the one who consummates all things and gives them their consistence."

—Pierre Teilhard De Chardin (1881–1955)

"To the early Christians Jesus was the central theme of the Old Testament revelation, which indeed reached its fulfillment in him as the Messiah."

—F. F. Bruce (1910–1990)

"Jesus is the thread that holds all Scripture together. He is the prism that breaks forth its multifaceted colors. He is the lens that puts all of it in focus, the switch that sheds light on its dimly lit quarters, and the key that unlocks its meaning and riches."[18]

—Leonard Sweet (1961–) and Frank Viola (1964–)

QUESTIONS FOR REFLECTION AND DISCUSSION

1. Did you learn something new about Jesus in this chapter? Describe what you learned.

2. Did something you already knew about Jesus become strengthened or reinforced? Describe it.

3. Do you agree with this chapter's premise, that Jesus is the central theme of Scripture? With so many themes in the Bible, how would you explain this statement to someone else?

4. This chapter presented Jesus being greater than Abraham, Jacob, Solomon, etc. How would you explain to someone seeking truth or to a new believer as to why Jesus is greater than all other biblical characters?

5. Review the bullet point list breaking down Paul's teaching about Jesus in Colossians 1:15-20. Of all those descriptions, which is most powerful to you? Are any of those descriptions challenging or difficult to comprehend?

6. A premise of this chapter is that Jesus, relative to all other beings, is in a class by himself and is the unique person of the universe. Do you agree? How would you explain that to someone else?

7. Did anything you read in this chapter change the way you will relate to Jesus? If so, how?

Chapter Five

FORETOLD: PROPHETIC WORDS AND PICTURES

"The beloved prophets made their proclamations with a view toward him."
—Ignatius of Antioch (?–117)

Expectant parents often share their joy with friends, telling in advance the wonderful news that a baby will be welcomed into their home. Parents, though, usually don't try to spell out details about the baby's future life. While they may have certain hopes and dreams, they realize they simply don't know all that will unfold as the child grows into adulthood. After all, they are only human and are not omniscient.

In contrast, God not only foreknew and announced the coming of his Son to earth but possessed and articulated precise knowledge regarding the intricate details of all that Jesus would accomplish, and he did this hundreds of years prior to Jesus' arrival here on earth. He supernaturally communicated numerous details about Jesus' life over many centuries leading up to his birth. These communications took place through two primary means, *prophetic words* and *prophetic pictures*.

Let's examine how God revealed—generation after generation—pieces of the puzzle that would eventually come together to provide a vivid and unerring depiction of why he would be sending his Son into the earth and what he would achieve.

PROPHETIC WORDS

Many people think that prophecy in the Old Testament was exclusively about the prediction of future events, but while some prophecies involved *foretelling*, a much larger percentage involved *forthtelling*. In other words, many of the declarations and teachings of the Old Testament prophets addressed current situations facing the people of God in the very day in which they lived.

We learn a very valuable lesson about the nature of prophecy—the foretelling kind—from what Jesus told his disciples in John 14:29: *"I have told you these things before they happen so that when they do happen, you will believe."* It seems like Jesus is saying that some things will be better understood through the rearview mirror, but God communicates enough information ahead of time so that we will later understand that he knew all the time what was happening.

When it comes to predictions about Jesus prior to his birth, we would like it if a single prophet had said something like, "On [exact date], the Messiah will be born in in a stable at [exact address] in Bethlehem of Judea to a young couple from Nazareth named Joseph and Mary. At the age of thirty, he will begin his public ministry and will preach, teach, and heal until religious authorities become incensed at him, make false accusations, and collaborate with the civil leaders who will carry out his execution by means of crucifixion. He will later be resurrected and ascend into Heaven."

If you know the Bible, you know that prophecy doesn't work that way. Rather, multiple hints or clues were given through various prophets over centuries. None of the prophecies communicated everything that could have been said, but all of them provided a piece of the puzzle. Paul also taught something important about the nature of prophecy when he said, *"Now our knowledge is partial and incomplete"* (1 Corinthians 13:9).

I'm sure you've heard the phrase, "Hindsight is 20/20." Today, as we look back at the life of Jesus as recorded in the four Gospels, it is easy to marvel at God's wisdom and foreknowledge in providing so many predictions about what his Son was to accomplish during his years on earth. When we study Scripture and recognize these things, we understand that Jesus was walking out a master plan and that nothing caught him or the Father by surprise.

In Matthew's Gospel, nine times we find the phrase, *"that it might be fulfilled"* relative to various happenings in Jesus' life.[19] Jesus knew he was fulfilling various prophecies from the Old Testament as indicated by another statement he made relative to his impending death: *"For the Son of Man must die, as the Scriptures declared long ago"* (Matthew 26:24).

Peter understood that the assignment the apostles received from Jesus was simply a continuation, not only of Jesus' ministry but of the entire prophetic scenario that had been building and developing for centuries. Consider what Peter said when he spoke to those of Cornelius' household.

And he ordered us to preach everywhere and to testify that Jesus is the one appointed by God to be the judge of all—the living and the dead.

He is the one all the prophets testified about, saying that everyone who believes in him will have their sins forgiven through his name

(Acts 10:42-43).

Just how many prophecies were there in the Old Testament about Jesus coming as the Savior? Author Doug Powell notes:

By some counts there are 300 to 400 messianic prophecies in the Old Testament. Other scholars believe that this number is a bit high. They certainly see that number of allusions to the Messiah, but count the major prophecies as less than 100. *The Holman Illustrated Bible Dictionary* lists 121 fulfilled messianic prophecies.[20]

What did the prophets testify concerning Jesus, and what are some of the specific prophecies that Jesus fulfilled? Here are just a few examples.

I. THE MESSIAH WILL BE THE SEED OF ABRAHAM

PROPHESIED:

In your seed all the nations of the earth shall be blessed

(Genesis 22:18 NKJV).

FULFILLED:

Now to Abraham and his Seed were the promises made. He does not say, "And to seeds," as of many, but as of one, "And to your Seed," who is Christ

(Galatians 3:16 NKJV).

2. THE MESSIAH WILL BE BORN INTO THE ROYAL LINE OF DAVID

PROPHESIED:

For a child is born to us, a son is given to us. The government will rest on his shoulders. And he will be called: Wonderful Counselor, Mighty God, Everlasting Father, Prince of Peace. His government and its peace will never end. He will rule with fairness and justice from the throne of his ancestor David for all eternity

(Isaiah 9:6-7).

FULFILLED:

This is a record of the ancestors of Jesus the Messiah, a descendant of David and of Abraham

(Matthew 1:1).

And it is one of King David's descendants, Jesus, who is God's promised Savior of Israel!

(Acts 13:23)

3. THE MESSIAH WILL BE BORN IN BETHLEHEM

PROPHESIED:

Bethlehem Ephrathah, though you are little among the thousands of Judah, yet out of you shall come forth to Me the One to be Ruler in Israel

(Micah 5:2 NKJV).

FULFILLED:

Jesus was born in Bethlehem of Judea in the days of Herod the king

(Matthew 2:1 NKJV).

4. THE MESSIAH WILL BE BORN OF A VIRGIN

PROPHESIED:

The Lord himself will give you the sign. Look! The virgin will conceive a child! She will give birth to a son and will call him Immanuel (which means "God is with us")

(Isaiah 7:14).

FULFILLED:

"Don't be afraid, Mary," the angel told her, "for you have found favor with God. You will conceive and give birth to a son, and you will name him Jesus." …Mary asked the angel, "But how can this happen? I am a virgin." The angel replied, "The Holy Spirit will come upon you, and the power of the Most High will overshadow you. So the baby to be born will be holy, and he will be called the Son of God"

(Luke 1:30-31, 34-35).

5. THE MESSIAH WILL BE PRECEDED BY A FORERUNNER

PROPHESIED:

Listen! It's the voice of someone shouting, "Clear the way through the wilderness for the Lord! Make a straight highway through the wasteland for our God!"

(Isaiah 40:3)

FULFILLED:

In those days John the Baptist came to the Judean wilderness and began preaching. His message was, "Repent of your sins and turn to God, for the Kingdom of Heaven is near." The prophet Isaiah was speaking about John when he said, "He is a voice shouting in the wilderness, 'Prepare the way for the Lord's coming! Clear the road for him!'"

(Matthew 3:1-3)

6. THE MESSIAH'S ANOINTING WILL RESULT IN MANY BEING SET FREE

PROPHESIED:

The Spirit of the Sovereign Lord is upon me, for the Lord has anointed me to bring good news to the poor. He has sent me to comfort the brokenhearted and to proclaim that captives will be released and prisoners will be freed

(Isaiah 61:1).

FULFILLED:

The scroll of Isaiah the prophet was handed to him. He unrolled the scroll and found the place where this was written: "The Spirit of the Lord is upon me, for he has anointed me to bring Good News to the poor. He has sent me to proclaim that captives will be released, that the blind will see, that the oppressed will be set free"

(Luke 4:17-19).

It could be argued that anyone could cite an Old Testament prophecy and claim to be its fulfillment. The difference is that Jesus backed up his words with his actions. His were not empty words, but the countless people who were liberated, set free, delivered, and healed were living testimonies to Jesus being exactly who he claimed to be. Even today, millions can still testify of Jesus' saving and liberating power.

7. THE MESSIAH WILL HAVE A TRIUMPHAL ENTRY INTO JERUSALEM

PROPHESIED:

Rejoice, O people of Zion! Shout in triumph, O people of Jerusalem! Look, your king is coming to you. He is righteous and victorious, yet he is humble, riding on a donkey—riding on a donkey's colt

(Zechariah 9:9).

FULFILLED:

The next day, the news that Jesus was on the way to Jerusalem swept through the city. A large crowd of Passover visitors took palm branches and went down the road to meet him. They shouted, "Praise God! Blessings on the one who comes in the name of the Lord! Hail to the King of Israel!" Jesus found a young donkey and rode on it

(John 12:12-14).

8. THE MESSIAH WILL BE REJECTED BY MEN

PROPHESIED:

He was despised and rejected—a man of sorrows, acquainted with deepest grief

(Isaiah 53:3).

The stone that the builders rejected has now become the cornerstone

(Psalm 118:22).

FULFILLED:

He came to his own people, and even they rejected him

(John 1:11).

You are coming to Christ, who is the living cornerstone of God's temple.
He was rejected by people, but he was chosen by God for great honor

(1 Peter 2:4).

9. DAVID PORTRAYED THE MESSIAH'S SUFFERINGS

PROPHESIED:

My God, my God, why have you abandoned me? …My enemies sur-
round me like a pack of dogs; an evil gang closes in on me. They have
pierced my hands and feet. I can count all my bones. My enemies stare
at me and gloat. They divide my garments among themselves and throw
dice for my clothing

(Psalm 22:1,16-18).

Another prophet confirmed David's words that Messiah's hands
and feet would be pierced:

They will look on me whom they have pierced and mourn for him as
for an only son

(Zechariah 12:10).

FULFILLED:

At about three o'clock, Jesus called out with a loud voice, "Eli, Eli,
lema sabachthani?" which means "My God, my God, why have you
abandoned me?"

(Matthew 27:46)

Jesus referenced his pierced hands and feet after his crucifixion when
he said:

Look at my hands. Look at my feet. You can see that it's really me

(Luke 24:39).

When the soldiers had crucified Jesus, they divided his clothes among the four of them. They also took his robe, but it was seamless, woven in one piece from top to bottom. So they said, "Rather than tearing it apart, let's throw dice for it." This fulfilled the Scripture that says, "They divided my garments among themselves and threw dice for my clothing." So that is what they did

(John 19:23-24).

10. ISAIAH PORTRAYED THE MESSIAH'S SUFFERINGS

PROPHESIED:

Yet it was our weaknesses he carried; it was our sorrows that weighed him down. And we thought his troubles were a punishment from God, a punishment for his own sins! But he was pierced for our rebellion, crushed for our sins. He was beaten so we could be whole. He was whipped so we could be healed. …He was oppressed and treated harshly, yet he never said a word. He was led like a lamb to the slaughter. And as a sheep is silent before the shearers, he did not open his mouth

(Isaiah 53:4-5,7).

FULFILLED:

He did not retaliate when he was insulted, nor threaten revenge when he suffered. He left his case in the hands of God, who always judges fairly. He personally carried our sins in his body on the cross so that we can be dead to sin and live for what is right. By his wounds you are healed

(1 Peter 2:23-24).

The clarity and thoroughness of Isaiah's prophetic statements, including what is referenced above, are worth expanding upon. Anyone who knows the story of Jesus' crucifixion will marvel at Isaiah's laser precision in describing what Jesus would be experiencing more than 700 years before he would stand trial before Pilate. For example:

- His face will be disfigured (Isaiah 52:14).
- He will be hated and rejected (Isaiah 53:3).
- He will be a man of sorrows and acquainted with intense grief (Isaiah 53:3).
- He will carry our weaknesses and our sorrows (Isaiah 53:4).
- He will be *"pierced for our rebellion"* and *"crushed for our sins"* (Isaiah 53:5).
- He will be beaten and whipped so we could be whole and healed (Isaiah 53:5).
- God will lay all on him all of our sins (Isaiah 53:6).
- In spite of oppressive, harsh treatment, he will remain silent (Isaiah 53:7).
- He will be condemned unfairly (Isaiah 53:8).
- He will be pure and innocent (Isaiah 53:9).
- *"They intended to bury him with criminals, but he ended up in a rich man's tomb"* (Isaiah 53:9 NET).
- His life will be a sin offering (Isaiah 53:10).
- He will bear the sins of people so they could be made righteous (Isaiah 53:11).
- He will pray for rebels and transgressors (Isaiah 53:12).

In those fourteen powerful statements, Isaiah painted a prophetic masterpiece that Jesus would fulfill in a level of detail that only God could have foreseen.

II. THE MESSIAH WILL BE RESURRECTED

PROPHESIED:

For you will not leave my soul among the dead or allow your holy one to rot in the grave

(Psalm 16:10).

FULFILLED:

He isn't here! He is risen from the dead, just as he said would happen
(Matthew 28:6).

God released him from the horrors of death and raised him back to life, for death could not keep him in its grip

(Acts 2:24).

12. THE MESSIAH WILL BECOME THE FOUNDATION OF A GREAT NEW WORK OF GOD

PROPHESIED:

David said, "The stone that the builders rejected has now become the cornerstone. This is the Lord's doing, and it is wonderful to see"
(Psalm 118:22-23).

Isaiah reiterated this theme.

Therefore, this is what the Sovereign Lord says: "Look! I am placing a foundation stone in Jerusalem, a firm and tested stone. It is a precious cornerstone that is safe to build on. Whoever believes need never be shaken"
(Isaiah 28:16).

FULFILLED:

Jesus applied the Psalm 118 passage to himself in Matthew 21:42. Paul referred to Jesus as the cornerstone in Ephesians 2:20, and Peter did the same multiple times (see 1 Peter 2:4,6-7).

> *You are coming to Christ, who is the living cornerstone of God's temple.*
> *He was rejected by people, but he was chosen by God for great honor.*
> (Acts 4:11).

The cornerstone was the first, largest, and most important stone laid in the foundation. From the cornerstone, all the direction and measurements for the building were established. In order for the walls, corners, and all aspects of the building to be correct, everything had to be properly aligned with the cornerstone. Likewise, for the church to be solid and healthy, all must be properly aligned to the Lord Jesus Christ.

PROPHETIC PICTURES

Imagine with me that a couple is going to give their child a bicycle for Christmas. Though they might not tell the child outright that he is going to receive a bicycle, perhaps for fun they might drop some hints. A few weeks before Christmas, for example, they might get the child a miniature toy replica of a bike. They might also point out similar bicycles as they are driving in the car together. When the child actually receives the bicycle on Christmas day, he would recognize that his parents' "teases" and the hints they had dropped were simply foretastes of the gift he had just received.

Just like the miniature toy replica of the bicycle spoke of the future gift, God also provided many "prophetic pictures" of Jesus long before his arrival in Bethlehem. Often referred to as "types and shadows," these are not verbally articulated promises (like the prophecies we've examined), but are like object lessons or visual illustrations given in advance. They painted pictures that spoke powerfully of the anticipated Messiah and his mission.

The author of Hebrews writes, *"The old system under the law of Moses was only a shadow, a dim preview of the good things to come, not the good things themselves"* (Hebrews 10:1). A "preview" is a good way to think of these prophetic pictures. We are talking about someone (or something) who appears in the Old Testament who prefigures someone (or something) who would later appear in the New Testament. In other words, a type "is an actual historical event or person that in some ways symbolizes or anticipates a later occurrence; particularly an Old Testament foreshadowing of a New Testament event."[21]

Noted Bible teacher of yesteryear Arthur T. Pierson (1837–1911) shared rich insights about the prophetic pictures of Christ in the Old Testament.

> The Word of God is a picture gallery, and it is adorned with tributes to the blessed Christ of God the Savior of mankind. Here a prophetic portrait of the coming One, and there an historic portrayal of Him who has come, here a typical sacrifice, and there the bleeding Lamb to whom all sacrifice looked forward; here a person or an event that foreshadowed the greatest of persons and the events that are the turning points of history; now a parable, a poem, an object lesson, and then a simple narration or exposition or explanation, that fills

with divine meaning the mysteries that have hid their meaning for ages, waiting for the key that should unlock them.

But, in whatever form or fashion, whatever guise of fact or fancy, prophecy or history, parable or miracle, type or antitype, allegory or narrative, a discerning eye may everywhere find Him—God's appointed Messiah, God's anointed Christ… All that is glorious is but a phase of His infinite excellence, and so all truth and holiness, found in the Holy Scripture, are only a new tribute to Him who is the Truth, the Holy One of God.[22]

With all this in mind, let's explore some of the prophetic pictures in the Old Testament that prefigured and prophetically illustrated the person and work of the Lord Jesus Christ.

ADAM PROPHETICALLY FORESHADOWED CHRIST

Adam foreshadows Christ in that he was the head of a race—the human race. Jesus is also the head of a race—all those born of God as new creatures. Sin came into the world through Adam. Righteousness came into the world through Jesus.

Now Adam is a symbol, a representation of Christ, who was yet to come. But there is a great difference between Adam's sin and God's gracious gift. For the sin of this one man, Adam, brought death to many. But even greater is God's wonderful grace and his gift of forgiveness to many through this other man, Jesus Christ

(Romans 5:14-15).

Just as everyone dies because we all belong to Adam, everyone who belongs to Christ will be given new life. ...The Scriptures tell us, "The first man, Adam, became a living person." But the last Adam—that is, Christ—is a life-giving Spirit

(1 Corinthians 15:22,45).

In short, Adam's disobedience brought death to mankind, while Jesus' obedience brings life to all who believe in him.

NOAH'S ARK PROPHETICALLY FORESHADOWED CHRIST

Jesus said that when he returns, conditions on earth will be like they were in the days of Noah (see Matthew 24:37). This paints a grim picture because in Noah's time, wickedness, violence, and corruption were rampant (see Genesis 6:5, 12). God used Noah, through the building of a great boat, to save his family when the rest of humanity was destroyed in a flood (see 2 Peter 2:5; Hebrews 11:7).

Peter indicates that Noah's Ark brought salvation to all who entered it, typifying the saving work Christ accomplished through his death, burial, and resurrection (see 1 Peter 3:18-22). Just as God used a wooden boat to rescue all who entered it in the ancient world, God used a wooden cross to save all who put their faith in Christ today. Then, only those who entered into the Ark were saved. Today, only those who enter into Christ through faith are saved.

ABRAHAM OFFERING UP ISAAC PROPHETICALLY FORESHADOWED CHRIST

In the fourth chapter of Romans, Paul gives an overview of how Abraham and Sarah believed God's promise for a son even when they were beyond the age of child-bearing (see also Hebrews 11:7).

Several years after Isaac was born, God issued a remarkable challenge. He told Abraham, *"Take your son, your only son—yes, Isaac, whom you love so much—and go to the land of Moriah. Go and sacrifice him as a burnt offering on one of the mountains, which I will show you"* (Genesis 22:2).

As Abraham sought to obey God in this most unusual case, the angel of the Lord told Abraham to stop—to not go through with it. Abraham had passed the test in showing that he was willing to obey God completely, and in doing so he had pre-enacted God offering his only Son on Calvary. Abraham was willing to offer his only son as a sacrifice, but God actually did offer his only Son, Jesus, as a sacrifice for all of our sins.

JOSEPH PROPHETICALLY FORESHADOWED CHRIST

There are many parallels between the lives of Joseph, the son of Jacob, and that of Jesus.

BOTH WERE HIGHLY FAVORED OF THEIR FATHER.

- Joseph: *"Jacob loved Joseph more than any of his other children because Joseph had been born to him in his old age"* (Genesis 37:3).
- Jesus: *"This is my dearly loved Son, who brings me great joy"* (Matthew 3:17).

BOTH EXPERIENCED CHALLENGES FROM THEIR BROTHERS.

- Joseph: *"His brothers hated Joseph because their father loved him more than the rest of them. They couldn't say a kind word to him"* (Genesis 37:4).
- Jesus: *"When his family heard what was happening, they tried to take him away. 'He's out of his mind,' they said"* (Mark 3:21); *"even his brothers didn't believe in him"* (John 7:5).

BOTH RESISTED TEMPTATION.

- Joseph: "*How could I do such a wicked thing? It would be a great sin against God*" (Genesis 39:9).
- Jesus: "[Jesus] *was tempted in every way, just as we are—yet he did not sin*" (Hebrews 4:15 NIV).

BOTH EXPERIENCED BETRAYAL AND FALSE ACCUSATIONS.

- Joseph: His brothers sold him into slavery (see Genesis 37:26-28). Potiphar's wife accused him falsely (see Genesis 39:1-20).
- Jesus: Judas betrayed Jesus with a kiss (see Luke 22:47-48). False accusations were leveled against Jesus at his trial (see Mark 14:55-59).

BOTH WERE SOLD (BETRAYED) FOR A PRICE.

- Joseph: Twenty pieces of silver (see Genesis 37:28)
- Jesus: Thirty pieces of silver (see Matthew 26:15)

BOTH WERE EXALTED AFTER MASSIVE SETBACKS.

- Joseph: "*So Pharaoh put Joseph in charge of all Egypt*" (Genesis 41:43).
- Jesus: "*God elevated him to the place of highest honor and gave him the name above all other names*" (Philippians 2:9).

BOTH WERE A SOURCE OF RESCUE AND SALVATION.

- Joseph: After executing his plan and in the midst of great famine:

Joseph opened up the storehouses and distributed grain to the Egyptians, for the famine was severe throughout the land of Egypt. And people from all around came to Egypt to buy grain from Joseph because the famine was severe throughout the world

(Genesis 41:56-57).

- Jesus: Through his death, burial, and resurrection, Jesus made eternal life, acceptance, and all the blessings of God available to all who receive him.

THE SACRIFICIAL LAMB PROPHETICALLY FORESHADOWED CHRIST

John the Baptist referred to Jesus as *"the Lamb of God who takes away the sin of the world!"* (John 1:29). All those who heard that would have immediately thought of the sacrificial lambs that had been offered up through the Old Testament sacrificial system. Before the Israelites departed Egyptian slavery, God had each family select a lamb, and its blood was placed on the sides and tops of the doorframes of their homes (see Exodus 12). As a result, their families were spared from the plague of death that struck the Egyptians.

Hundreds of years after Israel's departure from Egypt, the prophet Isaiah wrote of a future "Suffering Servant" who would come. The 53rd chapter of this prophetic book presents a graphic portrait describing Jesus' death 700 years before he was born in Bethlehem. His description includes this statement:

He was oppressed and treated harshly, yet he never said a word. He was led like a lamb to the slaughter. And as a sheep is silent before the shearers, he did not open his mouth

(Isaiah 53:7).

The New Testament distinctly connects Jesus with these prophetic pictures. Paul wrote, *"Christ, our Passover Lamb, has been sacrificed for us"*

(1 Corinthians 5:7). Peter wrote to believers and said their redemption was based on *"the precious blood of Christ, the sinless, spotless Lamb of God"* (1 Peter 1:19). Later, the apostle John referred to Jesus as *"the Lamb who was slaughtered before the world was made"* (Revelation 13:8).

THE BRONZE SNAKE PROPHETICALLY FORESHADOWED CHRIST

Jesus spoke of a particular prophetic picture that was used to foreshadow himself and his work. *"And as Moses lifted up the bronze snake on a pole in the wilderness, so the Son of Man must be lifted up, so that everyone who believes in him will have eternal life"* (John 3:14-15).

In Numbers 21, many Israelites were dying from poisonous snake bites. At God's direction, *"Moses made a snake out of bronze and attached it to a pole. Then anyone who was bitten by a snake could look at the bronze snake and be healed!"* (Numbers 21:9).

This can seem odd to readers. Why would Jesus (at his own acknowledgement) be symbolized by a bronze serpent? Being held up on a pole seems obvious enough; that speaks of Jesus when he was lifted up on the cross. But a lamb (which was also used to represent Jesus) seems like a far more logical symbol than a serpent. After all, God pronounced a curse on the serpent because of its role in the fall of man (see Genesis 3:14-15).

Jesus certainly was the sinless, spotless Son of God, but on the cross, he was our substitute. Paul writes:

> But Christ has rescued us from the curse pronounced by the law. When he was hung on the cross, he took upon himself the curse for our wrongdoing. For it is written in the Scriptures, "Cursed is everyone who is hung on a tree"

> (Galatians 3:13).

God made him who had no sin to be sin for us, so that in him we might become the righteousness of God

(2 Corinthians 5:21 NIV).

Though Jesus was personally without sin, he represented us on the cross—he was our substitute. He was bearing the punishment and the penalty that our sins deserved. He took upon himself the curse that was ours so we could receive blessing. He took upon himself our sin so that we could become recipients of his righteousness.

MANNA FROM HEAVEN PROPHETICALLY FORESHADOWED CHRIST

As Israel traveled from Egypt, through the wilderness, and toward the Promised Land, God supernaturally fed them and provided for them (see Exodus 16). The manna God provided for them literally was "their daily bread," and it continued to be so until they stepped foot into the land of their inheritance.

The people to whom Jesus ministered requested a miraculous sign, and mentioned that Moses had given the people bread to eat in the wilderness. Jesus clarified who had really provided the manna, and used that to illustrate what God was giving them now.

Moses didn't give you bread from heaven. My Father did. And now he offers you the true bread from heaven. The true bread of God is the one who comes down from heaven and gives life to the world

(John 6:32-33).

Jesus proceeded to tell them that he was, in fact, "*the bread of life*" (John 6:35). What God had provided for the Israelites during their journey through the wilderness was good; it met their natural needs. What God provided through Jesus, the true bread of life, is even better. He meets the deepest and most profound needs of our lives.

THE HIGH PRIEST PROPHETICALLY FORESHADOWED CHRIST

Aaron, the first High Priest, received specific directions about offering sacrifices for the forgiveness of sins on the Day of Atonement (see Leviticus 16). Every year on that day, he and his successors would follow the Lord's instructions and enter the Most Holy Place with blood to secure forgiveness for the people of God. This was only a temporary solution, though, as it had to be done time and again. It was really only a foreshadowing of the ultimate solution that would come through the sacrifice of the Lord Jesus Christ. He is now our true High Priest forever.

> *For Christ did not enter into a holy place made with human hands, which was only a copy of the true one in heaven. He entered into heaven itself to appear now before God on our behalf. And he did not enter heaven to offer himself again and again, like the high priest here on earth who enters the Most Holy Place year after year with the blood of an animal. If that had been necessary, Christ would have had to die again and again, ever since the world began. But now, once for all time, he has appeared at the end of the age to remove sin by his own death as a sacrifice*
>
> (Hebrews 9:24-26).

MELCHIZEDEK PROPHETICALLY FORESHADOWED CHRIST

After Abraham successfully rescued Lot, his nephew, he encountered an intriguing figure named Melchizedek. He is described as *"the king of Salem and a priest of God Most High"* (Genesis 14:18). Notice that he was both a king *and* a priest. Melchizedek brought Abraham bread and wine, and spoke words of blessing over him. In return, *"Abram gave Melchizedek a tenth of all the goods he had recovered"* from the battle (Genesis 14:20). Later, David spoke prophetically and indicated that the Messiah would be *"a priest forever in the order of Melchizedek"* (Psalm 110:4). As a contemporary of Abraham, Melchizedek lived long before the Aaronic priesthood was established; he was not of Jewish lineage.

Though Melchizedek is mentioned limitedly in the Old Testament, he is referred to extensively in the book of Hebrews (chapters 5–7). Aaron was the first high priest in the Levitical system of the Old Testament, and he pre-figured Christ, but only limitedly. There are other aspects of Christ's ministry that are more fully portrayed by the priesthood of Melchizedek, and that is the point made in the book of Hebrews.

The Jews kept meticulous genealogical records regarding the priestly line. For centuries, the priests who were descended from Aaron served, died, and were replaced by successive generations. In that sense, they were all temporary, and the Aaronic priesthood itself was a temporary system. But Jesus, of course, is an eternal High Priest, and that is why Melchizedek, in that sense, prefigured him more accurately.

Regarding Melchizedek, we read, *"There is no record of his father or mother or any of his ancestors—no beginning or end to his life. He remains a priest forever, resembling the Son of God"* (Hebrews 7:3). Some believe that Melchizedek was actually the pre-existent Christ appearing to Abraham. Others believe that Melchizedek was simply *like* Christ, and that his unknown genealogy presents a similarity to Christ having existed from eternity past through eternity future.

Jesus also differed from the Aaronic priesthood in that he was from the tribe of Judah, not from the tribe of Levi. The author of Hebrews states *"Jesus became a priest, not by meeting the physical require-ment of belonging to the tribe of Levi, but by the power of a life that cannot be destroyed"* (Hebrews 7:16). It is in this sense that Melchizedek was a prophetic picture of Christ, and why David prophesied that Jesus would be a priest forever. The perpetuity of Jesus and his priesthood is highlighted further in Hebrews 7:23-24: *"There were many priests under the old system, for death prevented them from remaining in office. But because Jesus lives forever, his priesthood lasts forever."*

As important as Melchizedek's priesthood was, it is important to remember that he was also a king. Aaron and his descendants were limited in how much they could pre-figure Christ because of their temporary tenure as priests, and because they were not royalty. Christ is both our eternal High Priest and our eternal King; thus, he is well represented and concisely pre-figured by Melchizedek. The one who blessed Abraham gave us a beautiful prophetic picture of Jesus.

JONAH PROPHETICALLY FORESHADOWED CHRIST

Jesus referenced Jonah from the Old Testament as an illustration of himself when he said:

> *For as Jonah was in the belly of the great fish for three days and three nights, so will the Son of Man be in the heart of the earth for three days and three nights*
>
> (Matthew 12:40).

In addition to their respective "three days and three nights" experi-ences, both were missionaries sent to people in need of repentance.

Jonah went reluctantly, but Jesus went willingly. Jonah was angry when people received mercy, but Jesus rejoices as people accept God's mercy.

QUOTES

"There is a God in heaven who reveals secrets, and he has shown… what will happen in the future."

—The Prophet Daniel (Daniel 2:28)

"In the person of Moses there is a prefiguring of Christ, who intercedes with the Father, and offers his own soul for the saving of the people."

—Tertullian (160–225)

"If you turn to the Old Testament, you can see him in a vast variety of forms. You can see him as the paschal lamb and as the scapegoat; you can see him at one time as the bullock, strong to labor, and at another time as the lamb, patient to endure; you can see him as the dove, full of innocence; you can see him in the blood sprinkled, in the incense burning, in the laver filled with water, in Aaron's rod that budded, in the golden pot that was full of manna; in the ark, you can see him having the law within his heart; and over the ark, you can see the golden light of the Shekinah above the mercy-seat, and say, 'Christ is here.' In every type, you may see Christ, and in so many different shapes, too, that you can say, 'Turn this whichever way I like, there is always something fresh in it.' Christ, if I may compare so glorious a Person to so humble a thing, is like the kaleidoscope. As often as you look through it, you see a fresh arrangement of colors, and a new design, and, in like manner, as often as you look at the Lord Jesus Christ, you always discover some new beauty in him."[23]

—Charles H. Spurgeon (1834–1892)

"The Bible is God's declaratory revelation to man containing the great truths about God, about man, about history, about salvation, and about prophecy that God wanted us to know. The Bible could be trusted just as much as if God had taken the pen and written the words Himself."

—John Walvoord (1910–2002)

"Peter Stoner, former Professor Emeritus of Science at Westmont College, calculated the probability of one person fulfilling just eight of the major prophecies concerning Messiah. His conservative estimate was one chance in 100,000 trillion (100,000,000,000,000,000). In another calculation, Stoner used 48 prophecies and arrived at the conservative estimate that the probability of 48 prophecies being fulfilled by one person is 10^{157}—that's 1 with 157 zeros trailing behind it! Could Jesus have fulfilled all of the Messianic prophecies by chance? Not a chance!"[24]

—from the *Apologetics Study Bible for Students*

QUESTIONS FOR REFLECTION AND DISCUSSION

1. Did you learn something new about Jesus in this chapter? Describe what you learned.

2. Did something you already knew about Jesus become strengthened or reinforced? Describe it.

3. What does it mean to you that God knows the end from the beginning and is able to prophetically declare what he will do in the future? How does that strengthen your faith?

4. How would you describe the difference between "prophetic words" and "prophetic pictures"? Give an example of each.

5. Review the portion entitled "Isaiah Portrayed the Messiah's Sufferings." How convincing is it to you that God prophetically foretold Jesus' suffering on the cross? How impacting should that be to someone who reads it?

6. Arthur T. Pierson said that "the Word of God is a picture gallery." Describe what you think he meant by that statement.

7. Did anything you read in this chapter change the way you will relate to Jesus? If so, how?

Chapter Six

WITHOUT BEGINNING: THE PRE-EXISTENCE OF JESUS

"Jesus was unique among men in that his birth did not mark His origin, but only his appearance as a man on the stage of time. Of no other person would it be possible to distinguish His birth and His origin....Jesus was the meeting place of eternity and time, the blending of deity and humanity, the junction of heaven and earth."[25]

—Oswald Sanders (1902–1992)

WHAT IS THE ISSUE?

Was Jesus created? Did he only begin existing when he was born in Bethlehem, or has he always existed? Long before Christ took on flesh in Mary's womb and was manifested on earth, he had been active in his pre-incarnate state. This correlates perfectly with John's statements telling us that *"He existed in the beginning with God"* (John 1:2) and that *"God created everything through him"* (John 1:3).

Paul's reiterates the declaration that Jesus had a vital role in the creation of all things. How could that be true had Jesus not pre-existed with the Father?

> *For through him* [Christ] *God created everything in the heavenly realms and on earth. He made the things we can see and the things we can't see—such as thrones, kingdoms, rulers, and authorities in the unseen world. Everything was created through him and for him*
>
> (Colossians 1:16).

Further, Paul makes a remarkable statement revealing that Christ actually accompanied the children of Israel as they journeyed from Egypt to the Promised land. He writes, *"they drank from the spiritual rock that traveled with them, and that rock was Christ"* (1 Corinthians 10:4).

THE CHRISTMAS CARD VERSE

Micah 5:2 often appears on Christmas cards because it predicts Bethlehem as the place of the Messiah's birth. Although known as the city of David, Bethlehem was a relatively small town in Judea. Naturally speaking, as the center of Judaism, nearby Jerusalem might have been considered a more logical choice, but that is not where Christ was born. Some perhaps would have thought Rome, the seat of imperial political and military power, to be a more auspicious place for the Messiah to be born, but neither was Rome selected by God to be the place of the Savior's nativity. Others might have thought that Athens, associated with western philosophy, was the was the ideal location for Jesus to be born, but it was not the place God had in mind.

When King Herod heard that a new ruler—a prophesied king—had been born, he went into panic mode and inquired of the religious leaders where the Jewish Messiah was to be born. They referred him to Bethlehem as the predicted location (see Matthew 5:1-6). Here is what Micah had written more than 700 years before Jesus' birth:

But you, Bethlehem Ephrathah, though you are little among the thousands of Judah, yet out of you shall come forth to Me the One to be Ruler in Israel, whose goings forth are from of old, from everlasting

(Micah 5:2 NKJV).

Jesus' birth in Bethlehem is one of three hundred Old Testament prophecies that he fulfilled, and that is a very conservative estimate. The small town's name means "house of bread," and how fitting that was for someone who would present himself as *"the bread of life"* (John 6:35,48).

As wonderful as the prediction of Jesus' birth in Bethlehem is, many miss something very powerful and profound in Micah's prophecy. The last part of that verse speaks of the very nature of who Christ is, specifically, his pre-existence and his activities prior to being manifested in the flesh. Consider the latter part of Micah 5:2 in a few different translations.

- (NKJV): *"Whose goings forth are from of old, from everlasting."*
- (NASB): *"His times of coming forth are from long ago, from the days of eternity."*
- (ESV): *"Whose coming forth is from of old, from ancient days."*
- (SEPT): *"His goings forth were from the beginning, from eternity."*

One commentary sheds great light on this passage: "The terms convey the strongest assertion of infinite duration of which the

Hebrew language is capable. Messiah's generation as man coming forth unto God to do His will on earth is from Bethlehem; but as Son of God, His goings forth are from everlasting."[26]

At the time Micah wrote this, he referred not only to a future birth, but also to ancient activity. What does this mean to us? What activities was this individual—the Messiah—involved in before he was born in Bethlehem? What did these "goings forth" look like? How many times did he go forth? We've already seen that he was active in creation and that he was with Israel throughout their wilderness wanderings, but is there more?

As I've studied this, I must admit that there is an element of mystery to all of this, but I don't think Micah wrote what he did without reason. I believe our answer to this can be found in examining certain "divine appearances" in the Old Testament. In some of these, the Being showing up *appears* to be a man or an angel—sometimes he is referred to as "the Angel of the Lord." However, there are typically strong indications that the One appearing is no ordinary man or angel—that he is something significantly more than that.

One reason I believe that many of the appearances of a divine being in the Old Testament involved the preincarnate Christ is because Jesus himself said that *"No one has ever seen God"* (John 1:18) and *"No one has seen the Father except the one who is from God"* (John 6:46 NIV). Paul was also clearly describing the Father when he referred to God as the one *"whom no one has seen or can see"* (1 Timothy 6:16 NIV). So if the Father has not been seen by mortal man, who is the person who was seen at various times and places throughout the Old Testament?

How are we to understand Exodus 6:2-3? *"God also said to Moses, 'I am the Lord. I appeared to Abraham, to Isaac and to Jacob as God*

Almighty'" (NKJV). It would seem we have a contradiction unless we understand something about Jesus and his role in the Trinity. Author and Bible teacher Elmer Towns states that "Jesus is the only member of the Trinity to have taken on a physical body at any time."[27] Of course, in the Incarnation, the Son of God literally became flesh, and in Bethlehem he was born as a human and will remain in that humanity forever. But prior to that, in the Old Testament, it appears that he took on different forms in order to appear to and relate to certain people whom he visited.

One commentary provides the following insight:

> It is very probable that the theophanies (divine appearances) of the Old Testament were in reality "Christophanies," since in His preexistent state, Christ's brief encounters with people to reveal God's will would be in perfect accord with His office work as Revealer. Consider for example such passages as Genesis 21:17–20; 48:16; and Exodus 23:20. In these passages "the angel of the Lord" is clearly identified as Deity, yet distinguished from God the Father. Genesis 48:16 specifically refers to the heavenly messenger as one who "redeemed" (KJV), or "delivered" (NIV). In other passages where the angel of the Lord is both identified with God and distinguished from Him, or where the angel of the Lord receives worship (as in Judges 13:16–22), it seems obvious that the angel was a manifestation of Christ. Such Old Testament manifestations of the Second Person of the Trinity point forward to the Incarnation, when Christ would come to make His dwelling among the people of this world.[28]

You'll note the use of the word *Christophany* in the previous quote. This theological term refers to an appearance of Christ prior to his birth in Bethlehem (the Incarnation) or after the Resurrection. In the remainder of this chapter, we'll be focusing on what likely may have been appearances of Christ prior to his birth. These are perhaps some of the "goings forth" to which Micah alluded.

CHRIST—THE ONE WHO SAW HAGAR

One referred to as "the angel of the Lord" came to Hagar, the mother of Ishmael, at her point of deepest need. After this heavenly messenger spoke meaningfully to her, Hagar responded in a way that reveals the uniqueness of her visitor.

> *Thereafter, Hagar used another name to refer to the Lord, who had spoken to her. She said, "You are the God who sees me." She also said, "Have I truly seen the One who sees me?" So that well was named Beer-lahai-roi (which means "well of the Living One who sees me")*
> (Genesis 16:13-14).

This wasn't Gabriel or any other created being who spoke to Hagar; it was the Lord himself, and I believe it was a Christophany—a pre-nativity appearance of the Son of God.

CHRIST—THE ONE WHO WENT FORTH TO MEET ABRAHAM

According to Micah, Messiah's goings forth were from the days of eternity. In Genesis 18, we see what I believe is one of those expeditions. In the very first verse we read that *"the Lord appeared to*

Abraham" and in the very next verse, Abraham sees three men stand-ing nearby and engages them (see Genesis 18:1-2). One might be inclined to think of the Trinity when they see the reference to three men, but the rest of the text in chapters 18 and 19 does not support that notion.

After a meal and conversation, we read that *"The other men turned and headed toward Sodom, but the Lord remained with Abraham"* (Genesis 18:22). After Abraham's conversation with and intercession before the Lord, we read the following:

> *When the Lord had finished his conversation with Abraham, he went on his way, and Abraham returned to his tent. That evening the two angels came to the entrance of the city of Sodom*
>
> (Genesis 18:33–19:1).

Here is a very plausible breakdown of what happened:

1. The pre-existent Christ and two angels show up and meet with Abraham. By appearance, they are described simply as "three men."
2. After that visit, the two angels (still described as men) depart while the Lord stays and communicates further with Abraham.
3. After the Lord concludes his conversation with Abraham, two angels—probably the exact same two "men" that were with the pre-incarnate Christ and Abraham—show up at the home of Lot in Sodom and begin dealing with him about the impending destruction of that city.

This explanation also makes sense of the encounter Jesus had with the Pharisees in his earthly ministry:

Unless you believe that I AM who I claim to be, you will die in your sins. "Who are you?" they demanded. Jesus replied, "The one I have always claimed to be. . . . When you have lifted up the Son of Man on the cross, then you will understand that I AM he. . . . Your father Abraham rejoiced as he looked forward to my coming. He saw it and was glad." The people said, "You aren't even fifty years old. How can you say you have seen Abraham?" Jesus answered, "I tell you the truth, before Abraham was even born, I AM!" At that point they picked up stones to throw at him. But Jesus was hidden from them and left the Temple

(John 8:24-25, 28, 56-59).

Notice that Jesus' audience understood that he was claiming to have seen Abraham. Why would Jesus make such a claim? Because he had seen Abraham, had a meal with him, and had an in-depth conversation. Beyond that, Jesus claimed that he had also existed before Abraham was even born.

Why did this interaction end with the people wanting to kill Jesus? Because Jesus had identified himself as the I AM, and this was blasphemy in their understanding. These religious people knew the Scripture well. They clearly recognized that Jesus was appropriating for himself the very name that God gave himself when Moses asked God about his identity (we'll address this shortly).

This was not the only time that people in Jesus' day clearly understood him to be equating himself with the eternal God. Having declared his union with the Father in John 10:30, we read:

Once again the people picked up stones to kill him. Jesus said, "At my Father's direction I have done many good works. For which one are you going to stone me?" They replied, "We're stoning you not for any good work, but for blasphemy! You, a mere man, claim to be God"

(John 10:31-33).

The people simply could not wrap their heads around the fact that the Eternal God had become human and was living among them. They could not comprehend that the Great I AM who had appeared to Abraham and later to Moses was living and walking among them.

CHRIST—THE ONE WHO WRESTLED WITH JACOB

Abraham's grandson, Jacob, had a most unusual experience that is recorded in Genesis 32:24-30. The story begins by stating that *"a man came and wrestled with him until the dawn began to break"* (Genesis 32:24) and ends with *"Jacob named the place Peniel (which means 'face of God'), for he said, 'I have seen God face to face, yet my life has been spared'"* (Genesis 32:30).

Apparently, Jacob believed this was no ordinary man, even though he may have had a human appearance. John Chrysostom, who died in 407 AD and served as the Bishop of Constantinople, noted the connection between the Being who conversed with Abraham and the One who wrestled with Jacob. Chrysostom wrote:

> Remember that with the patriarch as well, when Abraham was sitting by the oak tree, God came in human form as the good man's guest in the company of the angels, giving us a premonition from on high at the beginning that he would one day take

human form to liberate all human nature by this means from the tyranny of the devil and lead us to salvation.[29]

CHRIST—THE ONE WHO SPOKE TO MOSES FROM THE BURNING BUSH

Not only did Christ travel with the children of Israel through the wilderness, but one of his "goings forth" involved appearing to Moses to initiate Israel's deliverance. The "I AM" who spoke to Moses from the burning bush was Christ himself. Look at the original story:

> *God replied to Moses, "I AM WHO I AM. Say this to the people of Israel: I AM has sent me to you." God also said to Moses, "Say this to the people of Israel: Yahweh, the God of your ancestors—the God of Abraham, the God of Isaac, and the God of Jacob—has sent me to you. This is my eternal name, my name to remember for all generations"*
> (Exodus 3:14-15).

Again, this "I AM" terminology links us directly to Jesus' statement to the Pharisees, *"I tell you the truth, before Abraham was even born, I AM!"* (John 8:58). No wonder that in the very next verse, they picked up stones with the intention of killing Jesus. They clearly understood that Jesus was declaring himself to be the preexistent and eternal God.

In addition to Christ communicating with Moses through the burning bush, and being the Rock that journeyed with Israel during the exodus, we also read that *"Inside the Tent of Meeting, the Lord would speak to Moses face to face, as one speaks to a friend"* (Exodus 33:11).

When you put all these pieces together, you begin to realize that centuries later, on the Mount of Transfiguration, when *"Moses and Elijah appeared and began talking with Jesus"* (Matthew 17:3), it wasn't the first time that Moses and Jesus had met or communicated.

CHRIST—THE ONE WHO APPEARED TO JOSHUA

Another pre-nativity appearance of Christ occurred in the book of Joshua. After the Israelites had crossed over the Jordan River into the Promised Land, Joshua *"looked up and saw a man standing in front of him with sword in hand"* (Joshua 5:13). After Joshua's inquiry, this individual identified himself as *"the commander of the Lord's army"* (Joshua 5:14).

This Person will give Joshua instructions regarding the conquest of Jericho, but this fascinating exchange takes place first:

> *At this, Joshua fell with his face to the ground in reverence. "I am at your command," Joshua said. "What do you want your servant to do?" The commander of the Lord's army replied, "Take off your sandals, for the place where you are standing is holy." And Joshua did as he was told*
> (Joshua 5:14-15).

How many times had Joshua heard the story of the Great I AM telling Moses to take his shoes off at the burning bush because he was standing on holy ground?

This appearance of Christ is different in form—here he appears as the Commander of the army of the Lord—and yet Joshua bows before him and worships him. This could not have been an ordinary angel as only God is to be worshiped, and no holy angel or man of God would have allowed such reverence from Joshua.

CHRIST—THE ONE WHO ANNOUNCED SAMSON'S BIRTH

Manoah and his wife were childless. "The angel of the Lord" appeared to his wife and told her she would have a son who would rescue Israel from the Philistines. He also gave her directions about raising this son as a Nazirite. She described this encounter to her husband by saying, *"A man of God appeared to me! He looked like one of God's angels, terrifying to see"* (Judges 13:6).

Later, when Manoah was able to speak to this being, he asked him his name. *"'Why do you ask my name?' the angel of the Lord replied. 'It is too wonderful for you to understand'"* (Judges 13:18). The New International Version renders the latter part of the answer as *"It is beyond understanding"* and *The Message* states, *"You wouldn't understand—it's sheer wonder."* One commentary observes that this "too wonderful" name "expresses the peculiarity of his nature also. It is to be understood in an absolute sense—'absolutely and supremely wonderful.'"[30]

This is clearly not a typical angel such as Gabriel, and what happens next is even more remarkable. After Manoah prepared a sacrifice, *"the Lord did an amazing thing. As the flames from the altar shot up toward the sky, the angel of the Lord ascended in the fire. When Manoah and his wife saw this, they fell with their faces to the ground"* (Judges 13:19-20). After this, Manoah expressed his realization that they had seen God (see Judges 13:22).

CHRIST—THE ONE WHO SPOKE TO SAMUEL

The prophet Samuel had been dedicated to the Lord as a small child by his parents, Elkanah and Hannah. Young Samuel served Eli the priest, and *"was sleeping in the Tabernacle near the Ark of God"* (1 Samuel 3:3). The Lord began calling out to Samuel, but he thought it was Eli who was calling him. The third time, Eli told Samuel to inquire of the Lord if he called out to him again.

What happens next is most interesting. *"And the Lord came and called as before, 'Samuel! Samuel!'"* (1 Samuel 3:10). Notice that the Lord didn't just call Samuel, but he *"came and called."* This was a Christophany because the Lord came, just as Micah had predicted. The Messiah, the one to be born in Bethlehem, is the one whose *"goings forth are from of old, from everlasting"* (Micah 5:2 NKJV).

CHRIST—THE FOURTH MAN IN THE FURNACE

While the Jews were in Babylonian captivity, King Nebuchadnezzar had a ninety-foot-tall golden statue of himself erected and commanded all of the people to bow down in worship to it. However, three faithful, God-honoring Jews named Shadrach, Meshach, and Abednego refused to participate in such idolatry.

Though threatened with death in a blazing furnace, they replied:

If we are thrown into the blazing furnace, the God whom we serve is able to save us. He will rescue us from your power, Your Majesty. But even if he doesn't, we want to make it clear to you, Your Majesty, that we will never serve your gods or worship the gold statue you have set up
(Daniel 3:17-18).

The king's threat was not an idle one, and when the three men persisted in their resolve, he had them thrown into a flaming furnace that had been heated to an extraordinary temperature. God was faithful, and the king cried out in shock, *"I see four men, unbound, walking around in the fire unharmed! And the fourth looks like a god!"* (Daniel 3:25).

Other translations render that last part of the verse as:

- (NKJV): *"the form of the fourth is like the Son of God."*
- (NASB): *"the appearance of the fourth is like a son of the gods!"*
- (NRSV): *"the fourth has the appearance of a god."*
- (CEB): *"the fourth one looks like one of the gods."*

Nebuchadnezzar was polytheistic, and would not have known the One True God, the God of the Bible, the God of Abraham, Isaac, and Jacob. We can't trust his theology, but we can recognize that he saw something radically supernatural, and that he saw someone other than a normal human being in the furnace with the other three men.

One commentator notes, "From the Christian perspective, we know that the preincarnate Christ did appear to individuals in the Old Testament. Most likely the fourth man in the fire was the angel of the Lord, God himself in the person of his Son Jesus Christ, a view held by many expositors."[31]

CONCLUDING THOUGHTS

Though Christ was manifested in the flesh at Bethlehem, he had existed eternally with the Father and the Holy Spirit. Much of what we've discussed can be challenging to wrap our minds around, and I recognize an element of mystery to it all. Some things are very clear in Scripture, and in other places we see suggestions and hints that may lead us to believe certain things, yet humility is in order as we recognize our human limitations.

There are numerous statements in Scripture that make no sense unless Jesus existed as the eternal Son of God prior to his manifestation in human flesh in Bethlehem. In terms of their birth dates, naturally speaking, John the Baptist was six months older than Jesus, and yet remarkably he said about Jesus:

This is the one I was talking about when I said, "Someone is coming after me who is far greater than I am, for he existed long before me"

(John 1:15).

Naturally speaking, that was not true—John was older than Jesus. But John knew that there was more to Jesus than what met the eye. Even today, Jesus exceeds our highest imaginations and ideals. He is more wonderful than we realize. Paul was right when he wrote:

Now we see things imperfectly, like puzzling reflections in a mirror, but then we will see everything with perfect clarity. All that I know now is partial and incomplete, but then I will know everything completely, just as God now knows me completely

(1 Corinthians 13:12).

QUOTES

"Jesus Christ was with the Father before the ages, and in the end, He was revealed."

—Ignatius of Antioch (?–117)

"But the Son has been eternally co-existing with the Father. From of old, yes, from the beginning, He always reveals the Father."

—Irenaeus of Lyon (125–202)

"If Christ was only man, how did he say, 'Before Abraham was, I am?' For no man can be before someone from whom he himself has descended. Nor can it be that anyone could have been prior to him of whom he himself has taken his origin. Yet, Christ, although He was born of Abraham, says that He is before Abraham."

—Novatian (200–258)

"I said that the plant… is different from the [seed or root] from which it sprouted. Yet, it is absolutely of the same nature. Similarly, a river flowing from a spring takes another form and name. For neither is the spring called the river, nor the river the spring… The spring is the father, so to speak, and the river is the water from the spring. …God is the spring of all good things, but the Son is called the river flowing from Him."

—Dionysius of Alexandria (?–265), as quoted by Athanasius

"How astonished I am that there is laid before me a Child who is older than all things!"

—Ephrem the Syrian (306–373)

"His birth in Bethlehem was not His origin, only His incarnation… Christ's preexistence is not a matter of purely academic interest, it is the foundation on which the whole superstructure of the Christian faith rests. If He is not preexistent, He cannot be God, and if He is not God, He cannot be Creator and Redeemer."[32]

—Oswald Sanders (1902–1992)

"In orthodox Christian understanding, Jesus is fully divine and fully human. His preexistence relates to his divinity and his virgin birth to his humanity. The Word, the Second Person of the Trinity has always been. At a finite point in time he assumed humanity, however, and was born as the man Jesus of Nazareth."[33]

—Millard J. Erickson (1932–)

QUESTIONS FOR REFLECTION AND DISCUSSION

1. Did you learn something new about Jesus in this chapter? Describe what you learned.

2. Did something you already knew about Jesus become strengthened or reinforced? Describe it.

3. When did you realize that Jesus existed before he was manifested on earth in the manger? Was that hard for you to accept? To grasp?

4. After identifying Bethlehem as the future birthplace of the Messiah, Micah wrote of him, *"whose goings forth are from of old, from everlasting"* (Micah 5:2 NKJV). What does that last phrase mean to you?

5. Review the portion entitled "Christ—The One Who Went Forth to Meet Abraham," especially the passages from John 8 and 10. What conclusions do you make about the identity of Jesus from those verses?

6. Under "Concluding Thoughts," we read where John the Baptist said Jesus *"is far greater than I am, for he existed long before me'"* (John 1:15). Relative to the birth dates, John was approximately six

months older than Jesus. What did John understand about Jesus which caused him to say that?

7. Did anything you read in this chapter change the way you will relate to Jesus? If so, how?

Chapter Seven

NOTHING LESS THAN GOD: THE DEITY OF JESUS

"Jesus that I know as my Redeemer cannot be less than God."

—Athanasius of Alexandria (AD 297–373)

Some have suggested that Jesus was merely an exceptionally godly person, or that he was a man who evolved into godhood or some highly elevated, spiritual status. Such speculations are erroneous and fall terribly short. The Bible teaches that Jesus is and has always been far more; Jesus was God the Son who became a man. He left the eternal realm, stepped into our space and time world, and lived as a man. But in doing so, he never ceased being God.

Perhaps some of the most profound words ever written about Jesus were penned by John, the disciple *"whom Jesus loved"* (John 13:23). The other three gospel accounts—those of Matthew, Mark, and Luke—had been written many years before. Those three are sometimes call the "Synoptic Gospels" because they tend to look at

Jesus through a similar lens. John's Gospel, however, does not begin with a genealogy or a manger. Rather, John begins in eternity past and presents a more transcendent view of Jesus.

> *In the beginning the Word already existed. The Word was with God, and the Word was God. He existed in the beginning with God. God created everything through him, and nothing was created except through him. ...So the Word became human and made his home among us. He was full of unfailing love and faithfulness. And we have seen his glory, the glory of the Father's one and only Son. ...No one has ever seen God. But the unique One, who is himself God, is near to the Father's heart. He has revealed God to us*
>
> (John 1:1-3, 14, 18).

Let's unpack these infinitely rich verses just a bit.

WHAT DID JOHN TEACH IN THESE FIVE VERSES?

I. JOHN TAUGHT THE PRE-EXISTENCE OF JESUS:

In the beginning the Word already existed

(John 1:1).

He existed in the beginning with God

(John 1:2).

Jesus' life did not begin when he was conceived in the womb of Mary or when he was born in the manger in Bethlehem. He pre-existed all of that, and his pre-existent state was *with* God. Because of verses like the two above, you will often hear that Jesus is co-eternal with the Father. The Father had no origin, and neither did Jesus. Jesus' pre-existence was the focus of Chapter Six in this book.

2. JOHN ALLUDED TO THE TRINITY:

The Word was with God

(John 1:1).

The word *with* indicates there was more than one person in this scenario. There was fellowship and partnership. We learn elsewhere in Scripture that there are not three Gods. Rather, there is one God who eternally exists in three persons: the Father, the Son, and the Holy Spirit. We should not be troubled that this is beyond our human comprehension. There is an element of mystery in the Trinity, or the triune nature of God. The Trinity will be the focus of Chapter Thirteen of this book.

3. JOHN AFFIRMED THE DEITY OF JESUS:

And the Word was God

(John 1:1)

The unique One, who is himself God

(John 1:18).

The Word was not only in the beginning with God but was God himself. This will be the focus of this chapter.

4. JOHN IDENTIFIED JESUS' ROLE AS CREATOR:

God created everything through him, and nothing was created except through him

(John 1:3).

If you ask the average Christian who created the Universe, the answer will simply be "God." That person might cite Genesis 1:1 as the basis of their assertion: *"In the beginning God created the heavens and the earth."* It is certainly true that God the Father took part in creation, but so did Jesus. Paul says of the Father, *"by whom all things were created,"* and of the Son, *"through whom all things were created"* (1 Corinthians 8:6).

All of this can be clarified and expanded upon by looking further into the New Testament. Paul clearly identifies Jesus as the agent in creation.

Christ is the visible image of the invisible God. He existed before anything was created and is supreme over all creation, for through him God created everything in the heavenly realms and on earth. He made the things we can see and the things we can't see—such as thrones, kingdoms, rulers, and authorities in the unseen world. Everything was created through him and for him. He existed before anything else, and he holds all creation together. ...For God in all his fullness was pleased to live in Christ...For in Christ lives all the fullness of God in a human body

(Colossians 1:15-17, 19; 2:9).

The author of Hebrews also states that *"through the Son he created the universe"* (Hebrews 1:2).

5. JOHN REFERRED TO THE HUMANITY OF JESUS:

So the Word became human and made his home among us

(John 1:14).

Jesus was fully human as well as fully God. This will be the focus of Chapter Nine in this book.

A MULTITUDE OF WITNESSES TO CHRIST'S DEITY

THE "THEOS" FACTOR

Theos is the Greek word for God. It is where we get our word *theology*. Though it typically is used regarding God the Father, it is also used at times of the Lord Jesus. Let's look at some of these New Testament instances.

1. "*The Word was with God, and the Word was God [theos]*" (John 1:1).
2. "*No one has ever seen God. But the unique One, who is himself God [theos], is near to the Father's heart. He has revealed God to us*" (John 1:18).
3. "*Thomas said to him, 'My Lord and my God [theos]!'*" (John 20:28 NIV).
4. Paul told the elders of the church of Ephesus to "*Be shepherds of the church of God [theos], which he bought with his own blood*" (Acts 20:28 NIV). We know that it was Jesus who died and bled on the cross, but Paul refers to the payment as being that of God's own blood. The simplest explanation of this is that God had become a man in the Person of Jesus, and had shed his blood for us.

5. Paul also referred to Jesus as *"the Messiah, who is God [theos] over all, forever praised! Amen"* (Romans 9:5 NIV).

6. *"Though he [Jesus] was God [theos], he did not think of equality with God as something to cling to"* (Philippians 2:6).

7. *"We look forward with hope to that wonderful day when the glory of our great God [theos] and Savior, Jesus Christ, will be revealed"* (Titus 2:13).

8. Regarding the Father speaking to Jesus, the author of Hebrews wrote, *"But to the Son he says, 'Your throne, O God [theos], endures forever and ever'"* (Hebrews 1:8).

9. After identifying himself, Peter begins his second epistle with these words, *"I am writing to you who share the same precious faith we have. This faith was given to you because of the justice and fairness of Jesus Christ, our God [theos] and Savior"* (2 Peter 1:1).

10. *"We live in fellowship with the true God because we live in fellowship with his Son, Jesus Christ. He is the only true God [theos], and he is eternal life"* (1 John 5:20).

THE EQUATION FACTOR

Jesus repeatedly equated himself with the Father. In John 10:30, Jesus said, *"The Father and I are one."* When Jesus said this, it outraged the people listening and they picked up stones to kill him. When Jesus asked them why they were doing this, they accused him of blasphemy and said, *"You, a mere man, claim to be God"* (John 10:33). Jesus challenged them, *"believe in the evidence of the miraculous works I have done, even if you don't believe me. Then you will know and understand that the Father is in me, and I am in the Father"* (John 10:38). Even then, the people sought to arrest him.

Jesus' claim of being one with the Father was repeated consistently throughout John's Gospel in different ways—really to an astonishing degree.

1. The Son does the Father's work (John 5:17-19, 36; 9:4; 10:25).
2. People are to honor the Son just as they honor the Father (John 5:23).
3. Knowing the Son is the same as knowing the Father (John 8:19).
4. Trusting in Jesus is trusting in the Father who sent him (John 12:44; 14:1).
5. Seeing Jesus is seeing the Father (John 12:45; 14:9).
6. Jesus spoke the Father's authorized words (John 12:50; 14:10; 17:8).
7. Anyone who welcomes Jesus is welcoming the Father (John 13:20).
8. Jesus is in the Father and the Father is in Jesus (John 14:10-11).
9. Anyone who hates the Son also hates the Father (John 15:23).
10. Jesus experienced glory with the Father before the world began (John 17:5).

Luke adds to this equation factor when he quotes Jesus' words, *"And anyone who rejects me is rejecting God, who sent me"* (Luke 10:16).

Only Jesus could legitimately make these kinds of statements. He said them, and they are true. Can you imagine the (rightful) uproar that would occur if a preacher stood in the pulpit today and said, "You are to honor me just as you honor the Father; if you know me you know the Father; if you've seen me you've seen the Father; you need to believe in me just like you believe in the Father." People would (and should) denounce that as craziness and as "ego run wild." We would rightfully assume that such a person is a delusional narcissist. And yet, when Jesus says these things, they are true; he truly is one with the Father.

THE WORSHIP FACTOR

When Moses received the Ten Commandments, the very first decree dealt with the fact that only God is to be worshiped.

> *You must not have any other god but me. You must not make for yourself an idol of any kind or an image of anything in the heavens or on the earth or in the sea. You must not bow down to them or worship them, for I, the Lord your God, am a jealous God who will not tolerate your affection for any other gods*
>
> (Exodus 20:3-5).

Ancient civilizations and cultures were heavily polytheistic, meaning that they believed in and worshiped many gods. The God of Abraham, Isaac, and Jacob wanted his followers to know that he was the one true God, and that all other "gods" were frauds and counterfeits. God spoke these words through another prophet:

> *For there is no other God but me, a righteous God and Savior. There is none but me. Let all the world look to me for salvation! ... For I am God; there is no other*
>
> (Isaiah 45:21-22).

As long as God's people feared and honored him, idolatry—worshiping anything or anyone other than the true God—was resisted with vehemence. When a ninety-foot statue of King Nebuchadnez-zar was erected and all were commanded to bow and worship it, Shadrach, Meshach, and Abednego absolutely refused. When told to bow or burn, these three Hebrews said, *"We want to make it clear to you, Your Majesty, that we will never serve your gods or worship the gold statue you have set up"* (Daniel 3:18).

When Satan tempted Jesus, showing him the kingdoms of the world and offering them to him in exchange for worship, Jesus relied on and used the Scripture to resist. For Jesus, the worship of God only was crystal clear and unalterable.

> *"Get out of here, Satan," Jesus told him. "For the Scriptures say, 'You must worship the Lord your God and serve only him'"*
>
> (Matthew 4:10).

In the book of Revelation, John was so overwhelmed at the grandeur of all he was seeing and hearing that he fell down at the feet of an angel to worship. The angel immediately stopped John:

> *No, don't worship me. I am a servant of God, just like you and your brothers and sisters who testify about their faith in Jesus. Worship only God*
>
> (Revelation 19:10; see also Revelation 22:8-9).

Likewise, men of God in the Bible refused to be worshiped. When Peter showed up at the home of Cornelius (see Acts 10:25-26), Cornelius fell at his feet to worship, but Peter *"pulled him up and said, 'Stand up! I'm a human being just like you!'"* (Acts 10:26). When God used Paul and Barnabas in the healing of a lame man in Lystra, the people falsely believed the men to be Zeus and Hermes and were going to offer a sacrifice to them. Paul and Barnabas refused such misguided worship and admonished them, instead, to *"turn to the living God, who made heaven and earth, the sea, and everything in them"* (Acts 14:15).

So far, we've established three premises in this section: 1) only God is to be worshiped, 2) God's angels refuse to be worshiped, and 3) men of God refuse to be worshiped. In studying further, we must now examine the occasions when Jesus was worshiped. This was never subtle or vaguely alluded to. It was blatant and overt, and most importantly, Jesus never refused such worship.

JESUS IS WORSHIPED!

Throughout Jesus' earthly ministry and on into eternity, he is worshiped. How can this be unless in some way he truly is God? In any of the situations during his ministry when people came and knelt before him, he could have stopped them and told them only to direct their worship to the heavenly Father. If he were not deity, he was scripturally obligated to correct them and insist they not worship him, but he never did that. Consider the following:

1. Jesus was worshiped by the wise men. They came from distant lands to worship him (see Matthew 2:2). When they saw Jesus, *"they bowed down and worshiped him"* (Matthew 2:11).

2. A leper *"came and worshiped Him, saying, 'Lord, if You are willing, You can make me clean'"* (Matthew 8:2 NKJV).

3. A ruler of the synagogue worshiped Jesus as he sought help for his daughter (see Matthew 9:18).

4. Of the Canaanite woman seeking deliverance for her daughter, we read *"she came and worshiped Him, saying, 'Lord, help me!'"* (Matthew 15:25 NKJV).

5. When the mother of James and John came to Jesus, desiring preferential treatment for them, *"she knelt respectfully to ask a favor"* (Matthew 20:20).

6. When the two Marys encountered Jesus after his resurrection, *"they ran to him, grasped his feet, and worshiped him"* (Matthew 28:9). When the eleven remaining disciples encountered Jesus later, *"they worshiped him—but some of them doubted!"* (Matthew 28:17).

7. We understand that some of the disciples had doubts and hesitations about Jesus' resurrection, but doubts gave way to faith. Thomas was not with the other disciples at one of Jesus' earlier post-resurrection appearances and expressed doubt. When he saw Jesus face to face, he said, *"My Lord and my God!"* (John 20:28).

8. Because God has elevated Jesus to the place of highest honor and given him the name above all other names, one day *"at the name of Jesus every knee should bow, in heaven and on earth and under the earth, and every tongue declare that Jesus Christ is Lord, to the glory of God the Father"* (Philippians 2:10-11).

9. As remarkable as all these statements are, it seems even more amazing that God the Father commanded the angels to worship Jesus. *"And when he brought his supreme Son into the world, God said, 'Let all of God's angels worship him'"* (Hebrews 1:6).

10. Peter instructed believers to *"worship Christ as Lord of your life"* (1 Peter 3:15).

11. Along with the Father, Jesus is worshiped freely in Heaven (Revelation 5:1-14; 7:9-10).

THE SHARING OF TITLES

In Chapter Three of this book, we looked at a myriad of titles and descriptions of the Lord Jesus. While that chapter focused on specific titles ascribed to Jesus, it is important to realize that in many cases, he shares those exact titles with the Father.

Consider the titles shared by the Father and the Son:

The Father	Title	Jesus
Genesis 17:1	Almighty	Revelation 1:8
Genesis 1:1	Creator	Colossians 1:16
Isaiah 44:6	First and Last	Revelation 1:17
Exodus 6:3	Jehovah (YHWH)	Hebrews 1:10[34]
Genesis 18:25	Judge	2 Timothy 4:1
1 John 1:5	Light	John 8:12
Psalm 110:1	Lord	Philippians 2:11
Deuteronomy 10:17	Lord of Lords	1 Timothy 6:15
Isaiah 12:2	Savior	Luke 2:11
Isaiah 40:11	Shepherd	John 10:11, 14

Jesus and the Holy Spirit also share a title—*paraklētos* in the Greek. This word referred to a person who was called alongside to help, strengthen, or comfort. It was specifically used of an Advocate or a defense attorney in a court setting. Why would we need someone to speak on our behalf? Perhaps because Satan is described as *"the accuser of our brothers and sisters, who accuses them before our God day and night"* (Revelation 12:10 NIV). Thank God that we have a helper and advocate both in Jesus and in the Holy Spirit.

> *And I will ask the Father, and he will give you another Advocate [paraklētos], who will never leave you. He is the Holy Spirit*
>
> (John 14:16–17).

My dear children, I am writing this to you so that you will not sin. But if anyone does sin, we have an advocate [paraklētos] who pleads our case before the Father. He is Jesus Christ, the one who is truly righteous

(1 John 2:1).

LET'S BE PERFECTLY CLEAR

I don't want there to be any vagueness about our terminology when we refer to the deity of the Lord Jesus Christ. Some groups have diluted the idea by referring to "the god within every person," or the "spark of divinity" within us all. Noted Bible teacher R.A. Torrey (1856-1928) dealt with this same issue in his day.

> When I was a boy, to say you believed in the Divinity of Christ, meant that you believed in the real Deity of Christ, that you believed that Jesus was actually a Divine Person, that He was God. It no longer means that. ...So our subject...is not the Divinity of Christ, but the Deity of Christ; and our question is not is Jesus Christ Divine, but is Jesus Christ God? Was that person who was born at Bethlehem nineteen hundred and twenty-one years ago, and who lived thirty-three or thirty-four years here upon earth as recorded in the four gospels of Matthew, Mark, Luke and John, who was crucified on Calvary's cross, who rose from the dead the third day, and was exalted from earth to heaven to the right hand of the Father, was He God manifested in the flesh, was He God embodied in a human being? Was He and is He a being worthy of our absolute faith, and supreme love, and our unhesitating obedience, and our whole-heart-

ed worship, just as God the Father is worthy of our absolute faith and supreme love and unhesitating obedience and our whole-hearted worship? Should all men honour Jesus Christ even as they honour God the Father (John 5:23)? Not merely is He an example that we can wisely follow, or a Master whom we can wisely serve, but is He a God Whom we can rightly worship?[35]

In modern times, Max Lucado also addressed the vital issue of clarity and precision when he said, "Jesus was not just godly, godlike, God hungry, God focused, or God worshipping. He was God. Not merely a servant of God, instrument of God, or friend of God, but Jesus was God."[36]

QUOTES ABOUT THE DEITY OF CHRIST

"Christ never used that familiar phrase of all the prophets, 'Thus saith the Lord.' For He was Himself the Lord, who openly spoke by His own authority, prefacing his words with the phrase, 'Truly, truly, I say unto you.'"

—Tertullian (160–220)

"I have had so many experiences of Christ's divinity, that I must say: either there is no God, or he is God."

—Martin Luther (1483–1546)

"He who…does not perceive Christ to be God…is blind amidst the brightness of noon day."

—John Calvin (1509–1564)

"Depend upon it, my hearer, you never will go to heaven unless you are prepared to worship Jesus Christ as God."

—Charles H. Spurgeon (1834–1892)

"Jesus Bar–Joseph, the carpenter of Nazareth, was in fact and in truth, and in the most exact and literal sense of the words, the God 'by whom all things were made'…He was in every respect a genuine living man. He was not merely a man so good as to be 'like God'—He was God."

—Dorothy L. Sayers (1893–1957)

"The deity of Christ is the key doctrine of the scriptures. Reject it, and the Bible becomes a jumble of words without any unifying theme. Accept it, and the Bible becomes an intelligible and ordered revelation of God in the person of Jesus Christ."[37]

—J. Oswald Sanders (1902–1992)

"If Jesus is not God, then there is no Christianity, and we who worship Him are nothing more than idolaters. Conversely, if He is God, those who say He was merely a good man, or even the best of men, are blasphemers. More serious still, if He is not God, then He is a blasphemer in the fullest sense of the word. If He is not God, He is not even good."[38]

—J. Oswald Sanders (1902–1992)

"The real issue…is this Jesus to be worshiped or only admired?"

—John Stott (1921–2011)

"Jesus Christ is what God does, and the cross where God did it."

—Frederick Buechner (1926–2022)

QUESTIONS FOR REFLECTION AND DISCUSSION

1. Did you learn something new about Jesus in this chapter? Describe what you learned.

2. Did something you already knew about Jesus become strengthened or reinforced? Describe it.

3. How significant is it to you that Jesus was referred to as *theos* (God) ten different times in the New Testament?

4. Review the Scriptures listed under "The Equation Factor." Does it make sense that a person could make that many parallels between himself and the Father without asserting that he himself was deity?

5. Based on the number of times Jesus was worshiped during his earthly ministry, is there any other conclusion to arrive at other than that he really believed he was deity—co-equal with the Father?

6. What is the difference between Jesus being truly deity (God) as opposed to simply being godly or godlike?

7. Did anything you read in this chapter change the way you will relate to Jesus? If so, how?

Chapter Eight

HIS GRAND ENTRANCE: THE VIRGIN BIRTH AND INCARNATION

"The Son of God—He who made the universe—assumed flesh and was conceived in the virgin's womb."

—Clement of Alexandria (AD 150–215)

An examination of the Gospel accounts clearly reveals the virgin "conception" of Jesus by the Holy Spirit. Since most people refer to the virgin birth, we will stay with that terminology. The first chapter of Matthew's Gospel gives a brief account of Jesus' birth and says of Mary that *"while she was still a virgin, she became pregnant through the power of the Holy Spirit"* (Matthew 1:18). Further, he states that Joseph *"did not have sexual relations with her until her son was born"* (Matthew 1:25).

Luke's account of this miraculous event is more detailed, and he likely received the particulars by interviewing Mary herself (discussing the events of Jesus' life with witnesses is how Luke compiled his

Gospel). After all of the staggering events that led up to and followed Jesus' birth, Luke writes that *"Mary kept all these things in her heart and thought about them often"* (Luke 2:19).

When Luke interviewed Mary, it is possible that she shared certain details with him that she had never shared before. It was in that type of setting that she may have conveyed the precious truths she had been treasuring in her heart for decades. We don't know for sure, but we still marvel at the extensive richness of Luke's account of Jesus' conception and birth.

In the sixth month of Elizabeth's pregnancy, God sent the angel Gabriel to Nazareth, a village in Galilee, to a virgin named Mary. She was engaged to be married to a man named Joseph, a descendant of King David. Gabriel appeared to her and said, "Greetings, favored woman! The Lord is with you!"

Confused and disturbed, Mary tried to think what the angel could mean. "Don't be afraid, Mary," the angel told her, "for you have found favor with God! You will conceive and give birth to a son, and you will name him Jesus. He will be very great and will be called the Son of the Most High. The Lord God will give him the throne of his ancestor David. And he will reign over Israel forever; his Kingdom will never end!"

Mary asked the angel, "But how can this happen? I am a virgin."

The angel replied, "The Holy Spirit will come upon you, and the power of the Most High will overshadow you. So the baby to be born will be holy, and he will be called the Son of God."

…Mary responded, "I am the Lord's servant. May everything you have said about me come true." And then the angel left her

(Luke 1:26–35, 38).

Directly after this encounter, Mary traveled to visit her relative Elizabeth, the wife of Zechariah. In their old age, they had conceived and their soon-to-be-born son would later be known as John the Baptist. When Mary greeted her, *"Elizabeth's child leaped within her, and Elizabeth was filled with the Holy Spirit"* (Luke 1:41). Elizabeth called Mary *"the mother of my Lord"* and explained, *"When I heard your greeting, the baby in my womb jumped for joy"* (Luke 1:44). As adults, John would be the forerunner who prepared the way for Jesus and acknowledged him as *"the Lamb of God who takes away the sin of the world"* (John 1:29).

The virgin birth of Jesus is inextricably woven into the story of redemption—of God purchasing our forgiveness, delivering us from the penalty and the power of sin, and bringing us back into his family. Anti-supernaturalists may try to discount the virgin birth as mythical or unimportant, but it is absolutely essential to the completeness and cohesion of Scripture. I remember my mother sharing her faith in the Bible with me when I was very young. She said, "This is the Bible. If you can believe any of it, you can believe all of it."

Elmer Towns powerfully expressed the necessity of accepting the virgin birth as it is taught in Scripture:

> The virgin birth of Christ is not an independent doctrine which we can receive or reject without affecting our Christianity. It is one of the foundation stones of Christianity; our faith will crumble if it is removed. This doctrine is tied to biblical inerrancy, Christ's sinless character, the atonement, and other key doctrines of the Bible. If Jesus was not born of a virgin, he would be unable to save himself, because he would not be a sinless Savior. If we cannot accept the virgin birth of Christ, very little credibility remains in the Bible.[39]

WHY WAS THE VIRGIN BIRTH NECESSARY?

The death, burial, and resurrection of Jesus Christ are central to God redeeming us back to himself, but those epic events were preceded by the virgin birth and the Incarnation. Being conceived in the womb of Mary by the Holy Spirit, the eternal Son of God received a human body—was made flesh—and escaped the sin nature that had plagued the human race since the fall of man. Thus, Jesus was uniquely qualified to be our Savior and Redeemer.

In God's economy, it was necessary that a sinless human be the sacrifice for the sins of all humanity. In short, a sinful man got us into trouble and it would take a sinless man to get us out of trouble. A sinful man could not die redemptively for us, because he had his own sin to deal with. Paul addresses how the redemption of fallen man took place in the following passage.

> *When Adam sinned, sin entered the world. Adam's sin brought death, so death spread to everyone, for everyone sinned. ...Now Adam is a symbol, a representation of Christ, who was yet to come. But there is a great difference between Adam's sin and God's gracious gift. For the sin of this one man, Adam, brought death to many. But even greater is God's wonderful grace and his gift of forgiveness to many through this other man, Jesus Christ*
>
> (Romans 5:12, 14–15).

No other human qualified because all of humanity had partaken of Adam's sin and had sinned themselves. That's why Jesus came into the human race by means of a virgin birth. Someone had to die to redeem humanity and no one else qualified. God the Son, the second member of the Trinity, became human so he could redeem people back to himself. In his pre-incarnate state, he could not die, but as a man, he could.

> *Because God's children are human beings—made of flesh and blood—the Son also became flesh and blood. For only as a human being could he die, and only by dying could he break the power of the devil, who had the power of death. Only in this way could he set free all who have lived their lives as slaves to the fear of dying. We also know that the Son did not come to help angels; he came to help the descendants of Abraham. Therefore, it was necessary for him to be made in every respect like us, his brothers and sisters, so that he could be our merciful and faithful High Priest before God. Then he could offer a sacrifice that would take away the sins of the people. Since he himself has gone through suffering and testing, he is able to help us when we are being tested*
> (Hebrews 2:14-18).

The early part of the above passage stresses Jesus as our substitute—that he died on our behalf. Verse 18 talks about him being our helper—that because he was human and experienced suffering, he can identify with us and help us through our challenges. This is reinforced a few chapters later: *"This High Priest of ours understands our weaknesses, for he faced all of the same testings we do, yet he did not sin"* (Hebrews 4:15). Having come and lived in the flesh, we can take heart in knowing that Jesus understands every situation we could ever face.

THE VIRGIN BIRTH PROPHESIED

One of my favorite verses in all of Scripture, one that communicates God's infinite wisdom, reads, *"So the Word became human and made his home among us"* (John 1:14). So just how did the Word, who pre-existed with God and was himself God, become flesh—become human? The bold answer from the Bible is that *"the Lord himself will give you the sign. Look! The virgin will conceive a child! She will give birth to a son and will call him Immanuel (which means 'God is with us')"* (Isaiah 7:14).

Some have tried to detract from the significance of this passage by stressing that the word rendered *virgin* can also be translated *young lady*. Linguistically, that may true, but contextually, such an assertion makes no sense. Isaiah said that was to be a "sign." In Israel and in every part of the world, young women were constantly conceiving children. That is how the human race has always been perpetuated. It would only have been a sign if it was an exceptional conception, not an everyday occurrence. A virgin conceiving a child is the only rendering that makes sense in this verse. Besides that, the Holy Spirit himself interprets it to mean a virgin in the New Testament (see Matthew 1:22-23), not simply as a young lady.

Isaiah's prophecy, given around 700 years before the birth of Christ, was not the first indication of a special offspring of a woman. Immediately after the fall of man, God informs the serpent about the future work of the Seed of a woman:

> *And I will put enmity between you and the woman, and between your seed and her Seed; He shall bruise your head, and you shall bruise His heel*

> (Genesis 3:15 NKJV).

The Seed of woman—and we believe this to be a prophetic description of Jesus—would be the one who would bring complete destruction to the kingdom of darkness, just as the serpent had brought great harm to the human race. This promise of the triumph of the "Seed of woman" has long been called the *protoevangelium*, the first gospel.

When Charles Wesley penned his magnificent hymn, "Hark the Herald Angels Sing," he recognized Christ as the Seed of woman in the lyric, "Rise the woman's conquering Seed, bruise in us the serpent's head." Not only does Paul refer to Christ as *"the Seed"* in the book of Galatians (3:16,19 NKJV), but John writes that *"the Son of God came to destroy the works of the devil"* (1 John 3:8).

It seems that during his earthly life, there may have been rumors about the unusual nature of his birth, and people who only thought naturally could have come to horribly wrong conclusions. In a heated exchange with the Pharisees (see John 8), they asked Jesus questions about his identity and that of his father. They became quite testy with him as they defended their Abrahamic lineage, and then they made what could be a very snide remark to Jesus, *"We aren't illegitimate children! God himself is our true Father"* (John 8:41).

Noted commentator William Barclay says of this verse:

> It is certainly true in later times that the Jews spread abroad a most malicious slander against Jesus. The Christians very early preached the miraculous birth of Jesus. The Jews put it about that Mary had been unfaithful to Joseph; that her paramour had been a Roman soldier called Panthera; and that Jesus was the child of that adulterous union. It is just possible that the Jews were flinging at Jesus even then an insult over his birth, as if to say: "What right have you to speak to the like of us as you do?[40]

If Barclay's assessment is accurate, it not only proves how crass the religious people were to make such an insinuation, but it also indicates that perhaps false rumors had been circulating about the unique nature and timing of Jesus' birth for some time.

As a believer, I embrace the plain teaching of Scripture and of the Apostles' Creed regarding Jesus, "Who was conceived of the Holy Spirit, born of the Virgin Mary."

The apostle Paul comments, "*But when the right time came, God sent his Son, born of a woman, subject to the law. God sent him to buy freedom for us who were slaves to the law, so that he could adopt us as his very own children*" (Galatians 4:4–5). Later, he quoted an early Christian hymn or creed when he tells Timothy about the great mystery of godliness:

> *He was **manifested in the flesh**, vindicated by the Spirit, seen by angels, proclaimed among the nations, believed on in the world, taken up in glory*
>
> (1 Timothy 3:16 ESV).

Jesus' conception was anything but the norm. He was conceived by the Holy Spirit in the womb of Mary without a natural, biological father. He was "born of a woman" and was "manifested in the flesh."

Had Jesus not been miraculously conceived of the Holy Spirit, he would not have been qualified to be our Savior. To represent God in the work of redemption, he had to be fully God. To represent man in the same transaction, he had to be fully man. This is what the virgin birth made possible.

There will certainly be people who simply accepted Jesus—put their faith in him—without ever hearing detailed doctrine about the virgin birth, and they no doubt were born again when they put their faith in Jesus who died on the cross for their sins and was raised from the dead. In that sense, an uninformed person might not believe in the virgin birth, and yet they are saved. However, had Jesus not been born of a virgin, nothing he did could have produced our salvation. A regular, sinful man could not effectively die vicariously on behalf of others.

I appreciate the brilliant insight reflected in Oswald Sanders' statement:

> It is conceded that the Bible does not demand belief in the virgin birth as a prerequisite for salvation, but it does indicate that the fact of the virgin birth must be true if we are to be saved. It is possible for a man to be saved without knowing details of the process, just as babies are born without any knowledge of embryology. It is the integrity of the fact, not our knowledge of it, that lays the basis for our salvation.[41]

Someone who rejects the supernatural claims of the Bible will not only reject the virgin birth, but they will also reject the resurrection of Christ and all the miracles of the Bible. The truth is that the Christian faith is a supernatural faith. Jesus physically entered the earth through a supernatural act (the virgin birth), and he left the earth through another supernatural act (the ascension).

To truly celebrate Christ, we must embrace the fact that God has supernaturally intervened on our behalf to do everything that was necessary to rescue us from the grip of sin and death. This involved God the Son being born of a virgin and Jesus being raised from the dead after he had died for our sins. This is what the Bible teaches. This is what we can believe with wonder, amazement, and thanksgiving.

GREAT STATEMENTS ABOUT THE VIRGIN BIRTH

"He was truly born of a virgin… He is God existing in flesh, true Life in death. He is both of Mary and of God."

—Ignatius of Antioch (?–117)

"We even affirm that He was born of a virgin."

—Justin Martyr (100–165)

"Christ Jesus, the Son of God, because of His surpassing love towards His creation, humbled Himself to be born of the virgin. Thereby, He united man through Himself to God."

—Irenaeus of Lyon (125–202)

"This ray of God, then, as it was always foretold in ancient times, descended into a certain virgin. And He was made flesh in her womb. So, in His birth, God and man were united."

—Tertullian (160–220)

"He in the last times divested Himself and became a man, and was incarnate although still God. While He was made a man, He remained the God that He was. He assumed a body like our own, differing in only one respect: that the body was born of a virgin and of the Holy Spirit. This Jesus Christ was truly born, truly suffered…and truly died."

—Origen (184–253)

"He enters into a virgin. Through the Holy Spirit, He is clothed with flesh. God is mingled with man."

—Cyprian (210–258)

"Neither is there any other cause of the Incarnation except this alone: He saw us bowed down to the ground, perishing, tyrannized by death; and He had mercy."

—John Chrysostom (349-407)

"Rejoice that the immortal God is born that mortal men may live in eternity."

—Jan Hus (1369-1415)

"I believe that Jesus Christ, true God, begotten of the Father from eternity, and also true man, born of the Virgin Mary, is my Lord."

—Martin Luther (1483–1546)

"The mystery of the humanity of Christ, that He sunk Himself into our flesh, is beyond all human understanding."

—Martin Luther (1483–1546)

"The Son of God did not want to be seen and found in heaven. Therefore he descended from heaven into this humility and came to us in our flesh, laid himself into the womb of his mother and into the manger and went on to the cross. This was the ladder that he placed on earth so that we might ascend to God on it. This is the way you must take."

—Martin Luther (1483–1546)

"For, first, the birth of Christ was the incarnation of God: it was God taking upon himself human—a mystery, a wondrous mystery, to be believed in rather than to be defined."

—Charles H. Spurgeon (1834–1892)

"Christ is the humility of God embodied in human nature; the Eternal Love humbling itself, clothing itself in the garb of meekness and gentleness, to win and serve and save us."

—Andrew Murray (1828–1917)

"Some things strange and tragic have been happening in recent years within Christianity. For one, some ministers have advised their congregations not to be greatly concerned if theologians dispute the virgin birth of Jesus. The issue, they say, is not important. For another thing, some professing Christians are saying they do not want to be pinned down as to what they really believe about the uniqueness and reality of the deity of Jesus, the Christ."[42]

—A. W. Tozer (1897–1963)

"If we accept that Jesus was the incarnate Son of God, does not belief in the virgin birth become logically inevitable? Who could be the Father of the Son of God but God Himself?"[43]

—Oswald Sanders (1902–1992)

"The virgin birth of Christ is a key doctrine; for if Jesus Christ is not God come in sinless human flesh, then we have no Savior. Jesus had to be born of a virgin, apart from human generation, because He existed before His mother. He was not just born in this world; He came down from heaven into the world. Jesus was sent by the Father and therefore came into the world having a human mother but not a human father."[44]

—Warren Wiersbe (1929–2019)

"What we celebrate at Christmas is not so much the birth of a baby, but the incarnation of God Himself."

—R. C. Sproul (1939–2017)

"Emmanuel. God with us. He who resided in Heaven, co–equal and co–eternal with the Father and the Spirit, willingly descended into our world. He breathed our air, felt our pain, knew our sorrows, and died for our sins. He didn't come to frighten us, but to show us the way to warmth and safety."[45]

—Charles Swindoll (1934–)

"Of all the great sages and prophets throughout world history, Jesus alone claimed to be God-become-man."

—Luis Palau (1934–2021)

"Jesus was conceived by the Holy Spirit (Luke 1:35), and not by Joseph, in order that His human nature might be sinless. This is why He would be called 'the Son of God' at His birth."[46]

—Tony Evans (1949–)

"The Virgin Birth alone insured both the full deity and full humanity of Jesus. If God had created Jesus a complete human being in heaven and sent him to earth apart from any human parent, it is difficult to see how he could be truly a man. If God had sent his Son into the world through both a human father and mother, it is difficult to see how he could be truly God."[47]

—Sam Storms (1951–)

"The omnipotent, in one instant, made himself breakable. He who had been spirit became pierce-able. He who was larger than the universe became an embryo. And he who sustains the world with a word chose to be dependent upon the nourishment of a young girl."[48]

—Max Lucado (1955–)

QUESTIONS FOR REFLECTION AND DISCUSSION

1. Did you learn something new about Jesus in this chapter? Describe what you learned.

2. Did something you already knew about Jesus become strengthened or reinforced? Describe it.

3. What would you say to someone who claimed that it really doesn't matter whether Jesus was born of a virgin or not?

4. This chapter contains the statement, "Had Jesus not been miraculously conceived of the Holy Spirit, he would not have been qualified to be our Savior." What is your assessment of that statement, and why?

5. In Genesis 3:15, a prophecy is given regarding the future "Seed of woman" that would crush the head of the serpent. Charles Wesley wrote of Jesus, "Rise the woman's conquering Seed, bruise in us the serpent's head." Why do you think Charles Wesley made this connection?

6. How far in the Christian faith do you believe a person can advance if they reject the supernatural claims of the Bible? Why?

7. Did anything you read in this chapter change the way you will relate to Jesus? If so, how?

Chapter Nine

LIKE US: THE HUMANITY OF JESUS

"Man's maker was made man,
That He, Ruler of the stars,
Might nurse at His mother's breast;
That the Bread might hunger,
The Fountain thirst,
The Light sleep,
The Way be tired on its journey;
That the Truth might be accused of false witness,
The Teacher be beaten with whips,
The Foundation be suspended on wood;
That Strength might grow weak;
That the Healer might be wounded;
That Life might die."

—Augustine (354–430)

No understanding of Jesus is complete without understanding his humanity. Yes, he was God, and yes, he existed from all eternity, but he also became completely human through the Incarnation. This word is from the Latin word *carne*, which means flesh or body. Theologically speaking, Incarnation refers to the eternal Son of God taking on flesh and becoming fully human without forfeiting his Deity.

Let's revisit the apostle John's remarkable statement:

In the beginning the Word already existed. The Word was with God, and the Word was God. He existed in the beginning with God. God created everything through him, and nothing was created except through him. ...So the Word became human and made his home among us. He was full of unfailing love and faithfulness. And we have seen his glory, the glory of the Father's one and only Son

(John 1:1-3, 14).

The portion we are going to focus on in this chapter is found in verse 14, *"So the Word became human and made his home among us."*

John taught the deity of Christ, but not to the exclusion of his humanity. In his first epistle, he expanded on this emphasis and drove home Jesus' physicality while still advocating for his divine nature.

We proclaim to you the one who existed from the beginning, whom we have heard and seen. We saw him with our own eyes and touched him with our own hands. He is the Word of life. This one who is life itself was revealed to us, and we have seen him. And now we testify and proclaim to you that he is the one who is eternal life. He was with the Father, and then he was revealed to us

(1 John 1:1-2).

John's expression that he and his fellow disciples *"touched him with our own hands"* no doubt goes back to the emphasis Jesus himself placed on the bodily nature of his resurrection when he told his questioning disciples, *"Look at my hands. Look at my feet. You can see that it's really me. Touch me and make sure that I am not a ghost, because ghosts don't have bodies, as you see that I do"* (Luke 24:39). Immediately after this, Jesus ate in front of them to further demonstrate the reality of his humanity.

It might seem strange to some in the twenty-first century that Jesus' humanity was ever in question. People who have heard about him being born to a human mother and eventually bleeding and dying on a cross would, of course, assume that Jesus was a man. But people in the first few centuries, especially those who had been influenced by Greek philosophy, had an entirely different perspective.

Those who had been influenced by Gnostic beliefs presupposed that matter was inferior to that which was spiritual and that, in some cases, matter was evil. They even believed that the material world had been created by an inferior "god." If Jesus, then, was as wonderful as people thought, he could not have really been flesh and blood. He must have been some kind of mystical being, perhaps only *appearing* to be human. Maybe, they speculated, he was some kind of spiritual being but not really human.

Specifically, Docetism (from the Greek word, *dokeo*, "to seem") presented the idea that Jesus only *appeared* to be human, but that he really was not—that he was just a spirit who gave the impression of being a man. While Greek philosophy advocated escaping from the flesh, Jesus Christ willingly and intentionally took on flesh and lived among us.

The apostle John understood the Gnostic line of thinking and saw how dangerous it was to the truth of the gospel. If Jesus wasn't fully human, then he couldn't really die, and if he wasn't human then maybe his blood wasn't real either. If his blood was only imaginary, then there really was no price paid for our sins. In other words, denying the humanity of Jesus would completely undermine the story of redemption taught in Scripture.

Dear friends, do not believe everyone who claims to speak by the Spirit. You must test them to see if the spirit they have comes from God. For there are many false prophets in the world. This is how we know if they have the Spirit of God: If a person claiming to be a prophet acknowledges that Jesus Christ came in a real body, that person has the Spirit of God. But if someone claims to be a prophet and does not acknowledge the truth about Jesus, that person is not from God. Such a person has the spirit of the Antichrist, which you heard is coming into the world and indeed is already here

(1 John 4:1-3)

JOHN VS. CERINTHUS

In the early days of the New Testament, true ministers contended for the truth that Jesus had come and lived as a man upon the earth. False ministers were denying his full humanity. Much of what the apostle John wrote in his Gospel and in his epistles was designed to offset false, damnable heresies by a clear articulation of the truth. John had a disciple in Smyrna named Polycarp, who in turn had a disciple named Irenaeus.

In his work, *Against Heresies*, Irenaeus shares about the erroneous beliefs of a theological opponent of John.

Cerinthus, again, a man who was educated in the wisdom of the Egyptians, taught that the world was not made by the primary God, but by a certain Power far separated from him, and at a distance from that Principality who is supreme over the universe, and ignorant of him who is above all. He represented Jesus as having not been born of a virgin, but as being the son of Joseph and Mary according to the ordinary course of human generation, while he nevertheless was more righteous, prudent, and wise than other men. Moreover, after his baptism, Christ descended upon him in the form of a dove from the Supreme Ruler, and that then he proclaimed the unknown Father, and performed miracles. But at last Christ departed from Jesus, and that then Jesus suffered and rose again, while Christ remained impassible [unable to suffer or experience pain], inasmuch as he was a spiritual being.[49]

Irenaeus also records how John once saw that Cerinthus was in the public bath facility, and urged his companions to leave immediately "lest even the bath-house fall down, because Cerinthus, the enemy of the truth, is within."[50]

John's dealings with Cerinthus give tremendous insight into a statement in John's second epistle:

Many deceivers have gone out into the world. They deny that Jesus Christ came in a real body. Such a person is a deceiver and an antichrist. ... If anyone comes to your meeting and does not teach the truth about Christ, don't invite that person into your home or give any kind of encouragement

(2 John 7,10).

Remember the statement referenced earlier from his first epistle where John stated that *"If a person claiming to be a prophet acknowledges that Jesus Christ came in a real body, that person has the Spirit of God"* (1 John 4:2). At the time John wrote his epistles, the humanity of Jesus was under such a severe attack that John put forth this issue as a litmus test. Essentially, John said that true teachers are affirming Christ's humanity; the false teachers are denying Jesus' humanity. If Jesus had not been human, his blood and his death were not real, and he could not have purchased salvation for anyone.

KENOSIS

As we explore another passage of Scripture dealing with Jesus' coming in the flesh, there is a particular word in the Greek language—*kenosis*—that we want to examine. Let's look at the entire passage first.

> *Though he was God, he did not think of equality with God as something to cling to. Instead, he* ***gave up his divine privileges*** *[kenosis]; he took the humble position of a slave and was born as a human being. When he appeared in human form, he humbled himself in obedience to God and died a criminal's death on a cross*
>
> (Philippians 2:6-8).

These verses teach the deity of Christ, the humanity of Christ, and the end result of him becoming human—to die a criminal's death even though he himself was pure, sinless, and spotless.

The Greek word we want to look at—*kenosis*—is translated differently in different versions of the New Testament. Each shows different shades of nuance and meaning. Here's how that word in Philippians 2:7 is rendered:

- (NLT): "*he gave up his divine privileges.*"
- (NKJV): "*made Himself of no reputation.*"
- (NASB): "*emptied Himself.*"
- (NIV): "*made himself nothing.*"
- (MSG): "*he set aside the privileges of deity.*"
- (AMPC): "*stripped Himself [of all privileges and rightful dignity].*"

So what are we to make of this? How are we to understand and interpret this idea of *kenosis* properly? Does this mean that Jesus was God before he became human, but once he became human he stopped being God? Not at all!

Keith Trump is a friend and Greek scholar who I consult periodically on questions relative to scriptural texts. One of his first remarks on this passage is that "in the consolidated totality of the New Covenant, Jesus consistently remained fully God and fully man." After studying this, he remarked that he would not translate *kenosis* "to empty" but would render it, "to completely pour something into something else." Keith proceeded:

> What Paul is saying in Philippians 2 is that Almighty God poured His entire self (κενόω) into the human body of Jesus. Furthermore, Jesus poured his entire self out as an offering via his death. In this context, Jesus certainly "laid aside" certain rights exclusive to his divinity while expressing his

humanity. Having said all of this, I would translate the Philippians 2:6-8 as:

"Although He has always existed as God, he did not cling to his divine rights, position, and location. Instead, He poured His entire self into the human body prepared for Him. Once manifested in human form, He took on the position of the lowest class of servanthood. Furthermore, He poured His entire life out for others, even the point of humbly accepting death by means of cruel crucifixion."

Keith's perspective is echoed by pastor and Bible teacher Tony Evans. He expounds regarding Philippians 2:7:

Does this mean that Jesus emptied himself of his deity? Not at all. It was impossible that Jesus Christ could cease being God. This famous verse is not about what Jesus emptied Himself of, but what He emptied Himself into. It's like pouring something from one pitcher into another. Jesus took all of His deity and poured it into another vessel, the "form of a bond-servant. He didn't stop being who He is, but He changed the form of who He is."[51]

Jesus became what he had not been (humanity), but he did not cease being what he had always been (deity). Jesus Christ never ceased being God. As someone said, "Remaining what he was, he became what he was not."

EVIDENCE FOR CHRIST'S HUMANITY

I. JESUS HAD A HUMAN ANCESTRY AND FAMILY.

Though Jesus did not have an earthly biological father, he did have a natural mother. Detailed genealogies for Jesus are provided in Scripture (see Matthew 1:1-17; Luke 3:23-38). In Paul's epistle to the Romans, he expresses both Christ's humanity and deity at the beginning of his letter. Note his reference to Jesus being from the lineage of David:

> *The Good News is about his Son. In his earthly life he was born into King David's family line, and he was shown to be the Son of God when he was raised from the dead by the power of the Holy Spirit. He is Jesus Christ our Lord*
>
> (Romans 1:3-4).

At various times, references to Jesus' natural family are made. In the following example, people from his hometown recognized that Jesus had grown up around them, but they were mystified by the spiritual power in which he walked.

> *He returned to Nazareth, his hometown. When he taught there in the synagogue, everyone was amazed and said, "Where does he get this wisdom and the power to do miracles?" Then they scoffed, "He's just the carpenter's son, and we know Mary, his mother, and his brothers—James, Joseph, Simon, and Judas. All his sisters live right here among us. Where did he learn all these things?" And they were deeply offended*

and refused to believe in him. Then Jesus told them, "A prophet is honored everywhere except in his own hometown and among his own family"

(Matthew 13:54-57).

Contrary to some mythical legends, Jesus did not do miracles prior to his being empowered by the Holy Spirit (see Luke 3:21-22; John 2:11; Acts 10:38). Had Jesus routinely walked on water, healed the sick, and raised the dead as a youth, the people in his hometown would not have reacted as they did when these things began happening in his ministry.

2. JESUS' JOURNEY THROUGH LIFE WAS THOROUGHLY HUMAN.

Jesus was born and raised in a family. His neighbors watched him grow up. He learned Scripture as was customary for young Jewish boys, and like Joseph, he became a carpenter. He faced temptations and challenges throughout life. He had friends, and wept at the tomb of Lazarus when he died. He was disappointed when people rejected him because he knew they were rejecting the hand of God stretched out to help them (see Luke 19:41-44).

Jesus experienced realities common to physical humanity. As a man, he experienced things he would not have had he remained exclusively in his deity.

- Jesus experienced hunger (Mark 11:2), but God does not (Psalm 50:12).

- After strenuous travel, Jesus was tired (John 4:6), but God is never weary (Isaiah 40:28).

- Jesus slept (Matthew 8:24), but God never sleeps (Psalm 121:4).

- Jesus was tempted (Hebrews 5:14), but God cannot be tempted (James 1:13).

- Jesus died (John 19:30), but God cannot die (1 Timothy 6:16).

All these things Jesus experienced because he had become human, had taken on flesh.

Jesus was not an emotionless robot. He was not an automaton that simply carried out its pre-programmed instructions. He had feelings, frustrations, and friendships. He experienced love, grief, and joy. Sometimes people think that Jesus cannot relate to them because he is too lofty and perfect—too far removed from them. Yet Scripture tells us that he is able to sympathize with us because he has faced all the same kinds of challenges we face in life (see Hebrews 4:15).

Jesus experienced the full range of human emotions during his life and earthly ministry:

PASSION

Passion for God's house will consume me

(John 2:17).

JOY

...the joy of your lord

(Matthew 25:21, 23 NKJV).

Jesus was filled with the joy of the Holy Spirit

(Luke 10:21).

...you will be filled with my joy

(John 15:11).

Jesus...for the joy set before him he endured the cross

(Hebrews 12:2 NIV).

WEEPING / TEARS

But as he came closer to Jerusalem and saw the city ahead, he began to weep

(Luke 19:41).

Jesus wept

(John 11:35).

Jesus...offered prayers and pleadings, with a loud cry and tears

(Hebrews 5:7).

COMPASSION

When he saw the crowds, he had compassion on them

(Matthew 9:36).

Jesus saw the huge crowd...and he had compassion on them and healed their sick

(Matthew 14:14).

I feel sorry for these people. They have been here with me for three days, and they have nothing left to eat

(Matthew 15:32).

Moved with compassion, Jesus reached out and touched him

(Mark 1:41).

When the Lord saw her, his heart overflowed with compassion

(Luke 7:13).

LOVE

Looking at the man, Jesus felt genuine love for him

(Mark 10:21).

Jesus loved Martha, Mary, and Lazarus

(John 11:5).

He had loved his disciples during his ministry on earth, and now he loved them to the very end

(John 13:1).

The disciple Jesus loved

(John 13:23; 19:26; 20:2; 21:7; 21:20).

I have loved you even as the Father has loved me

(John 15:9).

Love each other in the same way I have loved you

(John 15:12).

FRIENDSHIP

So the two sisters sent a message to Jesus telling him, "Lord, your dear friend is very sick"

(John 11:3).

Greater love has no one than this, than to lay down one's life for his friends. You are My friends.... No longer do I call you servants...but I have called you friends

(John 15:13-15 NKJV).

AMAZEMENT

When Jesus heard this, he was amazed

(Matthew 8:10).

DEEPLY MOVED / ANGER

He looked around at them angrily and was deeply saddened by their hard hearts

(Mark 3:5).

Looking up to heaven, he sighed

(Mark 7:34).

When he heard this, he sighed deeply in his spirit

(Mark 8:12).

When Jesus saw what was happening, he was angry with his disciples

(Mark 10:14).

He was deeply moved in spirit and troubled

(John 11:33 NIV).

Jesus, once more deeply moved, came to the tomb

(John 11:38 NIV).

DESIRE

With fervent desire I have desired to eat this Passover with you

(Luke 22:15).

DISTRESS / TROUBLED / ANGUISH

I have a baptism to be baptized with, and how distressed I am till it is accomplished!

(Luke 12:50 NKJV)

Now my soul is deeply troubled

(John 12:27).

Now Jesus was deeply troubled, and he exclaimed, "I tell you the truth, one of you will betray me!"

(John 13:21)

He became anguished and distressed

(Matthew 26:37).

He was in such agony of spirit that his sweat fell to the ground like great drops of blood

(Luke 22:44).

He told them, "My soul is crushed with grief to the point of death"

(Matthew 26:38).

3. JESUS EXPERIENCED HUMAN GROWTH AND LIMITATIONS.

- Luke 2:40 states that *"the child grew and became strong"* (NIV).
- A few verses later we read that *"Jesus grew in wisdom and in stature and in favor with God and all the people"* (Luke 2:52).

When Jesus was a baby, he looked like a baby. When he was a child, he looked like a child. He developed physically, emotionally, and intellectually. Some might find that difficult to accept because Jesus was God the Son. He was, but it's important to remember the *kenosis*—that Jesus willingly ceased operating in some of his divine privileges and prerogatives for a time.

People sometimes wonder why Jesus didn't know certain things if he was God. For example, when the woman with the issue of blood touched the hem of his garment and was healed, Jesus inquired as to who had touched his garment (see Mark 5:25-34). Speaking of his own future return, Jesus stated that neither he nor the angels knew when that would occur, but only the Father (see Matthew 24:36).

Apparently, Jesus had laid aside or chose not to operate from his omniscience; otherwise, he would have known those things. In other words, while he was a man on earth, Jesus was limited in what he knew. But what about today? Is he still limited in the ways described above? I don't think so. I say that because of what he prayed shortly before his death, burial, and resurrection. He asked that the Father would *"bring me into the glory we shared before the world began"* (John 17:5). I especially like the way the Amplified Bible, Classic Edition translates that part of his prayer: *"Glorify Me along with Yourself and restore Me to such majesty and honor in Your presence as I had with You before the world existed."*

In his pre-existent state, Jesus enjoyed all of these attributes with the Father—such as omnipresence, omnipotence, and omniscience. He laid those aside for his time on earth, but as he saw his time on earth ending, he anticipated being fully restored to all the privileges of deity. It seems reasonable to think that since Jesus has been restored to his former position, he now freely accesses and operates in all of the traits he enjoyed with the Father from eternity past.

4. JESUS WAS A FULLY CONSTITUTED HUMAN.

Paul gives us insight into the tripartite nature of humans when he prayed for believers, that their *"whole spirit and soul and body be kept blameless until our Lord Jesus Christ comes again"* (1 Thessalonians 5:23). It has often been said that man is a spirit, he has a soul, and he lives in a body. When Jesus was interacting with Nicodemus about the new birth, he said, *"Flesh gives birth to flesh, but the Spirit gives birth to spirit"* (John 3:6 NIV).

This is why, when we are born again, we become new creatures (spiritually speaking, see 2 Corinthians 5:17), but our minds[52] still need to be renewed (see Romans 12:2), and we will someday receive new, glorified bodies (see Philippians 3:21). If Jesus was made like us in all ways, except that he was without sin, we should expect to see Jesus having a spirit, soul, and body in the context of his humanity.

- His Human Spirit: The last words Jesus spoke on the cross were, *"Father, I entrust my spirit into your hands!"* (Luke 23:46). Jesus wasn't committing the Holy Spirit into the Father's hands; he said this in reference to his own human spirit. At the Last Supper, when Jesus thought about the impending betrayal by Judas, Scripture tells us that Jesus was *"troubled in spirit"* (John 13:21 NIV).

- His Human Soul: As Jesus began to sense the approaching pressure of the cross, He told his friends, *"My soul is crushed with grief to the point of death. Stay here and keep watch with me"* (Matthew 26:38).

- His Human Body: When Jesus was anointed in Bethany, he said, *"She has poured this perfume on me to prepare my body for burial"* (Matthew 26:12). After his resurrection, when the disciples were startled at seeing Jesus alive, he said to them, *"Look at my hands. Look at my feet. You can see that it's really me. Touch me and make sure that I am not a ghost, because ghosts don't have bodies, as you see that I do"* (Luke 24:39).

Sometimes people wonder if Jesus was fully human since he never sinned. Absolutely he was! Before Adam sinned, he was fully human. He didn't become more or less human when he sinned; he simply became a sinful human being. Jesus was fully human even though he never sinned.

Peter Lewis penned this magnificent description of Jesus' humanity:

> The eternal Logos assumed a full human psychology no less than a human physiology. He was—and is—not merely God in the form of man, but God in the nature of man; not God in disguise, but God in the flesh. He did not only come among us; He became one of us, possessing as His very own, a true and full human nature from its conception. In that nature He as the Second Person of the Trinity resided, and to Him that nature properly belonged, so that God the Son

consciously and experientially lived His life through that humanity. The mystery and message of the Incarnation is that in Jesus God acquired manhood and the Deity became a member of the human race.[53]

5. EVERYONE RECOGNIZED JESUS AS A MAN.

- The Woman at the Well: Even though she had a life-changing encounter with Jesus (and he had told her directly that he was the Messiah), she still recognized him as completely human. When she told others about him, she said, *"Come and see a man who told me everything I ever did! Could he possibly be the Messiah?"* (John 4:29).

- Pontius Pilate: *"Then Jesus came out, wearing the crown of thorns and the purple robe. And Pilate said to them, 'Behold the Man!'"* (John 19:5 NKJV).

- The Disciples: When his closest followers witnessed the sea becoming calm after Jesus' rebuke, they said, *"Who is this man? When he gives a command, even the wind and waves obey him!"* (Luke 8:25).

It is true that Jesus was a remarkable man, a powerful man, a unique man, but he was a man in every sense of the term. During his life, some may have recognized that he was more than a mere man, but he was still a man.

WHAT ABOUT HIS MIRACLES?

Another question that is often asked pertains to the miracles, healings, and mighty works Jesus performed. Did he do those because he was God, or did he do them as a man powerfully anointed by the Holy Spirit? While Jesus was God manifested in the flesh, I think there is a strong case to be made for the latter—that he did his works as a man anointed by the Holy Spirit.

John the Baptist said that God had given Jesus *"the Spirit without limit"* (John 3:34). He had an anointing like no one else and operated fully in every ministry office. He was the ultimate Apostle, the ultimate Prophet, the ultimate Evangelist, the ultimate Pastor, and the ultimate Teacher. By contrast, all of Jesus' followers—all of us—have *"gifts that differ according to the grace given to us"* (Romans 12:6 ESV).

In one of his sermons, the apostle Peter provided this description of the healings that took place under Jesus' ministry.

> *And you know that God anointed Jesus of Nazareth with the Holy Spirit and with power. Then Jesus went around doing good and healing all who were oppressed by the devil, for God was with him*
>
> (Acts 10:38).

Consider what noted Bible teacher A.W. Tozer said about the miraculous aspect of Jesus' ministry:

> I am persuaded that our Lord Jesus, while He was on earth, did not accomplish His powerful deeds in the strength of His deity. I believe He did them in the strength and authority of His Spirit-anointed humanity.
>
> My reasoning is this: If Jesus had come to earth and performed His ministry in the power of His deity, what He did would have been accepted as a matter of course. Cannot God do anything He wants to do? No one would have questioned His works as the works of deity. But Jesus veiled His deity and ministered as a man. It is noteworthy, however,

that He did not begin His ministry—His deeds of authority and power—until He had been anointed with the Holy
Spirit.

I know there are erudite scholars and theological experts
who will dispute my conclusion. Nevertheless, I hold it
true. Jesus Christ, in the power and authority of His Spirit-anointed humanity, stilled the waves, quieted the winds,
healed the sick, gave sight to the blind, exercised complete
authority over demons, and raised the dead. He did all the
miraculous things He was moved to do among men not as
God, which would not have been miraculous at all, but as a
Spirit-anointed man. Remarkable![54]

WHAT DID JESUS LOOK LIKE?

The Bible doesn't typically give a lot of detail about what people
looked like. Occasionally, though, Scripture sometimes includes such
information. For example:

- Esau *"was very red at birth and covered with thick hair like a fur coat"*
  (Genesis 25:25).
- Samson and Absalom both had long hair (see Judges 16:7;
  2 Samuel 14:26).
- King Saul was tall (see 1 Samuel 9:2).
- David *"was reddish, with beautiful eyes and a handsome appearance"*
  (1 Samuel 16:12 NASB).
- Zacchaeus was short (see Luke 19:3).
- Paul's detractors said that his bodily presence was unimpressive
  (see 2 Corinthians 10:10 NASB).

When it comes to Jesus, painters and artists throughout the centuries have used their imaginations to depict him, but there really is no biblical description to provide specifics. According to Isaiah, *"There was nothing beautiful or majestic about his appearance, nothing to attract us to him"* (Isaiah 53:2). I deduce from this that there was nothing extraordinary or unusual about Jesus' physical appearance.

To the woman at the well, he looked just like another Jewish man passing through her village. To the two disciples along the road to Emmaus, he looked like other fellow travelers. Even after his resurrection, Mary mistook him for the gardener. People marveled at his words, his love, and the spiritual power that operated in his life, but Jesus probably didn't look all that different from other Jewish men in the first century.

The apostle Paul may have given us a strong clue as to why the Bible says little about Christ's physical appearance. He wrote, *"So from now on we regard no one from a worldly point of view. Though we once regarded Christ in this way, we do so no longer"* (2 Corinthians 5:16 NIV). The world often "judges a book by its cover," evaluating people based on how they look and the clothes they wear.

Even though many early Christians would have seen Jesus and would have known of such externals, Paul indicates that is not what we are to do. We need to see Jesus for who he really is and for what he really accomplished. It is good to remember the counsel God gave to the prophet Samuel, *"The Lord doesn't see things the way you see them. People judge by outward appearance, but the Lord looks at the heart"* (1 Samuel 16:7).

Artistic and imaginative renditions of Jesus over time have often reflected the artist's perception. In other words, Jesus was imagined to be similar to the people from that artist's culture and time. This tendency to see Jesus similar to ourselves was beautifully captured in a song entitled, "Some Children See Him" by Wihla Hutson and Alfred S. Burt.

The lyrics state that "some children see him lily white…some children see him bronzed and brown…some children see him almond-eyed…some children see him dark as they." This insight reflects the fact that there is a natural desire to relate to Jesus and to know that Jesus relates to us. But far beyond the complexion of our skin, the authors proceed to call everyone to devotion and worship regardless of what any of us may look like externally.

> The children in each different place
> will see the baby Jesus' face
> like theirs, but bright with heavenly grace,
> and filled with holy light.
> O lay aside each earthly thing
> and with thy heart as offering,
> come worship now the infant King.
> 'Tis love that's born tonight![55]

TWO EXCEPTIONS: DESCRIPTIONS OF JESUS GLORIFIED

Isaiah gave description of Jesus' appearance relative to the severe beatings and abuse he underwent at the time leading up to his crucifixion. He provides this gruesome portrayal, *"His face was so disfigured he seemed hardly human, and from his appearance, one would scarcely know he was a man"* (Isaiah 52:14). *The Message* renders that, *"He didn't even look human—a ruined face, disfigured past recognition."*

There was another momentary glimpse of Jesus given in the gospels that did not involve his normal, day-to-day appearance. On the opposite end of the spectrum from the disfigurement he experienced from his harsh pummeling was his glorious appearance in what is called the Transfiguration. In this highly unique situation, *"Jesus' appearance was transformed so that his face shone like the sun, and his clothes became as white as light"* (Matthew 17:2).

This transfiguration moment gave Peter, James, and John a foretaste of Jesus' glory after he had been resurrected and had ascended to Heaven. In the Revelation, John saw Jesus this way:

He was wearing a long robe with a gold sash across his chest. His head and his hair were white like wool, as white as snow. And his eyes were like flames of fire. His feet were like polished bronze refined in a furnace, and his voice thundered like mighty ocean waves…his face was like the sun in all its brilliance

(Revelation 1:13-16).

The vision John had of Jesus in the first chapter of Revelation probably reminded him—at least somewhat—of the way he saw him on the Mount of Transfiguration. However, that is not how Jesus appeared through the vast majority of his life and ministry here on earth. At those times, he fit Isaiah's description of being quite normal in appearance.

A FINAL THOUGHT FROM PETER LEWIS

Having become man, God the Son will never cease to be man. Even in heaven and through all eternity He will be God-in-the-flesh, albeit glorified flesh. The humanity that

He has assumed on earth He has taken to heaven. There, it is no longer a penalized, suffering humanity, but a human body irradiated with the glory of God. The eternal Logos will forever know in Himself the joy of the redeemed as well as the triumph of the redeemer. He will live forever in His two natures.

The implications of this for our planet and its people are enormous. It means that there is a human being on the throne of the universe! In the place of supreme and central significance for all creation there is a man, a member of and the head of the human race.

Science has taught us something of the vastness of the created universe. But because of its alienation from God and its consequent deficient understanding of humankind as it should be, our society has felt shrunken and lost and insignificant in a vast cosmos. But it is in the teaching and life and redeeming work of Jesus Christ that we discover reconciled man's true significance and real destiny. It was not into an angelic race that God was born, but into the people of this "inconspicuous" planet. It is not an angelic nature that He now inhabits and lives through at the Father's right hand, but a human one.

Go to the spiritual heart of this created universe, and there you will find a man. Go to the place where angels bow who never fell, and you will find a man. Go to the very center of the manifested glory of the invisible God, and you will find a man: true human nature, one of your own race, mediating the glory of God.[56]

It seems almost unfathomable to our finite minds that the eternal God of the universe could pour himself into a human vessel and live among us, and yet that's what Jesus did. He became human to reveal the Father to us, to die as the ultimate sacrifice for our sin, and to redeem us back to God. In the next chapter, we'll explore the sufferings and the death of Christ, which his humanity made possible.

GREAT STATEMENTS ABOUT THE HUMANITY OF JESUS

"If God never became flesh, like us, he could neither redeem us nor reveal to us his promise of eternal life. It is only by becoming like us that God can make us like him, restoring us in his image."
—Irenaeus of Lyon (125–202)

"He became what we are that he might make us what he is."
—Athanasius of Alexandria (AD 297–373)

"How could Christ have died for sinners if he himself were in sin?"
—John Chrysostom (347–407)

"The Lord Jesus himself has not only, as God, given the Holy Spirit, but also, as man, he has received him."
—Augustine (354–430)

"But we say that the Lord Jesus Christ is very God and very man, one person in two natures, and two natures in one person."
—Anselm of Canterbury (1033–1109)

"Christ is the dazzling bright sun who covered himself with a cloud in order to be seen."

—Antony of Padua (1195–1231)

"Take hold of Jesus as a man and you will discover that he is God."

—Martin Luther (1483–1546)

"He ate, drank, slept, waked; was weary, sorrowful, rejoicing; he wept and he laughed; he knew hunger and thirst and sweat; he talked, he toiled, he prayed...so that there was no difference between him and other men, save only this, that he was God, and had no sin."

—Martin Luther (1483–1546)

"Christ, by highest heaven adored;
Christ, the everlasting Lord!
Late in time behold Him come,
Offspring of the Virgin's womb:
Veiled in flesh the Godhead see;
Hail the incarnate Deity
Pleased as man with men to dwell,
Jesus, our Emmanuel."

—Charles Wesley (1707–1788)

"Jesus was God and man in one person, that God and man might be happy together again."

—George Whitefield (1714–1770)

"God manifested in the flesh is eternity in the form of time."
—Samuel Taylor Coleridge (1772–1834)

"If ever man was God or God man, Jesus Christ was both."
—Lord Byron (1788–1824)

"Remember, Christ was not a deified man, neither was he a humanized God. He was perfectly God and at the same time perfectly man."
—Charles H. Spurgeon (1834–1892)

"Do not be ashamed of Christ —of the Man that bought us with His own blood."
—D. L. Moody (1837–1899)

"Jesus was God spelling himself out in language humanity could understand."
—S.D. Gordon (1859–1936)

"Christ was born in the first century, yet He belongs to all centuries. He was born a Jew, yet He belongs to all races. He was born in Bethlehem, yet He belongs to all countries."
—George Washington Truett (1867–1944)

"Jesus became man not by stepping down from deity into manhood, but by taking up manhood into God. The incarnation was not a degradation. God did not degrade himself. When Jesus Christ became man, he humbled himself but he did not degrade himself. The deity never degraded himself and never will. When the holy Son of God walked among sinful men, there was no degradation.... At the incarnation, Jesus became all that man is, except sin. But in doing that, he took the man up into all that God is, except deity."[57]

—A. W. Tozer (1897–1963)

"If Jesus Christ is not true God, how could he help us? If he is not true man, how could he help us?"

—Dietrich Bonhoeffer (1906–1945)

"He came in complete human form to meet a universal need in a way that is adequate for all times and places and is without parallel or substitute."

—H. D. Lewis (1910–1992)

"Because in no other person but the historic Jesus of Nazareth has God become man and lived a human life on earth, died to bear the penalty of our sins, and been raised from death and exalted to glory, there is no other Savior, for there is no other person who is qualified to save."

—John Stott (1921–2011)

"If God is infinite, he is beyond us. If he is beyond us, we cannot know him unless he chooses to make himself known. If he were to make himself known, he would surely do so in the highest terms intelligible to us, namely through human personality. It is exactly this that Christians believe he has done."[58]

—John Stott (1921–2011)

"The really staggering Christian claim is that Jesus of Nazareth was God made man.... The more you think about it, the more staggering it gets. Nothing in fiction is so fantastic as is this truth of the Incarnation."

—J.I. Packer (1926–2020)

QUESTIONS FOR REFLECTION AND DISCUSSION

1. Did you learn something new about Jesus in this chapter? Describe what you learned.

2. Was there something you already knew about Jesus that became strengthened and reinforced? Describe it.

3. What does the *kenosis* of Philippians 2:7 mean to you? What does it mean to you that the Son of God poured his entire self into a human body?

4. Review the description of emotions Jesus experienced and expressed. Have you perceived Jesus that way, or have you tended to see him as stoic and emotionless?

5. The Bible teaches that Jesus was completely sinless. Do you think he could be fully human if he never sinned? Why or why not?

6. Do you agree with Tozer's statement that Jesus performed his miracles in the strength and authority of His Spirit-anointed humanity?

7. Did anything you read in this chapter change the way you will relate to Jesus? If so, how?

Chapter Ten

THE DEATH OF JESUS: IT IS FINISHED!

"It was love that motivated his self-emptying, that led him to become a little lower than angels, to be subject to parents, to bow his head beneath the Baptist's hands, to endure the weakness of the flesh, and to submit to death even upon the cross."

—Bernard of Clairvaux (1090–1153)

Andrew David Naselli presents a fascinating breakdown of the four Gospels relative to their intense focus on the week leading up to Jesus' death. He writes:

> What is striking about the Gospels is that they focus on one week in Jesus' life—the final week in his life up to his death on the cross. Everything points to that one week, and the Gospels devote about a third of their words to that final week.
> Matthew 21–28 = ⅓ of book
> Mark 11–16 = ⅓ of book
> Luke 19–24 = ¼ of book

John 12–20 = nearly ½ of book (John 13–19 is devoted to one day = ⅓ of book)

One-third (twenty-nine of the eighty-nine chapters) of the Gospels is devoted to Jesus' final week, and the other two-thirds prepares readers for that final week. The heart of the Bible is the Gospels, and the heart of the Gospels is the sacrificial, redemptive work of Christ. The Gospels are essentially passion narratives with extended introductions.[59]

What are we to make of this concentrated focus on the events leading up to and following the death of Christ? The amount of Gospel material dedicated to the final week of Jesus' earthly life expresses how central his death is to the overall message of the New Testament. In this chapter, we will be exploring the overall context and purpose of Jesus' death, the physical, emotional, and spiritual aspects of his suffering, and what all of this means to us.

THE BIG PICTURE

Why did Jesus suffer and what did his sufferings accomplish? What is the big picture, the overall context? And what do we as believers have as a result of his death, burial, and resurrection? Let's explore several important aspects of the Savior's death.

I. JESUS' DEATH WAS PRE-PLANNED AND INTENTIONAL

Jesus was not an unfortunate victim of mob violence, nor was he simply in the wrong place at the wrong time. His death was not the result of an accident or of an unfortunate turn of events. His crucifixion had been predicted manifold times through prophetic words and pictures throughout the Old Testament (refer back to Chapter Five of this book). On the day of Pentecost, Peter recognized the natural role that certain ones had played in Jesus' death, but went even further. He referred to Jesus' death as being God's "prearranged plan."

> *But God knew what would happen, and **his prearranged plan** was carried out when Jesus was betrayed. With the help of lawless Gentiles, you nailed him to a cross and killed him*
>
> (Acts 2:23).

Other translations refer to:

- (NKJV): "*the determined purpose and foreknowledge of God.*"
- (NASB): "*the predetermined plan and foreknowledge of God.*"
- (NIV): "*God's deliberate plan and foreknowledge.*"
- (AMPC): "*the definite and fixed purpose and settled plan and foreknowledge of God.*"

John the Revelator described Jesus in a heavenly vision as *"the Lamb who was slaughtered before the world was made"* (Revelation 13:8). From a natural, chronological perspective, this could not be; Jesus wasn't slain until 2,000 years ago. However, from an eternal perspective, relative to the mind of God, Jesus was marked for death before any aspect of creation had taken place.

2. JESUS PREDICTED HIS OWN DEATH REPEATEDLY

When the eternal Son of God came into this earth, and as Jesus grew and stepped into his ministry, Scripture demonstrates abundantly that Jesus was crystal clear in understanding that his assignment from the

Father included dying for the sins of the world. Six times in Matthew's Gospel alone, Jesus tells his disciples that he is going to die.

For as Jonah was in the belly of the great fish for three days and three nights, so will the Son of Man be in the heart of the earth for three days and three nights

(Matthew 12:40).

From then on Jesus began to tell his disciples plainly that it was necessary for him to go to Jerusalem, and that he would suffer many terrible things at the hands of the elders, the leading priests, and the teachers of religious law. He would be killed, but on the third day he would be raised from the dead

(Matthew 16:21).

As they went back down the mountain, Jesus commanded them, "Don't tell anyone what you have seen until the Son of Man has been raised from the dead"

(Matthew 17:9).

After they gathered again in Galilee, Jesus told them, "The Son of Man is going to be betrayed into the hands of his enemies. He will be killed, but on the third day he will be raised from the dead." And the disciples were filled with grief

(Matthew 17:22-23).

As Jesus was going up to Jerusalem, he took the twelve disciples aside privately and told them what was going to happen to him. "Listen," he said, "we're going up to Jerusalem, where the Son of Man will be betrayed to the leading priests and the teachers of religious law. They will sentence him to die. Then they will hand him over to the Romans to be mocked, flogged with a whip, and crucified. But on the third day he will be raised from the dead"

(Matthew 20:17-19).

But after I have been raised from the dead, I will go ahead of you to Galilee and meet you there

(Matthew 26:32).

Jesus made other statements concerning his impending death in such places as John 12:7-8, 23-24, 27; 14:25.

At this point, it is reasonable to wonder how his disciples responded to these statements Jesus made concerning his death. Regarding Jesus declaring his upcoming death, Luke writes, *"But they didn't understand any of this. The significance of his words was hidden from them, and they failed to grasp what he was talking about"* (Luke 18:34). That's hard to imagine, but such was the case.

3. JESUS' DEATH WAS VOLUNTARY

Jesus' foreknowledge of his death and his own words lead us to understand that Jesus voluntarily submitted to the Father's will in becoming the ultimate sacrifice for the sins of the world.

The Father loves me because I sacrifice my life so I may take it back again. No one can take my life from me. I sacrifice it voluntarily. For I have the authority to lay it down when I want to and also to take it up again. For this is what my Father has commanded

(John 10:17-18).

We also see the voluntary nature of Jesus' death in the following:

- At a moment when Jesus could have walked away from his arrest, he prayed, *"My Father! If it is possible, let this cup of suffering be taken away from me. Yet I want your will to be done, not mine"* (Matthew 26:39).

- When the Roman soldiers came to arrest Jesus, he asked them who they were looking for. When they said that they were seeking Jesus, he responded, *"I AM he"* (John 18:5). John then relates, *"As Jesus said 'I AM he,' they all drew back and fell to the ground!"* (John 18:6). The very power of Jesus identifying himself caused all of them to fall over backwards. Had Jesus wished, he could have simply walked away to freedom as he had done at other times when facing hostile crowds (see Luke 4:30; John 8:59).

- In the Garden of Gethsemane, when Peter saw that Jesus was to be arrested, he drew his sword and went on the offensive. Jesus told him to put up his sword and told Peter, *"Do you think I cannot call on my Father, and he will at once put at my disposal more than twelve legions of angels?"* (Matthew 26:53 NIV). A legion in that day could have been as many as 6,000 soldiers. This means that 72,000 angelic warriors were at Jesus' disposal had he wished to request them from the Father, but he did not. He was committed to carrying out the Father's will by dying on the cross.

Jesus' death was entirely voluntary. As the author of Hebrews states, *"Christ offered himself to God as a perfect sacrifice for our sins"* (Hebrews 9:14).

4. JESUS' DEATH WAS SUBSTITUTIONARY

A substitute is simply one who takes the place of another. In sports, when one player comes out of the game to rest, a substitute takes his or her place. In school, when a teacher is not able to be in the classroom on a certain day, a substitute teacher comes in for that day. On the cross, Jesus took our place; he was our substitute. He took the punishment our sins deserved.

Isaiah paints a perfect picture of what Jesus accomplished on the cross. In the following verses, note how Isaiah mentions the substitutionary nature of Jesus' suffering.

> Yet it was **our weaknesses** he carried; it was **our sorrows** that weighed him down. And we thought his troubles were a punishment from God, a punishment for his own sins! But he was pierced for **our rebellion**, crushed for **our sins**. He was beaten so we could be whole. He was whipped so we could be healed
>
> (Isaiah 53:4-5).

The New Testament emphatically stresses the substitutionary nature of Christ's death.

> God made him who had no sin to be sin for us, so that in him we might become the righteousness of God
>
> (2 Corinthians 5:21 NIV).

> You know the generous grace of our Lord Jesus Christ. Though he was rich, yet for your sakes he became poor, so that by his poverty he could make you rich
>
> (2 Corinthians 8:9).

But Christ has rescued us from the curse pronounced by the law. When he was hung on the cross, he took upon himself the curse for our wrong-doing. For it is written in the Scriptures, "Cursed is everyone who is hung on a tree." Through Christ Jesus, God has blessed the Gentiles with the same blessing he promised to Abraham, so that we who are believers might receive the promised Holy Spirit through faith

(Galatians 3:13-14).

He suffered death for us…by God's grace, Jesus tasted death for everyone

(Hebrews 2:9).

The substitutionary nature of Christ's death has been understood and expressed by others throughout church history. Martin Luther stated, "Either sin is with you, lying on your shoulders, or it is lying on Christ, the Lamb of God. Now if it is lying on your back, you are lost; but if it is resting on Christ, you are free, and you will be saved. Now choose what you want." In his commentary on Galatians, Luther also remarked, "When we hear that Christ was made a curse for us, let us believe it with joy and assurance. By faith Christ changes places with us. He gets our sins, we get His holiness."

Another reformer, John Calvin (1509–1564), shared this insight into the substitutionary nature of Christ's death:

Having become with us the Son of Man, he has made us with himself sons of God. By his own descent to the earth he has prepared our ascent to heaven. Having received our mortality, he has bestowed on us his immortality. Having undertaken our weakness, he has made us strong in his strength. Having submitted to our poverty, he has transferred to us his riches. Having taken upon himself the burden of unrighteousness with which we were oppressed, he has clothed us with his righteousness.[60]

Likewise, Scottish minister Horatius Bonar (1808–1889) said:

> If Christ be not the Substitute, he is nothing to the sinner. If he did not die as the Sin-bearer, he has died in vain. Let us not be deceived on this point, or misled by those who, when they announce Christ as the Deliverer, think they have preached the Gospel. If I throw a rope to a drowning man, I am a deliverer. But is Christ no more than that? If I cast myself into the sea, and risk my life to save another, I am a deliverer. But is Christ no more? Did he but risk his life? The very essence of Christ's deliverance is the substitution of himself for us, his life for ours. He did not come to risk his life; He came to die! He did not redeem us by a little loss, a little sacrifice, a little labor, a little suffering. *"He redeemed us to God by his blood," "the precious blood of Christ"* (Revelation 5:9; 1 Peter 1:19). He gave all he had, even his life, for us."[61]

In a simpler yet still profound statement, A. W. Tozer remarked, "The only sin Jesus ever had was ours. And the only righteousness we can ever have is his." Jesus truly was our substitute, and by faith we receive the benefits of what he did for us.

5. JESUS' DEATH WAS EFFECTIVE

Concisely stated, Jesus' death worked. It accomplished what it was intended to accomplish and produced the intended results. A person lacking illumination from Scripture might think that Jesus' death was a great tragedy, that Jesus could have accomplished far more had he not died so young. Yet one who understands Scripture realizes that his death in his early thirties perfectly and masterfully accomplished his life's intended purpose.

Earthly rulers thought they were silencing Jesus and bringing his influence to an end when they crucified him. Spiritual principalities may have thought they were destroying the plan of God by influencing the masses to call for Jesus' crucifixion. But behind it all, God's design was perfectly achieved. Paul writes of *"the mystery of God—his plan that was previously hidden, even though he made it for our ultimate glory before the world began. But the rulers of this world have not understood it; if they had, they would not have crucified our glorious Lord"* (1 Corinthians 2:7-8). What was intended for Jesus' demise was turned by God for his glory and our benefit.

There is overwhelming consensus in Scripture about what was accomplished when Jesus hung on the cross, shed his blood, and died. The following three sections will highlight what Scripture says about the cross, Jesus' blood, and his death.

BIBLE STATEMENTS ABOUT THE CROSS

- **Endured**: *"Because of the joy awaiting him, he [Jesus] endured the cross, disregarding its shame"* (Hebrews 12:2).
- **The Curse Borne**: *"When he was hung on the cross, he took upon himself the curse for our wrongdoing"* (Galatians 3:13).
- **Sin Borne**: *"He personally carried our sins in his body on the cross"* (1 Peter 2:24).
- **Sin Cancelled**: *"He canceled the record of the charges against us and took it away by nailing it to the cross"* (Colossians 2:14).

- **Satan Defeated**: *"he disarmed the spiritual rulers and authorities. He shamed them publicly by his victory over them on the cross"* (Colossians 2:15).

- **God's Power**: *"The message of the cross is foolish to those who are headed for destruction! But we who are being saved know it is the very power of God"* (1 Corinthians 1:18).

- **Salvation Through the Cross**: *"If I were no longer preaching salvation through the cross of Christ, no one would be offended"* (Galatians 5:11).

- **The Christian's Boast**: *"As for me, may I never boast about anything except the cross of our Lord Jesus Christ"* (Galatians 6:14).

BIBLE STATEMENTS ABOUT THE BLOOD

Throughout the Old Testament, the blood of sacrificed animals spoke powerfully of deliverance and forgiveness. As Israel was preparing to depart Egypt, God instructed his people to roast a lamb or goat, one per family, and for them to eat it. They were also instructed to *"take some of the blood and smear it on the sides and top of the doorframes of the houses where they eat the animal"* (Exodus 12:7). This was the institution of Passover, and their obedience resulted in their safety and protection.

Blood was a major part of the entire Old Testament sacrificial system that was carried out in the tabernacle in the wilderness and later at the temple in Jerusalem. The book of Leviticus deals extensively with the priests and the sacrificial system, and *blood* is referenced repeatedly throughout the book. A key verse reads, *"For the life of the flesh is in its blood; and I have given it to you on the altar to take away your sin: for it is the blood which makes free from sin because of the life in it"* (Leviticus 17:11 BBE). Another time, Moses instructed Israel that *"the blood is the life"* (Deuteronomy 12:23).

The blood of Old Testament sacrifices provided a temporary covering for sin, but not a permanent solution. The New Testament teaches that *"it is not possible for the blood of bulls and goats to take away sins"* (Hebrews 10:4). Those sacrifices though, pointed to the future, toward the genuine *"Lamb of God who takes away the sin of the world!"* (John 1:29). We also read that *"our High Priest offered himself to God as a single sacrifice for sins, good for all time"* and that *"by that one offering he forever made perfect those who are being made holy"* (Hebrews 10:12,14).

What does Scripture teach about the power and significance of Jesus' blood? When we understand that "the life is in the blood" and "the blood is the life," it begins to be clear that when Jesus shed his blood for us, he was pouring out his life for us. What benefits are ours because of the blood of Jesus' sacrifice?

- **Forgiven**: *"He purchased our freedom with the blood of his Son and forgave our sins"* (Ephesians 1:7).
- **Justified**: *"We have been made right in God's sight by the blood of Christ"* (Romans 5:9). *"People are made right with God when they believe that Jesus sacrificed his life, shedding his blood"* (Romans 3:25).
- **Peace**: *"And through him God reconciled everything to himself. He made peace with everything in heaven and on earth by means of Christ's blood on the cross"* (Colossians 1:20).
- **Redeemed**: Speaking of our redemption, Peter says that it was accomplished by *"the precious blood of Christ, the sinless, spotless Lamb of God"* (1 Peter 1:19). John records the words of a song he heard

in heaven, "*your blood has ransomed people for God from every tribe and language and people and nation*" (Revelation 5:9).

- **Cleansed**: "*the blood of Jesus, his Son, cleanses us from all sin*" (1 John 1:7).

- **Remission**: "*for this is my blood, which confirms the covenant between God and his people. It is poured out as a sacrifice to forgive the sins of many*" (Matthew 26:28); and "*without the shedding of blood, there is no forgiveness*" (Hebrews 9:22).

- **Purified Conscience**: "*Just think how much more the blood of Christ will purify our consciences from sinful deeds*" (Hebrews 9:14).

- **Freed**: "*All glory to him who loves us and has freed us from our sins by shedding his blood for us*" (Revelation 1:5).

- **Washed**: "*They have washed their robes in the blood of the Lamb and made them white*" (Revelation 7:14).

- **Sanctification**: "*Therefore Jesus also, that He might sanctify the people with His own blood, suffered outside the gate*" (Hebrews 13:12 NKJV).

- **Covenant**: "*This is my blood, which confirms the covenant between God and his people*" (Matthew 26:28).

- **Purchased**: "*the church of God which He purchased with His own blood*" (Acts 20:28 NKJV).

- **Brought Near**: "*Once you were far away from God, but now you have been brought near to him through the blood of Christ*" (Ephesians 2:13).

- **Confidence**: "*we can boldly enter heaven's Most Holy Place because of the blood of Jesus*" (Hebrews 10:19).

- **Power**: "*And they have defeated him by the blood of the Lamb and by their testimony. And they did not love their lives so much that they were afraid to die*" (Revelation 12:11).

BIBLE STATEMENTS ABOUT JESUS' DEATH

The cross is where Jesus' death took place, and it was there that his redeeming blood was shed. But he didn't just suffer and bleed there; he died there. Scripture is replete with vivid descriptions of what his death accomplished and what we have as a result—through faith in him.

- **Died a Criminal's Death**:"*He humbled himself in obedience to God and died a criminal's death on a cross*" (Philippians 2:8).

- **Died for Sinners**:"*When we were utterly helpless, Christ came at just the right time and died for us sinners*" (Romans 5:6).

- **Broke the Power of Sin**:"*When he died, he died once to break the power of sin*" (Romans 6:10).

- **Removed Sin**:"*He has appeared at the end of the age to remove sin by his own death as a sacrifice*" (Hebrews 9:26).

- **Removed the Penalty**: "*Christ died to set them free from the penalty of the sins they had committed under that first covenant*" (Hebrews 9:15).

- **Made Us Holy**:"*So also Jesus suffered and died outside the city gates to make his people holy by means of his own blood*" (Hebrews 13:12).

- **Reconciled Us to God**:"*He has reconciled you to himself through the death of Christ in his physical body*" (Colossians 1:22).

- **Friendship Restored**:"*Our friendship with God was restored by the death of his Son while we were still his enemies*" (Romans 5:10).

- **No Condemnation**: "*Who then will condemn us? No one—for Christ Jesus died for us and was raised to life for us, and he is sitting in the place of honor at God's right hand, pleading for us*" (Romans 8:34).

- **Brought Us Home**: "*Christ suffered for our sins once for all time. He never sinned, but he died for sinners to bring you safely home to God*" (1 Peter 3:18).

- **A New Way Opened**: "*By his death, Jesus opened a new and life-giving way through the curtain into the Most Holy Place*" (Hebrews 10:20).

- **Life Together**: "*Christ died for us so that, whether we are dead or alive when he returns, we can live with him forever*" (1 Thessalonians 5:10).

THE UNTHINKABLE SUFFERING OF CHRIST

My enemies surround me like a pack of dogs; an evil gang closes in on me. They have pierced my hands and feet

(Psalm 22:16).

They will look on me whom they have pierced and mourn for him as for an only son. They will grieve bitterly for him as for a firstborn son who has died

(Zechariah 12:10).

If you watched Mel Gibson's *The Passion of the Christ*, you may have an idea of what this section is going to address. This movie graphically portrays the absolute nightmarish, brutal, and ghastly nature of the torture Jesus endured prior to his crucifixion and the extreme agony he experienced on the cross. The movie is difficult to watch, but to have personally witnessed it would have been even more gruesome. In speaking of Christ's unthinkable abuse, Isaiah prophesied that *"His face was so disfigured he seemed hardly human, and from his appearance, one would scarcely know he was a man. ...We turned our backs on him and looked the other way"* (Isaiah 52:14; 53:3).

225

Though there were no high-definition movies in biblical days, Paul told the Galatians that *"the meaning of Jesus Christ's death was made as clear to you as if you had seen a picture of his death on the cross"* (Galatians 3:1). Is it possible that Paul was intentionally verbally graphic so that early Christians would appreciate the magnitude of what Jesus suffered so they would appreciate their salvation? An early church leader in Constantinople, John Chrysostom (347–407), said, "By the cross we know the gravity of sin and the greatness of God's love towards us."

Before we address some of the issues of Jesus' suffering, may I encourage you to read the descriptions given by Matthew (26:57–27:50), Mark (14:53–15:37), Luke (22:54–23:49), and John (18:12–19:37)? These are true, historical accounts of his trial, beating and scourging, and death by crucifixion. As you do, remember that Jesus went through all of that because he loves us and did not want our sin to separate us from the Father. He wanted us to receive forgiveness and become the children of God.

What did the suffering of Jesus include?

- Spitting in his face (Matthew 26:67)
- Blindfolded (Mark 14:65)
- Beaten with fists (Matthew 26:67)
- Slapped (Matthew 26:67)
- Verbally abused (Matthew 26:68)
- Scourged with a lead-tipped whip (Matthew 27:26)
- A crown of thorns shoved into his scalp (Matthew 27:29)
- Mocked and taunted (Matthew 27:29)
- Spit on again—perhaps by hundreds of soldiers (Matthew 27:30)

- Beaten repeatedly on his head with a staff—a large stick (Matthew 27:30)
- Forced to carry his cross—probably the horizontal bar weighing approximately sixty pounds—to his place of execution (John 19:17). Simon of Cyrene relieved him of this task along the way (Matthew 27:32)
- Nailed to the cross and crucified (Matthew 27:35)
- Blasphemed and mocked (Matthew 27:39-44)
- Gave up his spirit and died (John 19:30)
- To ensure he was really dead, a soldier pierced his heart with a spear and water and blood flowed out (John 19:33-34).

It is possible that the Gospel writers did not provide more detail about what was involved in a scourging or crucifixion because these were widely known practices in those days. The people they were addressing at that time knew how repulsive and revolting these forms of torture and death were. It is also possible that the biblical writers felt it was far more important to focus on the meaning and the results of Jesus' suffering than highlighting the grotesque details of the physical process.

Having said that, it can still be insightful to understand the magnitude of Jesus' physical suffering to appreciate more fully what he endured on our behalf, for our benefit. Let's look in a bit more detail at what Jesus suffered before and during his crucifixion. As you read concerning what went on physically throughout Jesus' suffering, don't forget why he underwent it and what his suffering was for—it was for you and me.

THE SCOURGING

I offered my back to those who beat me and my cheeks to those who pulled out my beard. I did not hide my face from mockery and spitting

(Isaiah 50:6).

He was beaten so we could be whole. He was whipped so we could be healed

(Isaiah 53:5).

Matthew makes such a brief statement—that the Roman governor *"ordered Jesus flogged with a lead-tipped whip, then turned him over to the Roman soldiers to be crucified"* (Matthew 27:26). This scourging, or flogging, brought unimaginable pain and damage to the victim's body. There were the leather straps, usually knotted, and often having pieces of jagged bone and metal affixed to them. That way, when the straps came down on the back of the naked victim (and often, the rest of his body as well), it would not only cause deep lacerations, but the pieces of bone and metal would tear off chunks of flesh. It is likely that Jesus' hands were bound and tied to a pole above him so that his skin was stretched tightly to ensure maximum damage from the repeated blows.

Noted commentator William Barclay writes, "Such scourging always preceded crucifixion and 'it reduced the naked body to strips of raw flesh, and inflamed and bleeding welts.' Men died under it, and men lost their reason under it, and few remained conscious to the end of it."[62] Another commentary notes, "The backs of the prisoners were completely flayed by this process. They frequently fainted, and sometimes died. The soldiers would not inflict the punishment mildly, for they were the cruel ones who mocked Him afterward.

It was, moreover, the policy of Pilate that Jesus should be perfectly disfigured."[63]

It is likely that multiple soldiers participated in whipping Jesus. After the scourging, they *"twisted together a crown of thorns and set it on his head...they spit on him, and took the staff and struck him on the head again and again"* (Matthew 27:29-30 NIV). Jesus was severely injured and lost much blood before he was led away to the place of his execution. It is no wonder that he was unable to carry the patibulum (the cross bar) all the way to Calvary.

THE CRUCIFIXION

As horrible as scourging was, the worst for Jesus was yet to come. Cicero, the Roman statesman and philosopher called crucifixion "the most cruel and the most horrible torture" and said, "Let the very word 'cross,' be far removed from not only the bodies of Roman citizens, but even from their thoughts, their eyes, and their ears." Roman citizens were typically not crucified, but it was a powerful threat and tool of intimidation against non-citizens, against slaves and the lowest of criminals throughout the Empire.

In 1965, a medical doctor named C. Truman Davis wrote an outstanding piece on what Jesus experienced on the cross from a medical viewpoint. After describing the nails being driven through the hands and feet, and the cross-bar being affixed to the vertical beam, Davis writes:

> The Victim is now crucified. As He slowly sags down with more weight on the nails in the wrists, excruciating, fiery pain shoots along the fingers and up the arms to explode in the brain—the nails in the wrists are putting pressure on

the median nerves. As He pushes Himself upward to avoid this stretching torment, He places His full weight on the nail through His feet. Again there is the searing agony of the nail tearing through the nerves between the metatarsal bones of the feet.

At this point, as the arms fatigue, great waves of cramps sweep over the muscles, knotting them in deep, relentless, throbbing pain. With these cramps comes the inability to push Himself upward. Hanging by his arms, the pectoral muscles are paralyzed and the intercostal muscles are unable to act. Air can be drawn into the lungs, but cannot be exhaled. Jesus fights to raise Himself in order to get even one short breath. Finally, carbon dioxide builds up in the lungs and in the blood stream and the cramps partially subside. Spasmodically, he is able to push Himself upward to exhale and bring in the lifegiving oxygen.

After Jesus suffered like this for hours, Davis proceeds:

It is now almost over. The loss of tissue fluids has reached a critical level; the compressed heart is struggling to pump heavy, thick, sluggish blood into the tissue; the tortured lungs are making a frantic effort to gasp in small gulps of air. The markedly dehydrated tissues send their flood of stimuli to the brain.

With one last surge of strength, he once again presses His torn feet against the nail, straightens His legs, takes a deeper breath, and utters His seventh and last cry, *"Father! Into thy hands I commit my spirit."*

And then, following Jesus' death, Davis concludes:

> Apparently to make doubly sure of death, the legionnaire drove his lance through the fifth interspace between the ribs, upward through the pericardium and into the heart. The 34th verse of the 19th chapter of the Gospel according to St. John reports: "And immediately there came out blood and water." That is, there was an escape of water fluid from the sac surrounding the heart, giving postmortem evidence that Our Lord died not the usual crucifixion death by suffocation, but of heart failure due to shock and constriction of the heart by fluid in the pericardium.[64]

JESUS' SEVEN SAYINGS FROM THE CROSS

It is difficult to imagine that anyone, suffering as Jesus did, could maintain clarity and coherence, and yet his brief utterances during those six hours of excruciating pain reveal his majesty and mastery even in the face of death.

1. Regarding those who crucified him, Jesus prayed, *"Father, forgive them, for they don't know what they are doing"* (Luke 23:34). What a remarkable expression of the love and the mercy of God—the very love and mercy that Jesus had come to earth to reveal.

2. Jesus was crucified between two criminals. One reviled him and one requested mercy. To the repentant criminal, Jesus said, *"I assure you, today you will be with me in paradise"* (Luke 23:43).

3. At a time when a suffering person could have only thought of himself, Jesus spoke a kind and caring word regarding his mother.

He saw Mary standing next to John and said, *"'Dear woman, here is your son.' And he said to this disciple, 'Here is your mother.' And from then on this disciple took her into his home"* (John 19:26-27).

4. Jesus' fourth statement from the cross is one that we will examine much more closely in the following section. *"At about three o'clock, Jesus called out with a loud voice, 'Eli, Eli, lema sabachthani?' which means 'My God, my God, why have you abandoned me?'"* (Matthew 27:46).

5. *"I am thirsty"* (John 19:28). Thirst can be brought on by dehydration and blood loss, and Jesus had no doubt experienced both. How ironic that the one who offered living water (see John 4:10) is himself now thirsty.

6. Next, Jesus said, *"It is finished!"* (John 19:30). This word, *tetelestai* in the Greek, was language from commerce. When written on a receipt, it meant "paid in full." This was a cry of victory and accomplishment—the debt of sin had been satisfied. Note that Jesus said, "*It* is finished," not "*I* am finished." Much was yet ahead for him, including his resurrection, ascension into Heaven, and his future works. The price for sin, though, had been paid, once and for all.

7. And finally, *"Jesus shouted, 'Father, I entrust my spirit into your hands!' And with those words he breathed his last"* (Luke 23:46). He died as he had lived, with complete trust in the Father.

These moving statements are just another revelation of Jesus' remarkable magnificence. While his suffering is revealed in the sense of abandonment he felt and the thirst he experienced, we see him praying for forgiveness for those who crucified him, ministering assurance to the repentant criminal, expressing care and concern for his mother, triumphantly announcing the completion of his mission, and committing his spirit into the hands of his Father.

THE INWARD SUFFERINGS OF CHRIST

Having examined some physical descriptions of what Jesus experienced through his beatings, scouring, and crucifixion, let's look at another aspect of what he went through, namely, the agonies of his soul. Theologian John Calvin stated that "unless his soul shared in the punishment, he would have been the Redeemer of bodies alone."[65] Similarly, Jonathan Edwards wrote, "Besides what our Lord endured in this excruciating corporeal death, he endured vastly more in his soul."[66]

We begin to get a glimpse of the inward sufferings of Jesus in the Garden of Gethsemane. As he prepared himself spiritually for the coming hours, he told his three closest disciples, *"My soul is crushed with grief to the point of death"* (Matthew 26:38). Another version describes the scene: *"He began to show grief and distress of mind and was deeply depressed. Then He said to them, My soul is very sad and deeply grieved, so that I am almost dying of sorrow"* (Matthew 26:37–38 AMPC).

If those words don't convey the intensity of Christ's inward suffering, consider another phenomenon that occurred during this same time. Scripture tells us that *"He prayed more fervently, and he was in such agony of spirit that his sweat fell to the ground like great drops of blood"* (Luke 22:44). Luke, a physician, is the only Gospel writer who recorded this specific incident. Perhaps his background in medicine made this noteworthy to him.

In modern times, a medical doctor named Joseph W. Bergeron writes that "Sweating blood, called *hematidrosis* in medical terminology, is a rarely observed phenomenon. It is the spontaneous discharge of blood through the skin, *sweating blood.*"[67] Another team of medical doctors confirmed the rarity of the specific disorder and state that it "may occur in highly emotional states or in persons with bleeding disorders. As a result of hemorrhage into the sweat glands, the skin becomes fragile and tender. Luke's descriptions support the diagnosis of hematidrosis."[68]

Theologian John Calvin also commented on the spiritual, emotional, and mental agonies Jesus experienced in the Garden of Gethsemane, and he contrasts Jesus' death with what he calls "common death." While Jesus certainly experienced physical death on the cross, the insinuation seems to be that there was something unique in Jesus' death, something beyond what others experience, and this was due to him bearing the sin of the world on the cross. Calvin writes:

> What shameful softness would it have been (as I have said) for Christ to be so tortured by the dread of common death as to sweat blood, and to be able to be revived only at the appearance of angels? What? Does not that prayer, coming from unbelievable bitterness of heart and repeated three times—*"Father, if it be possible, let this cup pass from me"* (Matthew 26:39)—show that Christ had a harsher and more difficult struggle than with common death?
>
> For feeling himself, as it were, forsaken by God, he did not waver in the least from trust in his goodness. This is proved by that remarkable prayer to God in which he cried out in acute agony: *"My God, My God, why hast thou forsaken me?"* (Matthew 27:46). For even though he suffered beyond

measure, he did not cease to call him his God, by whom he cried out that he had been forsaken.[69]

John Maclaurin (1693–1754), a Scottish minister, contrasted the physical and spiritual sufferings of Christ with the following words:

> We may paint the outward appearance of his sufferings, but not the inward bitterness or invisible causes of them. Men can paint the cursed tree, but not the curse of the law that made it so. Men can paint Christ bearing the cross to Calvary, but not Christ bearing the sins of many. We may describe the nails piercing his sacred flesh, but who can describe eternal justice piercing both flesh and spirit? We may describe the soldier's spear, but not the arrows of the Almighty; the cup of vinegar which he but tasted, but not the cup of wrath, which he drank out to the lowest dregs; the derision of the Jews, but not the desertion of the Almighty forsaking his Son, that he might never forsake us who were his enemies.[70]

Charles H. Spurgeon, called the prince of preachers, pastored a Baptist church of 6,000 in London during the 1800s. In teaching on Christ *"being made sin"* and *"being made a curse,"* Spurgeon said the following:

> We would be very clear here, because very strong expressions have been used by those who hold the great truth which I am endeavouring to preach, which strong expressions have conveyed the truth they meant to convey, but also a great deal more. [In] Martin Luther's wonderful book on

the Galatians…he says plainly, but be assured did not mean what he said to be literally understood, that "Jesus Christ was the greatest sinner that ever lived; that all the sins of men were so laid upon Christ that he became all the thieves, and murderers and adulterers that ever were, in one." Now, he meant this, that God treated Christ as if he had been a great sinner; as if he had been all the sinners in the world in one; and such language teaches that truth very plainly: but, Luther-like in his boisterousness, he overshoots his mark, and leaves room for the censure that he has almost spoken blasphemy against the blessed person of our Lord.

Now, Christ never was and never could be a sinner; and in his person and in his character, in himself considered, he never could be anything but well-beloved of God, and blessed for ever and well-pleasing in Jehovah's sight; so that when we say to-day that he was a curse, we must lay stress on those words, *"He was made a curse"*—constituted a curse, set as a curse; and then again we must emphasize those other words, "for us"—not on his own account at all; but entirely out of love to us, that we might be redeemed, he stood in the sinner's place and was reckoned to be a sinner, and treated as a sinner, and made a curse for us.

Let us go farther into this truth. How was Christ made a curse? In the first place, he was made a curse because all the sins of his people were actually laid on him. Remember the words of the apostle—it is no doctrine of mine, mark you; it is an inspired sentence, it is God's doctrine—*"He made him to be sin for us"*; and let me quote another passage from the prophet Isaiah, *"The Lord hath laid on him the iniquity of us all"*; …and yet another from the same prophet, *"He shall bear their iniquities."* The sins of God's people were lifted from off them and imputed to Christ, and their sins were looked upon as if Christ had committed them. He was regarded as if he had been the sinner; he actually and in very deed stood in the sinner's place.

…So Christ was made a curse. Wonderful and awful words, but as they are scriptural words, we must receive them. Sin being on Christ, the curse came on Christ, and in consequence, our Lord felt an unutterable horror of soul. Surely it was that horror which made him sweat great drops of blood when he saw and felt that God was beginning to treat him as if he had been a sinner. …It was an anguish never to be measured, an agony never to be comprehended. It is to God, and God alone that his griefs were fully known.[71]

In another sermon, Spurgeon related a remarkable story about Martin Luther's honest struggle to understand what is most likely incomprehensible to the human mind.

I have read that once upon a time, Martin Luther sat down in his study to consider this text. Hour after hour, that mighty man of God sat still, and those who waited on him came into the room, again and again, and he was so absorbed in his meditation that they almost thought he was a corpse. He moved neither hand nor foot, and neither ate nor drank, but sat with his eyes wide open, like one in a trance, thinking over these wondrous words, *"My God, my God, why hast thou forsaken me?"* And when, after many long hours, in which he seemed to be utterly lost to everything that went on around him, he rose from his chair, someone heard him say, "God forsaking God! No man can understand that," and so he went his way.[72]

B.H. Carroll (1843–1914), former President of the Southwest Baptist Theological Seminary in Dallas, Texas, said the following:

> About the ninth hour, which would be three o'clock, the silence was broken, and we have the fourth voice of Jesus: *"My God, my God, why hast thou forsaken me?"* Physical death is the separation of the soul from the body, and spiritual death is the separation of the soul from God. So just before that darkness passed away, closing the ninth hour, Christ died the spiritual death.[73]

Jesus' overall anticipatory anguish is vividly described by Ralph Earle (1908–1995), the founding Professor of New Testament at the Nazarene Theological Seminary in Kansas City, Missouri. Earle writes:

> What did Jesus' death mean for Him? The answer is best suggested by His prayer in Gethsemane. There He cried out in agony of soul, *"O my Father, if it be possible, let this cup pass from me."* Then, He bowed his head in humble submission and said: *"Nevertheless not as I will, but as thou wilt."*
>
> What was this cup from which He prayed to be delivered? Carping critics have said that Jesus cringed with cowardly fear at the thought of death. But such cavilers are

utterly ignorant of the true significance of that hour. Jesus was not afraid to die!

What was it, then, from which He shrank in anguish of spirit? It was His Father's face turned away from Him in the awful hour when *"Him who knew no sin he made to be sin on our behalf; that we might become the righteousness of God in him."* Our Substitute took the torturous trail of a lost soul, walking out into the labyrinthine depths of outer darkness. He tasted death for every man. That means more than physical death. When Christ cried out on the cross, *"My God, my God, why hast thou forsaken me?"* He was experiencing something far deeper. He was paying the penalty for sin—not His, but ours. The penalty for sin is separation from God. This was the price that Jesus had to pay for our salvation. There was no alternative. The final words of Christ in the Garden were these: *"The cup which my Father hath given me, shall I not drink it?"* To secure man's salvation, the Son of God let the blow of divine justice fall on Himself. He who could say, *"I do always those things that please him"* had to endure the displeasure of the one He delighted to serve.

In those few but fateful hours on the cross Jesus tasted the unspeakable horror of eternal death. Spiritual darkness shrouded His soul. His cry of dereliction is the measure of His sacrifice. Olin A. Curtis has well expressed it thus: "And so, there alone, our Lord opens his mind, his heart, his personal consciousness, to the whole inflow of the horror of sin—the endless history of it, from the first choice of selfishness on, on to the eternity of hell; the boundless ocean and desolation he allows; wave upon wave, to overwhelm his soul."[74]

I recall hearing those desperate words as a child, usually the Sunday prior to Easter. As the pastor of my church told the story of the crucifixion he would always include Jesus crying out, *"My God, My God, why have You forsaken Me?"* (Matthew 27:46 NKJV). Not understanding the spiritual ramifications of what I was hearing, I wondered, "If God didn't come and help Jesus during his greatest hour of need, what reason would I have to expect God to help me if I was in trouble?" I did not realize that Jesus was suffering as my substitute on the cross. He was bearing the punishment and penalty for my sin so that I would never have to. He was experiencing alienation and rejection from the Father so that I could know his eternal acceptance and embrace.

Renowned evangelist Billy Graham wrote in his book *Peace with God*:

> Sometimes people have asked me why Christ died so quickly, in six hours, on the cross, while other victims agonized on the cross for two and three days—and longer. He was weak and exhausted when He came there. He had been scourged, He was physically depleted. But when Christ died, He died voluntarily. He chose the exact moment when He expired.
>
> There he hung between heaven and earth. Having suffered unspeakably.
>
> …The spikes never held Him—it was the cords of love that bound tighter than any nails that men could mold. *"But*

God commendeth his love toward us, in that, while we were yet sinners, Christ died for us" (Romans 5:8).

...But the physical suffering of Jesus Christ was not the real suffering. Many men before Him had died. Others had hung on a cross longer than He did. Many men had become martyrs. The awful suffering of Jesus Christ was His spiritual death. He reached the final issue of sin, fathomed the deepest sorrow, when He cried, *"My God, why hast thou forsaken me?"* This cry was proof that Christ, becoming sin for us, had died physically, and with it He lost all sense of the Father's presence at that moment in time.

...He who knew no sin was made to be sin on our behalf that we might become the righteousness of God in Him (Galatians 3:13; Mark 15:34; 2 Corinthians 5:21). On the cross He was made sin. He was God-forsaken. Because He knew no sin there is a value beyond comprehension in the penalty He bore, a penalty that He did not need for Himself.

...How it was accomplished in the depth of the darkness man will never know. I know only one thing—He bore my sins in His body upon the tree. He hung where I should have hung. The pains of hell that were my portion were heaped on Him, and I am able to go to heaven and merit that which is not my own, but is His by every right.[75]

I especially appreciate Billy Graham's humility in acknowledging there is something "beyond comprehension" about Christ's sufferings. He also said that "man will never know" exactly how Jesus accomplished all that he did relative to our redemption. It is perfectly appropriate if we sense an overwhelming awe relative to Jesus' amazing work.

In the light of the various scriptural indications and the remarkable statements from great servants of God through the ages, we assuredly say that Jesus' suffering involved his whole person. The author of Hebrews tells that in order for Jesus to represent us and to help us, *"it was necessary for him to be made in every respect like us, his brothers and sisters"* (Hebrews 2:17). Just like us, then, Jesus was spirit, soul, and body (see 1 Thessalonians 5:23).

Perhaps we can understand it this way: Jesus went to the cross in the entirety of his being—spirit, soul, and body. He bore the consequences of sin in the entirety of his being—spirit, soul, and body. He did all this so that he might redeem us back to God in the entirety of our being—spirit, soul, and body.

Nothing in the spiritual, emotional, and mental sufferings of Christ detracts from his physical death or the significance of his shed blood. All of redemption is a package, so to speak. All of these factors, along with his virgin birth, his sinless life, his resurrection and ascension—they are all a collective part of the redemptive work that God carried out through Christ.

GREAT STATEMENTS ABOUT THE DEATH OF JESUS

"By the cross we know the gravity of sin and the greatness of God's love towards us."

—John Chrysostom (347–407)

"Jesus became the greatest liar, perjurer, thief, adulterer and murderer that mankind had ever known—not because he committed these sins but because he was actually made sin for us."

—Martin Luther (1483–1546)

"When we hear that Christ was made a curse for us, let us believe it with joy and assurance. By faith Christ changes places with us. He gets our sins, we get His holiness."

—Martin Luther (commenting on Galatians 3:13) (1483–1546)

"Jesus died to save such as you, he is full of compassion."

—George Whitefield (1714–1770)

"When men sought to make Him a king He fled; now that they seek to put Him to death He goes out to meet them."

—Rudolph Stier (1800–1862)

"Christ took your cup of grief, your cup of the curse, pressed it to his lips, drank it to its dregs, then filled it with his sweet, pardoning, sympathizing love, and gave it back for you to drink, and to drink forever!"

—Octavius Winslow (1808–1878)

"When Christ cried out on Calvary, 'It is finished!' He meant what He said. All that men have to do now is just accept the work of Jesus Christ."

—D.L. Moody (1837–1899)

"Upon a life I did not live, upon a death I did not die, another's life, another's death, I stake my whole eternity."

—Hudson Taylor (1832–1905)

"We are told that Christ was killed for us, that His death has washed out our sins, and that by dying He disabled death itself. That is the formula. That is Christianity. That is what has to be believed."

—C.S. Lewis (1898–1963)

"O Lord Jesus Christ, who by thy death didst take away the sting of death."

—Book of Common Prayer, 1928

"The cross of Christ preaches…the blood of the cross speaks. It has something to say. Have you heard it?"

—D. Martyn–Lloyd Jones (1899–1981)

"Jesus was crucified, not in a cathedral between two candles, but on a cross between two thieves."

—George F. MacLeod (1895–1991)

"In the cross of Christ I see three things: First, a description of the depth of man's sin. Second, the overwhelming love of God. Third, the only way of salvation."

—Billy Graham (1918–2018)

"The single, overwhelming fact of history is the crucifixion of Jesus Christ. There is no military battle, no geographical exploration, no scientific discovery, no literary creation, no artistic achievement, no moral heroism that compares with it. It is unique, massive, monumental, unprecedented, and unparalleled.

The cross of Christ is the central fact to which all other facts are subordinate."[76]

—Eugene Peterson (1932–2018)

"He came to pay a debt he did not owe, because we owed a debt we could not pay."

—Unknown

QUESTIONS FOR REFLECTION AND DISCUSSION

1. Did you learn something new about Jesus in this chapter? Describe what you learned.

2. Did something you already knew about Jesus become strengthened or reinforced? Describe it.

3. Why do you think such a high percentage of the content of the Gospel accounts is dedicated to the immediate time window around the death of Jesus?

4. What does it mean to you that Christ was your substitute, and that his death for you was substitutionary?

5. In this chapter, three lists were given—bullet points listing multiple ramifications of the cross, the blood, and the death of Jesus. Which of these impacted you the most, and why?

6. Of Jesus' seven sayings from the cross, which one most impressed you the most, and why?

7. Did anything you read in this chapter change the way you will relate to Jesus? If so, how?

Chapter Eleven

ABSOLUTE VICTORY: JESUS' RESURRECTION AND ASCENSION

"For I know that after His resurrection also, He was still possessed of flesh. And I believe that He is so now."

—Ignatius of Antioch (?–117)

Those who think that all religions are the same miss a glaring difference between Christianity and other belief systems. What gloriously distinguishes the gospel of Jesus Christ from other faiths is the literal, physical resurrection of Christ himself. Not only is Christ's resurrection inextricably woven into the very fabric of Scripture, but it is the very basis for the uniqueness of our faith. Pastor and Bible teacher Tony Evans brilliantly explains:

> The Resurrection places Jesus Christ in a class by Himself. It makes Him unique. Other religions can compete with Christianity on some things. They can say, for example,

"Your founder gave you a holy book? Our founder gave us a holy book. Your founder has a large following? So does ours. You have buildings where people come to worship your God? We have buildings where people come to worship our god." But Christians can say, "All of that may be true, but our Founder rose from the dead!"[77]

The fact of Jesus' resurrection is monumentally important, and its implications are all-important to our temporal and eternal well-being. As we recognize and believe in the historical reality of Jesus' death and resurrection, we must not miss this vital fact: It was *for us* that Jesus died and was raised. His blood secured *our* forgiveness; his resurrection provides *our* justification. When we trust in Jesus and what he did for us, God places us in right standing with himself.

THE HISTORIC EVENT

After suffering an unimaginably violent death, Jesus' lifeless body was taken down from the cross and placed in the tomb of a wealthy man named Joseph of Arimathea (see Matthew 27:57-61). Chief priests and other religious leaders went to Pilate, saying *"Sir, we remember what that deceiver once said while he was still alive: 'After three days I will rise from the dead'"* (Matthew 27:63). As a result, Roman soldiers were assigned to seal the tomb and to guard the tomb where Jesus' body lay (see Matthew 27:65-66).

What a great miscalculation! They thought it would only take a few soldiers to protect a dead body from being stolen, but they were misguided in thinking the disciples would even make such an attempt. The disciples were terrified and in hiding; they posed no threat. The problem the authorities faced was that God himself resurrected Jesus from the dead, and they could not have stopped that with every soldier in the Roman Empire.

The details of Jesus' burial and resurrection are well detailed by the writers of the Gospels. What follows is not comprehensive, but conveys several important aspects.

> *Afterward Joseph of Arimathea, who had been a secret disciple of Jesus (because he feared the Jewish leaders), asked Pilate for permission to take down Jesus' body. When Pilate gave permission, Joseph came and took the body away. With him came Nicodemus, the man who had come to Jesus at night. He brought about seventy-five pounds of perfumed ointment made from myrrh and aloes. Following Jewish burial custom, they wrapped Jesus' body with the spices in long sheets of linen cloth. The place of crucifixion was near a garden, where there was a new tomb, never used before. And so, because it was the day of preparation for the Jewish Passover and since the tomb was close at hand, they laid Jesus there*
> (John 19:38-42).

Garden tombs were typically for the wealthy, and Nicodemus provided enough perfumed ointment for a royal burial. Matthew includes two additional details, telling us that the tomb was Joseph's own, and that he also *"rolled a great stone across the entrance and left"* (Matthew 27:60).

THEN COMES SUNDAY MORNING

The apostle Matthew records the startling events of resurrection morning this way:

*Early on Sunday morning, as the new day was dawning, Mary Magda-
lene and the other Mary went out to visit the tomb. Suddenly there was
a great earthquake! For an angel of the Lord came down from heaven,
rolled aside the stone, and sat on it. His face shone like lightning, and his
clothing was as white as snow. The guards shook with fear when they saw
him, and they fell into a dead faint. Then the angel spoke to the women.
"Don't be afraid!" he said. "I know you are looking for Jesus, who was
crucified. He isn't here! He is risen from the dead, just as he said would
happen. Come, see where his body was lying. And now, go quickly and
tell his disciples that he has risen from the dead, and he is going ahead of
you to Galilee. You will see him there. Remember what I have told you"*

(Matthew 28:1-7).

Jesus' resurrection from the dead changed everything.

PRIMARY, NOT PERIPHERAL

The apostle Paul lists the death and resurrection of Jesus as "most
important" when communicating to them the essentials of the Christian faith. He writes:

*I passed on to you what was most important and what had also been
passed on to me. Christ died for our sins, just as the Scriptures said. He
was buried, and he was raised from the dead on the third day, just as
the Scriptures said. He was seen by Peter and then by the Twelve. After
that, he was seen by more than 500 of his followers at one time, most of
whom are still alive, though some have died. Then he was seen by James
and later by all the apostles. Last of all, as though I had been born at the
wrong time, I also saw him*

(1 Corinthians 15:3-8).

The validity of Christ's resurrection is based on multiple eye-witnesses, several of whom surrendered their lives as martyrs instead of denying what they knew to be true. The early Christian martyrs could have saved their lives by renouncing their faith in Jesus, by declaring that he had not really been raised from the dead, and renouncing their faith in him, but they chose to die rather than to recant their faith.

Luke reinforces Paul's statement by explaining that *"During the forty days after he suffered and died, he appeared to the apostles from time to time, and he proved to them in many ways that he was actually alive"* (Acts 1:3). As we seek to synthesize what the different Gospel writers recorded, we can piece together the following proposed list of Jesus' post-resurrection appearances.

1. Jesus appeared to Mary Magdalene at the tomb on Sunday morning: *"After Jesus rose from the dead early on Sunday morning, the first person who saw him was Mary Magdalene"* (Mark 16:9).

2. Jesus appeared to *"Mary the mother of James, and Salome"* who were with Mary Magdalene at the tomb (Mark 16:1). According to Luke, Joanna and other women were also involved (see Luke 24:8).

3. Jesus appeared to Peter on Sunday as well (see Luke 24:34; 1 Corinthians 15:5).

4. Later that day, Jesus appeared to two unnamed disciples on the road to Emmaus (see Luke 24:13-36). Though they did not initially recognize him, they said their hearts had burned within them *"as he talked with us on the road and explained the Scriptures"* to them (Luke 24:32) and that *"they had recognized him as he was breaking the bread"* (Luke 24:35).

5. Jesus appeared that Sunday evening to the remaining disciples with the exception of Thomas (see Luke 24:36-43; John 20:19-25). It was during this meeting that Jesus emphasized his physicality by saying, "*Look at my hands. Look at my feet. You can see that it's really me. Touch me and make sure that I am not a ghost, because ghosts don't have bodies, as you see that I do*" (Luke 24:39). Further, he asked if they had any food, and he ate broiled fish in their presence (see Luke 24:41-43).

6. Eight days later, Jesus appeared to the disciples again, and this time Thomas was present (see John 20:26-29). At this encounter, Thomas said to Jesus, "*My Lord and my God!*" (John 20:28).

7. Later yet, Jesus visited with seven of his disciples again by the Sea of Galilee. It was during this appearance that Jesus had breakfast with them, reiterated Peter's calling, and even illustrated how Peter would die in old age (see John 21:1-24).

8. In yet another appearance in Galilee, this time on a mountain, Jesus commissioned his disciples to "*go and make disciples of all the nations*" (Matthew 28:16-20). Mark's version of the Great Commission is recorded in Mark 16:15-18.

9. Jesus appeared to his disciples again, had a meal with them, spoke to them about the power of the Spirit that was to come upon them, and then ascended into Heaven (see Acts 1:4-11; Luke 24:49-51).

10. Though not recorded in the Gospel accounts, Jesus appeared after his resurrection to "*more than 500 of his followers at one time*," to his half-brother James (see 1 Corinthians 15:6-7), to Stephen, the first martyr of the church (see Acts 7:55-60), to Paul (see Acts 9:1-20; 1 Corinthians 15:8), and to John (see Revelation 1:12-18).

NOT AN AFTERTHOUGHT

Jesus' resurrection was just as pre-planned and intentional as his crucifixion had been. Actually, his death *and* resurrection were as interconnected as the two sides of a coin. Both were part of the whole—part of God's master plan. Jesus being raised from the dead was the fulfillment of his own repeated predictions. In Chapter Ten of this book, we explored several instances of Jesus predicting his own death, and he typically coupled those with pronouncements of his coming resurrection as well (see Matthew 16:21; 17:9, 22; 20:19; 26:32).

During his earthly ministry, Jesus staked the validity of his ministry and his entire future on the simple promise, "I will rise again!" In a confrontation with the Pharisees, Jesus said, *"Destroy this temple, and in three days I will raise it up"* (John 2:19). They thought Jesus was referring to the physical edifice in Jerusalem, but John explained that *"when Jesus said 'this temple,' he meant his own body. After he was raised from the dead, his disciples remembered he had said this, and they believed both the Scriptures and what Jesus had said"* (John 2:21-22).

But it wasn't just Jesus who predicted his resurrection before it happened. It had actually been predicted long before in the Old Testament. When believers reflect on the Day of Pentecost detailed in Acts 2, they naturally think of the great outpouring of the Holy Spirit, which is understandable. What they tend to overlook, though, is a very important part of the message that Peter preached—a sermon that saw 3,000 people place their faith in Jesus the Messiah. Peter spoke convincingly of the death, burial, and resurrection of Jesus.

In his message, Peter proclaims, *"God released him from the horrors of death and raised him back to life, for death could not keep him in its grip"*

(Acts 2:24). Peter proceeds to quote an Old Testament prophecy from Psalm 16:10 in which King David states, *"You will not leave my soul among the dead or allow your Holy One to rot in the grave"* (Acts 2:27). Inspired by the Holy Spirit, Peter makes a revealing interpretation of that passage:

> *You can be sure that the patriarch David wasn't referring to himself, for he died and was buried, and his tomb is still here among us. But he was a prophet, and he knew God had promised with an oath that one of David's own descendants would sit on his throne. David was looking into the future and speaking of the Messiah's resurrection. He was saying that God would not leave him among the dead or allow his body to rot in the grave. God raised Jesus from the dead, and we are all witnesses of this. Now he is exalted to the place of highest honor in heaven, at God's right hand*
>
> (Acts 2:29-33).

Just as Jesus was the focal point and fulfillment of vast numbers of prophecies, his resurrection was also the fulfillment of David's prophetic word.

NOT METAPHORICAL OR METAPHYSICAL

Jesus was not raised as a ghost, a state of mind, a consciousness, or as some kind of vapor. He inhabited the same physical body in which he had lived during his time upon the earth, but his physical body was also a glorified and transformed body. Luke explains this concept in his written account of Jesus' appearance to his disciples after his resurrection:

Jesus himself was suddenly standing there among them. "Peace be with you," he said. But the whole group was startled and frightened, thinking they were seeing a ghost! "Why are you frightened?" he asked. "Why are your hearts filled with doubt? Look at my hands. Look at my feet. You can see that it's really me. Touch me and make sure that I am not a ghost, because ghosts don't have bodies, as you see that I do." As he spoke, he showed them his hands and his feet. Still they stood there in disbelief, filled with joy and wonder. Then he asked them, "Do you have anything here to eat?" They gave him a piece of broiled fish, and he ate it as they watched

(Luke 24:36-43).

Jesus further reinforces the physicality and reality of his resurrection when he speaks to Thomas (who is encountering the resurrected Jesus for the first time). Jesus tells Thomas, *"Put your finger here, and look at my hands. Put your hand into the wound in my side. Don't be faithless any longer. Believe!"* (John 20:27). Scripture clearly indicates that Jesus engaged in many normal human physical activities such as breathing, walking, standing, talking, and eating. The resurrection aimed to quicken his mortal body, not do away with it.

WHAT CHRIST'S RESURRECTION ACCOMPLISHED

Having examined the facts and the historicity of Jesus' resurrection, it is imperative to explore the meaning of his resurrection.

1. The resurrection proved Christ's divine Sonship: *"He was shown to be the Son of God when he was raised from the dead by the power of the Holy Spirit. He is Jesus Christ our Lord"* (Romans 1:4).

2. The resurrection of Jesus secured our justification: "*He was handed over to die because of our sins, and he was raised to life to make us right with God*" (Romans 4:25).

3. The resurrection of Jesus completed our release from sin: "*And if Christ has not been raised, then your faith is useless and you are still guilty of your sins*" (1 Corinthians 15:17). Everything in the previous chapter about the effectiveness of Christ's death is true, but it would not have been realized had it not been for Jesus' resurrection. The cross, the blood, the death, *and* the resurrection of Jesus all worked together for the completion of our redemption.

4. Jesus was raised so that we could have new life with him: "*He gave us life when he raised Christ from the dead. ...He raised us from the dead along with Christ and seated us with him in the heavenly realms because we are united with Christ Jesus*" (Ephesians 2:5-6).

5. Christ was raised to give us a new birth and hope: "*He has given us new birth into a living hope through the resurrection of Jesus Christ from the dead*" (1 Peter 1:3 NIV).

6. Christ's resurrection is the prototype for and guarantees our future resurrection: "*Christ has been raised from the dead. He is the first of a great harvest of all who have died. ...Christ was raised as the first of the harvest; then all who belong to Christ will be raised when he comes back*" (1 Corinthians 15:20, 23).

7. The resurrection of Jesus led to him becoming our intercessor: "*Who then will condemn us? No one—for Christ Jesus died for us and was raised to life for us, and he is sitting in the place of honor at God's right hand, pleading for us*" (Romans 8:34). This verse demonstrates that the resurrection of Jesus led him into a new dimension of work and ministry, not into retirement and passivity.

Ultimately, resurrection is more than just the reviving of the physical body. Remember, Jesus raised three people from the dead during his earthly ministry—and all of those people eventually died again. When Jesus was resurrected, it was something more than what others had experienced—he was raised to new life, *never to die again!*

The risen Jesus triumphantly declares, *"I am the living one. I died, but look—I am alive forever and ever!"* (Revelation 1:18). If there is no resurrection, there is no gospel. Let me state this plainly: Any form or version of Christianity that does not have Jesus' death, burial, and resurrection at its center and core represents a departure from the doctrine presented in the Bible.

THE ASCENSION: WAIT, THERE'S MORE...

But Christ's resurrection was not the end of the story. Jesus was only on earth physically after his resurrection for forty days—he had to go somewhere after that, and he knew exactly where he was headed—to reassume his rightful place beside the Father. Jesus ascending into Heaven does not receive as much attention as his resurrection, and yet, it was the next logical and necessary step. Consider the following Scriptures where advance notices were given of the ascension—that Jesus would be returning to the Father in Heaven after his resurrection.

> *Then what will you think if you see the Son of Man ascend to heaven again?*
>
> (John 6:62)

> *I will be with you only a little longer. Then I will return to the one who sent me*
>
> (John 7:33).

Before the Passover celebration, Jesus knew that his hour had come to leave this world and return to his Father

(John 13:1).

There is more than enough room in my Father's home. If this were not so, would I have told you that I am going to prepare a place for you?

(John 14:2)

I am going to be with the Father

(John 14:12).

But now I am going away to the one who sent me. …In fact, it is best for you that I go away, because if I don't, the Advocate won't come. If I do go away, then I will send him to you

(John 16:5,7).

Now, Father, bring me into the glory we shared before the world began. …Now I am departing from the world; they are staying in this world, but I am coming to you

(John 17:5,11).

I came from the Father into the world, and now I will leave the world and return to the Father

(John 16:28).

I am ascending to my Father and your Father, to my God and your God

(John 20:17).

Note that in several of these passages, Jesus indicates that he is *returning* to the Father. He is not simply going to Heaven, like we will when we go for the first time. Jesus spoke of returning because he had been there prior to his incarnation and his coming to earth. He had been with the Father from eternity past.

ANOTHER HISTORICAL EVENT

Just as with every other major element of Jesus' life, it was predicted and then it happened. After several prophetic announcements, Jesus literally and physically ascended into Heaven itself.

Mark reports it:

When the Lord Jesus had finished talking with them, he was taken up into heaven and sat down in the place of honor at God's right hand
(Mark 16:19).

Luke describes it in his Gospel:

Then Jesus led them to Bethany, and lifting his hands to heaven, he blessed them. While he was blessing them, he left them and was taken up to heaven
(Luke 24:50-51).

Luke then presents the most detailed description of Jesus' ascension at the beginning of the book of Acts.

After saying this, he was taken up into a cloud while they were watching, and they could no longer see him. As they strained to see him rising into heaven, two white-robed men suddenly stood among them. "Men of Galilee," they said, "why are you standing here staring into heaven? Jesus has been taken from you into heaven, but someday he will return from heaven in the same way you saw him go!"

(Acts 1:9-11)

This account not only establishes the historical reality of Jesus' ascension into Heaven, but also assures believers of the certainty of his future return.

The ascension of Christ is also included in Paul's description of "the great mystery of our faith."

Christ was revealed in a human body and vindicated by the Spirit. He was seen by angels and announced to the nations. He was believed in throughout the world and taken to heaven in glory

(1 Timothy 3:16).

Then, writing to the church in Ephesus, Paul refers to Jesus' ascension and remarks:

Notice that it says "he ascended." This clearly means that Christ also descended to our lowly world. And the same one who descended is the one who ascended higher than all the heavens, so that he might fill the entire universe with himself

(Ephesians 4:8-9).

He descended. He ascended. What amazing thoughts. My wife Lisa shared with me recently how impacted she was to consider that Jesus was born in a stable amongst livestock, and that he died on a cross among criminals. You can't get more earthy and gritty than that. However, from another perspective, Jesus came into humanity through the virgin birth, and he left the earth through the ascension. You can't get more glorious than that.

NOW WHAT?

Jesus ascended to Heaven, but what did he do then? He sat down. He didn't sit down because he was weary, nor did he sit down to retire—he is on a throne, not in a rocking chair. Having been restored to his pre-existent glory, he sat down to reign alongside his Father. Even this act had been prophesied in the Old Testament. David wrote, *"The Lord said to my Lord, 'Sit in the place of honor at my right hand until I humble your enemies, making them a footstool under your feet'"* (Psalm 110:1).

Did you notice that this verse mentions that to be at the Lord's right hand is considered to be the "place of honor"? Bible scholar Craig Keener notes that "The position to a ruler's right was a position of great honor and authority; to be seated at God's right hand was to be enthroned as a ruler of the cosmos, even if not all his enemies had yet been destroyed."[78]

A number of New Testament statements reflect the same theme of Jesus being seated in Heaven as found in Psalm 110:1. I have included some below, but there are others as well.[79]

He was taken up into heaven and sat down in the place of honor at God's right hand

(Mark 16:19).

Christ Jesus died for us and was raised to life for us, and he is sitting in the place of honor at God's right hand

(Romans 8:34).

He raised Christ from the dead and seated him at his right hand in the heavenly realms

(Ephesians 1:20 NIV).

Set your sights on the realities of heaven, where Christ sits in the place of honor at God's right hand

(Colossians 3:1).

When he had cleansed us from our sins, he sat down in the place of honor at the right hand of the majestic God in heaven

(Hebrews 1:3).

Now Christ has gone to heaven. He is seated in the place of honor next to God, and all the angels and authorities and powers accept his authority

(1 Peter 3:22).

Those who are victorious will sit with me on my throne, just as I was victorious and sat with my Father on his throne

(Revelation 3:21).

While Jesus is consistently portrayed sitting at the Father's right hand, he stood up to honor and welcome his servant Stephen when he was martyred (see Acts 7:55-56).

The resurrection and ascension of Jesus are continued steps in God's great eternal plan of redemption, but they are not the final finale. Once seated, Jesus began new dimensions of his work, and they will be explored in the next chapter that addresses his present-day and future work. What we've seen of Jesus so far has been magnificent in every regard, but more glorious things are still to be explored.

GREAT STATEMENTS ABOUT CHRIST'S RESURRECTION AND ASCENSION

"God has made the Lord Jesus Christ the firstfruits by raising Him from the dead."

—Clement of Rome (35–99)

"Yet it was only by his ascension to heaven that his reign truly commenced....The Lord, by his ascension to heaven, has opened up the access to the heavenly kingdom, which Adam had shut.... Christ, by his ascension, took away his visible presence from us, and yet he ascended that he might fill all things: now, therefore, he is present in the church, and always will be."

—John Calvin (1509–1564)

"The resurrection of Jesus Christ from the dead is one of the best attested facts on record. There were so many witnesses to behold it, that if we do in the least degree receive the credibility of men's testimonies, we cannot and we dare not doubt that Jesus rose from the dead."

—Charles H. Spurgeon (1834–1892)

As we consider Christ ascended, our hearts burn within us at the thought that he is the type of all his people. As he was, so are we also in this world; and as he is, so shall we also be. To us also there remain both a resurrection and an ascension."

—Charles H. Spurgeon (1834–1892)

"But we are to remember that the resurrection is not merely a historical fact, the transcendent miracle and mystery of the apostolic age. Certainly it is all that. But it is more. It is a moral event, a principle of spiritual energy, as well as a fact of human history."

—A.J. Gordon (1836–1895)

"The resurrection of Jesus Christ was necessary to establish the truth of his mission and put the stamp of all-conquering power on his gospel."

—E.M. Bounds (1835–1913)

"The most casual reader of the New Testament can scarcely fail to see the commanding position the resurrection of Christ holds in Christianity. It is the creator of its new and brighter hopes, of its richer and stronger faith, of its deeper and more exalted experience."

—E.M. Bounds (1835–1913)

"At His Ascension our Lord entered Heaven, and He keeps the door open for humanity to enter."

—Oswald Chambers (1874–1917)

"The resurrection of Jesus Christ from the dead is the cornerstone of Christian doctrine. The crucifixion loses its meaning without the resurrection. Without the resurrection, the death of Christ was only the heroic death of a noble martyr. With the resurrection, it is the atoning death of the Son of God. It shows that death to be of sufficient value to cover all our sins, for it was the sacrifice of the Son of God."

—R.A. Torrey (1856–1928)

"Jesus was born of a virgin, suffered under Pontius Pilate, died on the cross and rose from the dead to make worshipers out of rebels!"[80]

—A.W. Tozer (1897–1963)

"In the Christian story God descends to re-ascend. He comes down; down from the heights of absolute being into time and space, down into humanity...down to the very roots and seabed of the Nature He has created. But He goes down to come up again and bring the ruined world up with Him."[81]

—C.S. Lewis (1898–1963)

"The resurrection is not merely important to the historic Christian faith; without it, there would be no Christianity. It is the singular doctrine that elevates Christianity above all other world religions."

—Adrian Rogers (1931–2005)

"If Jesus had not risen from the dead, no right-minded person would have glorified anything so hideous and repulsive as a cross stained with the blood of Jesus. An unopened grave would never have opened heaven."

—Billy Graham (1918–2018)

"The Ascension was from one standpoint the restoration of the glory that the Son had before the Incarnation, from another the glorifying of human nature in a way that had never happened before, and from a third the start of a reign that had not previously been exercised in this form."[82]

—J.I. Packer (1926–2020)

"Christ didn't merely enter heaven but strode into it as its rightful owner and heir."[83]

—Erwin Lutzer (1941–)

"This is the message of the resurrection. Life springs forth from death. A desert becomes a garden. Beauty transcends the ugly. Love overcomes hatred. A tomb is emptied. The grim and haunting outline of a cross is swallowed in the glow of an Easter morning sunrise."[84]

—Max Anders (1947–)

QUESTIONS FOR REFLECTION AND DISCUSSION

1. Did you learn something new about Jesus in this chapter? Describe what you learned.

2. Did something you already knew about Jesus become strengthened or reinforced? Describe it.

3. Why do you think the writers of Scripture were diligent to list so many of the eye-witnesses to Jesus' resurrection?

4. Jesus made sure his disciples knew that he had been *physically* resurrected—showing them his hands and feet, and eating in front of them. Why do you think he emphasized this so much?

5. Review the list entitled "What Jesus' Resurrection Accomplished." Which the items listed has been the most impacting in your life and relationship with God?

6. Traditionally, the ascension of Jesus does not receive as much attention as the resurrection. Why do you think that is, and what aspects (or benefits) of Jesus ascending and being seated at the Father's right hand should receive more attention?

7. Did anything you read in this chapter change the way you will relate to Jesus? If so, how?

Chapter Twelve

NOW AND FOREVER: THE PRESENT-DAY AND FUTURE WORK OF JESUS

"Before the throne of God above
I have a strong, a perfect plea;
A great High Priest, whose name is Love
who ever lives and pleads for me."
—Charitie L. Bancroft (1841–1923)

In the previous chapter, we saw how Jesus, having been crucified and then resurrected, *"was taken up into heaven and sat down in the place of honor at God's right hand"* (Mark 16:19). But what did he do when he sat down? Some of us may think of coming into our homes after a long day with the thought, "I'm worn out. I just want to sit down and do nothing, or sit down and watch television." In other words, we may simply equate sitting with relaxing and going into a mode of inactivity.

MAGNIFICENT JESUS

Nothing could be further from the truth when it comes to Jesus taking his seat next to the Father in Heaven. Immediately after Mark tells us that Jesus was taken to Heaven and sat at God's right hand, he writes, *"And the disciples went everywhere and preached, and the Lord worked through them, confirming what they said by many miraculous signs"* (Mark 16:20). Did you catch that? Even after he sat down, Jesus *"worked through them, confirming what they said by many miraculous signs."*

On the cross, Jesus acquired our salvation through shedding his blood and dying. This is why he cried out at the end, *"It is finished!"* (John 19:30). Jesus' redemptive suffering as our Savior is completely finished, and yet he is still working on our behalf. We can rightly say that Christ's current work is entirely founded and based upon his finished work.

Jesus has not gone into early retirement nor is he on an extended leave of absence. He is active, alive, and doing far more than most can imagine. Paul described Jesus' current position and activity so eloquently:

Now he is far above any ruler or authority or power or leader or anything else—not only in this world but also in the world to come. God has put all things under the authority of Christ and has made him head over all things for the benefit of the church. And the church is his body; it is made full and complete by Christ, who fills all things everywhere with himself (Ephesians 1:21-23).

The reference to the church being Christ's body is fascinating, and it is important to understand that a part of Jesus' current-day ministry is done through his body—assemblies of born-again believers

270

throughout the earth (see Romans 12:4-5; 1 Corinthians 12:27; Ephesians 4:11-12).

When Luke made his initial remarks in the Book of Acts (which is a sequel to the Gospel of Luke), he said, *"In my first book I told you, Theophilus, about everything Jesus began to do and teach until the day he was taken up to heaven"* (Acts 1:1-2). It seems to me that Luke was saying (my paraphrase), "In my first book—the Gospel of Luke—I told you about what Jesus *began* to do until the time he was taken up into Heaven. Now I'm going to tell you about what Jesus has *continued* to do since he ascended into Heaven."

HOW IS JESUS WORKING TODAY?

I. JESUS IS WORKING TODAY AS OUR ADVOCATE, INTERCESSOR, AND HIGH PRIEST

Having already encouraged believers not to sin, the apostle John then said, *"But if anyone does sin, we have an advocate who pleads our case before the Father. He is Jesus Christ, the one who is truly righteous"* (1 John 2:1). The word *advocate* here is best understood by us today as a defense attorney. The "accuser" (Revelation 12:10) will no doubt slander and malign God's children, but Jesus defends us and speaks on our behalf.

Other translations describing righteous Jesus as our "advocate" include:

> *He speaks on our behalf when we come into the presence of the Father* (GW).
> *We have someone who pleads with the Father on our behalf* (GNT).
> *We have one who speaks to the Father for us. He stands up for us* (NIRV).

We have one who speaks to the Father in our defense (NIV).
We have a Priest-Friend in the presence of the Father (MSG).

Aren't you glad that Jesus is still working on our behalf?

Knowing that he is our advocate brings us the understanding that Jesus is for us, not against us. The apostle Paul asked a powerful question and then provided an even more powerful answer: *"Who then will condemn us? No one—for Christ Jesus died for us and was raised to life for us, and he is sitting in the place of honor at God's right hand, pleading for us"* (Romans 8:34). The New King James Version translates this as *"makes intercession for us."* The intercessory work of Jesus on our behalf is grounded in the fact that he is our High Priest.

The Book of Hebrews makes much of Jesus' role as our High Priest. By studying this portion of Scripture, we can discover what Jesus is currently doing for us and every believer.

- *"This High Priest of ours understands our weaknesses"* (Hebrews 4:15).
- *"God qualified him as a perfect High Priest...and God designated him to be a High Priest in the order of Melchizedek"* (Hebrews 5:9-10).
- Jesus' priesthood is perpetual because *"He lives forever to intercede with God on their behalf"* (Hebrews 7:25).
- Christ has *"entered into heaven itself to appear now before God"* as our advocate (Hebrews 9:24).

Robert Murray McCheyne, the renowned Scottish minister, once said, "If I could hear Christ praying for me in the next room, I would not fear a million enemies. Yet distance makes no difference. He is praying for me." I can't imagine anything more encouraging to a believer! Jesus sits at the right hand of God, and no matter our weakness or infirmity, He is interceding—pleading—on our behalf. When we have sinned, He is our advocate with the Father. What comfort! What security! What assurance![85]

2. JESUS IS WORKING TODAY AS OUR SHEPHERD

In one of the most beloved of all the psalms, David spoke timeless words of comfort: *"The Lord is my shepherd; I have all that I need"* (Psalm 23:1). Countless generations of people have drawn strength and consolation from these words, and it is good to know that Jesus is still the Shepherd who leads, guides, and consoles His people.

Jesus described himself as *"the good shepherd"* (John 10:11, 14), and he hasn't ceased being our shepherd since he ascended into Heaven. His nature and his heart toward us have never changed. Jesus made all of the following statements relative to him being our shepherd.

> *The sheep recognize his voice and come to him* (John 10:3).
> *He calls his own sheep by name and leads them out* (John 10:3).
> *He walks ahead of them, and they follow him because they know his voice* (John 10:4).
> *My purpose is to give them a rich and satisfying life* (John 10:10).
> *The good shepherd sacrifices his life for the sheep* (John 10:11).
> *I know my own sheep, and they know me* (John 10:14).
> *I sacrifice my life for the sheep* (John 10:15).
> *My sheep listen to my voice* (John 10:27).
> *I know them, and they follow me* (John 10:27).
> *I give them eternal life, and they will never perish* (John 10:28).
> *No one can snatch them away from me* (John 10:28).

Are you confident that Jesus loves you that much? He does—he is the good shepherd.

Jesus perfectly personifies the Father's love in the story he described about a man with one hundred sheep and one wanders off and becomes lost. Jesus asked, *"Won't he leave the ninety-nine others on the hills and go out to search for the one that is lost? And if he finds it, I tell you the truth, he will rejoice over it more than over the ninety-nine that didn't wander away!"* (Matthew 18:12-13). I once heard someone suggest that it doesn't make a lot of sense for a shepherd to leave the ninety-nine to pursue the one unless you happen to be that one. That is the beauty of God's love for us.

Peter described Jesus, in his present-day ministry, as *"the Great Shepherd"* (1 Peter 5:4) and as the *"Shepherd"* and *"Guardian"* of our souls (1 Peter 2:25). And the author of Hebrews referred to *"our Lord Jesus, the great Shepherd of the sheep"* who *"ratified an eternal covenant with his blood"* (Hebrews 13:20).

3. JESUS IS WORKING TODAY AS THE HEAD OF THE CHURCH

The Body of Christ is not without a Commander in Chief. Paul said that Jesus *"is also the head of the church, which is his body"* (Colossians 1:18). *The Message* renders this verse, *"When it comes to the church, [Jesus] organizes and holds it together, like a head does a body."* When Jesus took his rightful place beside the Father, he did not flop into a recliner to take a nap; he sits on a throne of authority, and he reigns as Lord of his Church.

Examples of Jesus being head of the Church include the following:

• He definitively stated, *"I will build my church"* (Matthew 16:18).

- In Acts 9:1-5, Jesus made a special "recruiting trip" to call Saul of Tarsus unto himself and to enlist him in Christian ministry.

- The Lord Jesus gives "gifts" (apostles, prophets, evangelists, pastors, and teachers) *"to equip God's people to do his work and build up the church, the body of Christ"* (Ephesians 4:11-12).

- Regarding the church, Jesus did everything necessary to *"present her to himself as a glorious church without a spot or wrinkle or any other blemish. Instead, she will be holy and without fault"* (Ephesians 5:27).

- When Paul was on trial for the faith, the Lord Jesus stood by him and gave him strength (see 2 Timothy 4:17).

- In the final book of the New Testament, Jesus reveals himself as one who is walking amidst the churches, as one who is holding the messengers of the churches—the pastors—in his mighty right hand (Revelation 1:12–2:1).

4. JESUS IS WORKING TODAY AS OUR HEALER

Even a casual reading of the Gospels provides numerous examples of Jesus' works in healing. Since Jesus is *"the same yesterday, today, and forever"* (Hebrews 13:8), it should come as no surprise that Jesus still works today in the arena of healing.

Mark made it very clear that Jesus did not discontinue his healing ministry after his ascension. Mark 16:20 says, *"And the disciples went everywhere and preached, and the Lord worked through them, confirming what they said by many miraculous signs."*

Peter said to the paralyzed man in Lydda:

Aeneas, Jesus Christ heals you! Get up, and roll up your sleeping mat!"
And he was healed instantly

(Acts 9:34).

James counseled believers:

Are any of you sick? You should call for the elders of the church to come and pray over you, anointing you with oil in the name of the Lord. Such a prayer offered in faith will heal the sick, and the Lord will make you well

(James 5:14-15).

5. JESUS IS WORKING TODAY AS THE SUSTAINER AND PERFECTER

In Hebrews 1:2-4, Jesus is referred to as the Son of God and the heir of all things. In addition to references regarding Jesus' past work (his role in creation and his role in redemption), we also read of Jesus that *"he sustains everything by the mighty power of his command."* The Amplified Bible says that Jesus is *"upholding and maintaining and guiding and propelling the universe by His mighty word of power."* This correlates to what Paul said of Jesus, that *"He existed before anything else, and he holds all creation together"* (Colossians 1:17).

Not only does Jesus have a present-day function of sustaining the universe, but he is also involved in perfecting us. Hebrews 12:2 tells us that we are to keep our eyes upon Jesus, *"the champion who initiates and perfects our faith."* Think about that. Jesus is not only the origin and source of our faith, but he is also the one who will perfect and bring to completion all that he started in our lives.

HOW WILL JESUS WORK IN THE FUTURE?

Referring to the Messiah, Isaiah said, *"His government and its peace will never end"* (Isaiah 9:7). It is safe to say that the works of

Christ are not only continuing today, but there are also vast future works yet to be seen. I cannot begin to do justice to this wonderful thought—volumes have been written regarding eschatology (the doctrine of last things)—but be assured that Jesus has works yet to carry out, and they will be glorious. What will a few of these works look like?

- We know that Jesus is preparing a place for us, and that He will come for us one day. He told His followers:

  There is more than enough room in my Father's home. If this were not so, would I have told you that I am going to prepare a place for you? When everything is ready, I will come and get you, so that you will always be with me where I am

  (John 14:2-3).

- We know that Jesus will appear in the future. Paul said that:

  We look forward with hope to that wonderful day when the glory of our great God and Savior, Jesus Christ, will be revealed

  (Titus 2:13; see also Matthew 24:36-44; Acts 1:11; Hebrews 9:28; 1 John 2:28).

- We know that Jesus will oversee a great and glorious reunion.

  For the Lord himself will come down from heaven with a commanding shout, with the voice of the archangel, and with the trumpet call of God. First, the believers who have died will rise from their graves. Then, together with them, we who are still alive and remain on the earth will be caught up in the clouds to meet the Lord in the air. Then we will be with the Lord forever

  (1 Thessalonians 4:16-17).

- We know that Jesus will orchestrate a beautiful transformation in us. Paul said that Jesus will *"take our weak mortal bodies and change them into glorious bodies like his own, using the same power with which he will bring everything under his control"* (Philippians 3:21). *The Message* renders it that Jesus: *Will transform our earthy bodies into glorious bodies like his own. He'll make us beautiful and whole with the same powerful skill by which he is putting everything as it should be, under and around him.*

- We know that Jesus will one day conduct a great judgment. *For we must all appear and be revealed as we are before the judgment seat of Christ, so that each one may receive [his pay] according to what he has done in the body, whether good or evil [considering what his purpose and motive have been, and what he has achieved, been busy with, and given himself and his attention to accomplishing]*
(2 Corinthians 5:10 AMPC; see also Acts 10:42; 17:31; 2 Timothy 4:1).

- We know that one of Jesus' future works is to reign forever. *The kingdoms of this world have become the kingdoms of our Lord and of His Christ, and He shall reign forever and ever!*
(Revelation 11:15 NKJV)

- We know that Jesus will ultimately turn the Kingdom over to God the Father. Paul writes: *After that the end will come, when he will turn the Kingdom over to God the Father, having destroyed every ruler and authority and power. For Christ must reign until he humbles all his enemies beneath his feet. And the last enemy to be destroyed is death. For the Scriptures say, "God has put all things under his authority." (Of course, when it says "all things are under his authority," that does not include God himself, who gave Christ his authority.) Then, when all things are under his authority, the Son will put himself under God's authority, so that God, who gave his Son authority over all things, will be utterly supreme over everything everywhere*

(1 Corinthians 15:24-28).

When we consider all the works of Jesus—what he's done in the past, what he's doing in his present-day ministry, and what he is yet to do in the future—what does it mean for us? It means that each of us can say, "I trust and rest in the finished work that Christ accomplished for me. I yield to and cooperate with the ongoing work of Christ in me and through me. In addition, I dedicate myself to the unfinished task—the Great Commission—assigned to me by Christ, the Head of the Church. And finally, I anticipate the ultimate consummation of Christ's works in his eternal kingdom, when he will reign forever and ever."

QUOTES

"He came the first time to die; He is coming again to raise the dead. When He came the first time, they questioned whether He was King; the next time the world will know that He is King of kings and Lord of lords. The first time He wore a crown of thorns; the next time He will be wearing a crown of glory. The first time He came in poverty; the next time He is coming in power. The first time He had an escort of angels; the next time He will come with ten thousands of His saints. The first time He came in meekness; He is coming again in majesty."

—Adrian Rogers (1931–2005)

"There are well over 300 references to the return of Christ in the 216 chapters of the New Testament."[86]

—Charles Swindoll (1934–)

QUESTIONS FOR REFLECTION AND DISCUSSION

1. Did you learn something new about Jesus in this chapter? Describe what you learned.

2. Did something you already knew about Jesus become strengthened or reinforced? Describe it.

3. This chapter contained a quote by Robert Murray McCheyne— "If I could hear Christ praying for me in the next room, I would not fear a million enemies." How does knowing that Jesus is your Advocate, Intercessor, and High Priest affect your faith?

4. In considering Jesus' present-day ministry as Shepherd, to what degree are you allowing him to lead, guide, and comfort you? What can you do to yield and respond to him more in that regard?

5. Relative to Jesus being the head of the church, how do you see him functioning that way? In the past, have you perceived Jesus as being passive or active in building and overseeing his church?

6. The last item in the Quotes section was Charles Swindoll saying there are more than 300 references to the return of Christ in the New Testament. How do these prophecies and promises affect your daily life, and how do you envision the future return and reign of Christ?

7. Did anything you read in this chapter change the way you will relate to Jesus? If so, how?

Chapter Thirteen

GOD IN THREE PERSONS: BLESSED TRINITY

"Every divine action begins from the Father, proceeds through the Son, and is completed in the Holy Spirit."

—Basil of Caesarea (330–379)

Believing in the Trinity seemed normal to me, as I grew up singing the Doxology every Sunday. It contained the words, "Praise him above ye heavenly host. Praise Father, Son, and Holy Ghost." Another hymn sung frequently in my church contained the words, "Holy, holy, holy! Merciful and mighty, God in three persons, blessed Trinity!"

While these are beautiful and powerful, we must ask the all-important question as to whether the doctrine of the Trinity is really taught in the Bible. Some have contended that the word *Trinity* never appears in Scripture, and that is true—it was first used by the early church father Tertullian (160–220). However, the *concept* of the Trinity is alluded to in the Old Testament and presented pervasively throughout the New Testament.

Some believe the word Triune (or Triunity) more accurately describes the relationship of the Father, Son, and Holy Spirit, while theologian Peter Enns states that "The German word *Dreieinigkeit* ('three-oneness') better expresses the concept."[87] Regardless of which term we use—Trinity, Triune, or Three-Oneness—we are endeavoring to communicate that there is One God who exists in three persons, the Father, the Son, and the Holy Spirit, and these are co-equal and co-eternal. We must be mindful that there are not three gods, neither is there one God (person) who merely takes on different roles at different times.

Pastor and Bible teacher Jack Hayford wrote, "It is clear that they are three-in-one, and also that they are entirely one-in-three. Don't be surprised if you find this concept mysterious. It is perfectly logical that the very essence of God's being would exceed our full capacity to understand!"[88] In the fourth century, Gregory of Nazianzus captured the profundity and mystery of the Trinity when he stated, "No sooner do I conceive of the One than I am illumined by the Splendor of the Three; no sooner do I distinguish Them than I am carried back to the One."[89]

THE TRINITY IN THE NEW TESTAMENT

Our analytical yet finite minds would love to have a clinical *definition* of the Trinity, but the Bible does not offer that. What Scripture does provide are multiple and repeated *demonstrations* of the Trinity in operation, vivid *portrayals* of the Father, Son, and Holy Spirit working together in seamless harmony for our salvation and our good. Consider how often we see the Trinity in operation in God's word:

THE ANNUNCIATION

The **Holy Spirit** *will come upon you, and the power of the* **Most High** *will overshadow you. So the baby to be born will be holy, and he will be called the* **Son of God**

(Luke 1:35).

THE LORD'S BAPTISM

After his baptism, as **Jesus** *came up out of the water, the heavens were opened and he saw the* **Spirit of God** *descending like a dove and settling on him. And a* **voice from heaven** *said, "This is my dearly loved* **Son**, *who brings me great joy"*

(Matthew 3:16-17).

INSIGHT FROM JOHN THE BAPTIST

For he is sent by **God**. *He speaks God's words, for* **God** *gives him the* **Spirit** *without limit. The* **Father** *loves his* **Son** *and has put everything into his hands*

(John 3:34-35).

JESUS' PRAYER

And **I** *will ask the* **Father**, *and he will give you another Advocate, who will never leave you. He is the* **Holy Spirit**, *who leads into all truth. …But when the* **Father** *sends the Advocate as my representative—that is, the* **Holy Spirit**—*he will teach you everything and will remind you of everything* **I** *have told you*

(John 14:16-17, 26).

THE INITIAL GIVING/RECEIVING OF THE SPIRIT

*Again **he** said, "Peace be with you. As the **Father** has sent me, so **I** am sending you." Then **he** breathed on them and said, "Receive the **Holy Spirit**"*

(John 20:21-22).

THE GREAT COMMISSION

*Therefore, go and make disciples of all the nations, baptizing them in the name of the **Father** and the **Son** and the **Holy Spirit***

(Matthew 28:19).

JESUS' MINISTRY

*And you know that **God** anointed **Jesus of Nazareth** with the **Holy Spirit** and with power. Then **Jesus** went around doing good and healing all who were oppressed by the devil, for **God** was with him*

(Acts 10:38).

A MINISTERIAL CHARGE

*Feed and shepherd **God's flock**—his church, purchased with his own **blood**—over which the **Holy Spirit** has appointed you as leaders*

(Acts 20:28).

PAUL'S APOSTOLIC GREETING

*This letter is from Paul, a slave of **Christ Jesus**, chosen by **God** to be an apostle and sent out to preach his Good News. ...The Good News is about his **Son**...he was shown to be the **Son of God** when he was raised from the dead by the power of the **Holy Spirit***

(Romans 1:1,3-4).

PAUL'S REQUEST FOR PRAYER

*Dear brothers and sisters, I urge you in the name of our Lord **Jesus Christ** to join in my struggle by praying to **God** for me. Do this because of your love for me, given to you by the **Holy Spirit***

(Romans 15:30).

SANCTIFICATION

*You were cleansed; you were made holy; you were made right with **God** by calling on the name of the Lord **Jesus Christ** and by the **Spirit of our God***

(1 Corinthians 6:11).

SPIRITUAL GIFTS

*There are different kinds of spiritual gifts, but the same **Spirit** is the source of them all. There are different kinds of service, but we serve the same **Lord**. God works in different ways, but it is the same **God** who does the work in all of us*

(1 Corinthians 12:4-6).

GOD'S ENABLEMENT

*It is **God** who enables us, along with you, to stand firm for **Christ**. He has commissioned us, and he has identified us as his own by placing the **Holy Spirit** in our hearts as the first installment that guarantees everything he has promised us*

(2 Corinthians 1:21-22).

AN APOSTOLIC BENEDICTION

*May the grace of the Lord **Jesus Christ**, the love of **God**, and the fellowship of the **Holy Spirit** be with you all*

(2 Corinthians 13:14).

ACCESS TO GOD

*Now all of us can come to the **Father** through the same **Holy Spirit** because of what **Christ** has done for us*

(Ephesians 2:18).

PRAYER FOR BELIEVERS

*I fall to my knees and pray to the **Father**, the Creator of everything in heaven and on earth. I pray that from his glorious, unlimited resources he will empower you with inner strength through his **Spirit**. Then **Christ** will make his home in your hearts as you trust in him*

(Ephesians 3:14-17).

TEACHING ON CHURCH UNITY

*For there is one body and one **Spirit**, just as you have been called to one glorious hope for the future. There is one **Lord**, one faith, one baptism, one **God and Father** of all, who is over all, in all, and living through all*

(Ephesians 4:4-6).

REDEMPTION

*But—When **God** our Savior revealed his kindness and love, he saved us, not because of the righteous things we had done, but because of his mercy. He washed away our sins, giving us a new birth and new life through the **Holy Spirit**. He generously poured out the **Spirit** upon us through **Jesus Christ** our Savior*

(Titus 3:4-6).

CLEANSING

*How much more the blood of **Christ** will purify our consciences from sinful deeds so that we can worship the living **God**. For by the power of* *the eternal **Spirit**, **Christ** offered himself to **God** as a perfect sacrifice for our sins*

(Hebrews 9:14).

PETER'S APOSTOLIC GREETING

*This letter is from Peter, an apostle of **Jesus Christ**. I am writing to **God's** chosen people... **God the Father** knew you and chose you long ago, and his **Spirit** has made you holy. As a result, you have obeyed him and have been cleansed by the blood of **Jesus Christ***

(1 Peter 1:1-2).

ASSURANCE

*And **God** has given us his **Spirit** as proof that we live in him and he in us. Furthermore, we have seen with our own eyes and now testify that the **Father** sent his **Son** to be the Savior of the world*

(1 John 4:13-14).

PRAYER AND PATIENCE

*Pray in the power of the **Holy Spirit**, and await the mercy of our Lord **Jesus Christ**, who will bring you eternal life. In this way, you will keep yourselves safe in **God's love***

(Jude 20-21).

IN HEAVEN

The book of Revelation refers to the ***"Lord God, the Almighty"*** who was "*sitting on the throne*" (Revelation 4:8-9). We also see, "*a **Lamb** that looked as if it had been slaughtered*" (Revelation 5:6). This Lamb is called, "*the Lion of the tribe of Judah*" and "*the heir to David's throne*" (Revelation 5:5). And in front of the throne is "*the **sevenfold Spirit** of God*" (Revelation 4:5).

What powerful depictions of the Triune God accomplishing our redemption, establishing us in our faith, gloriously sustaining us, and reigning in Heaven! This list would have been much longer had I included all the verses in the New Testament which include references to the Father, the Son, and the Holy Spirit, but these are sufficient to demonstrate how powerful and pervasive the Trinitarian emphasis is in Scripture.

WHY IS THE FATHER REFERRED TO AS GOD?

If you paid careful attention to the above list, you saw that the Father is frequently referred to as God, while Jesus and the Holy Spirit are typically referred to by their names, or simply as the Son and the Spirit. In Chapter Seven of this book, we focused on the deity of Christ, and earlier in this chapter I made the statement that the Father, Son, and Holy Spirit are co-equal and co-eternal. If they are in fact equal, then why does Scripture tend to give preeminence to the Father? Or, if we put this in a theological context, why has the Father been referred to historically as "the First member of the Trinity"?

To address this, it is helpful to examine two specific statements Jesus made. In one place, Jesus said, *"The Father and I are one"* (John 10:30) and shortly afterward he said that *"the Father is greater than I"* (John 14:28 NIV). Some might presume that Jesus contradicted himself, but he absolutely did not; these two statements are perfectly complementary.

In the first statement, he was speaking relationally of his essential nature or substance—he was describing the union and unity he shared with the Father. In the second instance he was referring functionally to his subordination and submission to the Father's will. In other words, "I and the Father are one" concerns their essential substance and nature, while "the Father is greater than I" refers to their roles and activities. For example, on a functional level, the Father sends the Son, but the Son never sends the Father.

Let me illustrate this with a less-than-perfect analogy. Imagine that a man is a general in the military. He is enjoying a meal at home with his wife and two sons. One of the sons is a colonel in the military, while the other son is a major. However, at this family gathering, they are "off duty" and not functioning militarily. They are all equally human and share all the same traits common to humanity and no one, speaking intrinsically of their human nature, is superior or inferior to another.

However, when they are on duty, on the military base, or on the battlefield, it is a very different story. In terms of their functional rank, the general is the highest, the colonel is subordinate to him, and the major is the lowest ranking of the three. When it comes to their jobs, their rank and positions are different, and they would all have different functions. The general could give orders to the colonel, but a colonel would never give orders to a general.

Every illustration breaks down somewhere, and this one is no exception. In this example, there was a time when the father existed but the two sons didn't, but Jesus and the Holy Spirit have existed eternally with the Father. Those who do not embrace the deity of the Lord Jesus Christ will try to read into Jesus' statement (*"the Father is greater than I"*) that Jesus is intrinsically inferior to the Father or that he was created by the Father, but an overwhelming amount of Scripture discredits such views.

We must see Jesus' "greater than" statement in the light of what Paul wrote of Jesus, *"Though he was God, he did not think of equality with God as something to cling to. Instead, he gave up his divine privileges; he took the humble position of a slave and was born as a human being"* (Philippians 2:6-8). Regarding John 14:28, one commentator wisely states, "Jesus is here not at all speaking of the inner Trinitarian relation of the Persons of the Godhead but only of his person in its present state."[90] Another writes, "The Father is greater than Jesus in the sense that the one who sends a messenger is greater than the messenger he sends."[91]

THE TRINITY IN THE OLD TESTAMENT

We have seen how frequently and powerfully the Trinity operated throughout the New Testament, but what about the Old Testament? Did the Trinity spontaneously emerge when Jesus showed up, or were there indications of a Triune God long before that?

It is important to understand the nature of what is called "progressive revelation." This means that God did not reveal everything about himself or his plan all at once or even throughout the period of the Old Testament. God progressively and increasingly revealed himself to us as more and more Scripture was given, and while nothing God revealed contradicted what he gave previously, further light brought greater clarity and depth of understanding to us.

Augustine (354–430) alluded to this when he said, "The new is in the old concealed; the old is in the new revealed." We still don't know everything (obviously), and even Paul declared, *"All that I know now is partial and incomplete, but then I will know everything completely"* (1 Corinthians 13:12).

Bible scholar B.B. Warfield (1851-1921) wrote:

> The Old Testament may be likened to a chamber richly fur-
> nished but dimly lighted; the introduction of light brings
> into it nothing which was not in it before; but it brings out
> into clearer view much of what is in it but was only dimly or
> even not at all perceived before. The mystery of the Trinity
> is not revealed in the Old Testament; but the mystery of the
> Trinity underlies the Old Testament revelation, and here and
> there almost comes into view. Thus the Old Testament reve-
> lation of God is not corrected by the fuller revelation which
> follows it, but only perfected, extended and enlarged.[92]

Even though we do not expect the full clarity that we see after
Jesus came, what do we see of the Trinity in the Old Testament?

God spoke through Isaiah regarding the coming Messiah and said,
*"Look at my servant, whom I strengthen. He is my chosen one, who pleases
me. I have put my Spirit upon him"* (Isaiah 42:1). In the New Testament,
Matthew (or it is better to say "the Holy Spirit through Matthew")
directly applied this prophecy to the Lord Jesus Christ. With that
being the case, we have God the Father speaking in the Old Testament about sending Jesus who would be anointed by the Holy Spirit.

Again Isaiah speaks of a messenger anointed by the Spirit. *"The
Spirit of the Sovereign Lord is upon me, for the Lord has anointed me to
bring good news to the poor"* (Isaiah 61:1). Again, you see three parties:
the God who anoints, one who is anointed, and the Spirit himself.
And Jesus claimed that this passage was about him and that he was the
fulfillment of it (see Luke 4:17-21).

From the whole of Scripture, we recognize that there is both unity and plurality within the Godhead. Sometimes the unity is emphasized and sometimes the plurality is the focus. Because God's people in the Old Testament were entirely surrounded by polytheistic people groups, it is not surprising that God emphasized his unity in that era. However, there are still hints at his plurality in the Old Testament.

Consider three examples where the word *one* is used in the Hebrew language.

> *This explains why a man leaves his father and mother and is joined to his wife, and the two are united into one*
>
> (Genesis 2:24).

> *And the Lord said, "Indeed the people are one"*
>
> (Genesis 11:6 NKJV).

> *Hear, O Israel: The Lord our God, the Lord is one!*
>
> (Deuteronomy 6:4 NKJV)

In the first two passages, can you see how there is a sense of plurality that flows into the unity?

Bible scholar William Evans (1870–1950) shares the following insights on this Hebrew word.

> The word "one" in these scriptures is used in a collective sense; the unity here spoken of is a compound one, like unto that used in such expressions as "a cluster of grapes," or "all the people rose as one man." The unity of the Godhead is not simple but compound. The Hebrew word for "one"

(yacheed) in the absolute sense, and which is used in such expressions as "the only one," is never used to express the unity of the Godhead. On the contrary, the Hebrew word "echad," meaning "one" in the sense of a compound unity, as seen in the above quoted scriptures, is the one used always to describe the divine unity.[93]

In Chapters Five and Eleven of this book, we expounded a bit on Psalm 110:1 where David writes, *"The Lord said to my Lord, 'Sit in the place of honor at my right hand until I humble your enemies, making them a footstool under your feet.'"* Here is a fascinating conversation in a clearly messianic psalm, and clearly there is more than one person involved. The recipient of this verbal expression is told in verse four, *"You are a priest forever in the order of Melchizedek."* Clearly, this is the Father speaking to Jesus, and the Father calls Jesus "Lord" (Adonai).

Finally, in the book of beginnings, we see plurality and unity in God's statement about creating mankind.

Then God said, "Let us make human beings in our image, to be like us...." So God created human beings in his own image. In the image of God he created them; male and female he created them

(Genesis 1:26-27).

Did you notice the back and forth between plural and singular? "Let us" and then "in his own image?" God used similar language when he said, *"Whom should I send... Who will go for us?"* (Isaiah 6:8).

Speaking of the Genesis account, one of the great church fathers, Gregory of Nyssa (335-395), wrote:

This same language was not used for (the creation) of other things. The command was simple when light was created; God said, "let there be light." Heaven was also made without deliberation....These, though, were before (the creation of) humans. For humans, there was deliberation. He did not say, as he did when creating other things, "Let there be a human." See how worthy you are! Your origins are not in an imperative. Instead, God deliberated about the best way to bring to life a creation worthy of honor.[94]

So what did this "divine deliberation" entail? John Calvin writes of Genesis 1:26 in his commentary, "Christians, therefore, properly contend, from this testimony, that there exists a plurality of Persons in the Godhead. God summons no foreign counsellor; hence we infer that he finds within himself something distinct; as, in truth, his eternal wisdom and power reside within him."[95]

PONDERINGS AND ASSESSMENTS

The members of the Trinity—as with the members of any team—fulfill different roles and responsibilities. They also exhibit unparalleled respect and love toward one another. The pattern of their workings seems to be better understood and explained in the following, simplified way. However, keep in mind that they do not act independently of each other, but in conjunction and in harmony with one another.

- The Father *plans*: He is the architect and the source of divine activity.
- The Son *performs*: He executes and carries out the Father's plan.

- The Holy Spirit *perfects*: He follows up and brings into reality that which the Father ordained and that which the Son has carried out.

While those statements are generally true, we always want to remember the partnership and cooperative elements of the Trinity's working. Again, no member of the Trinity works in isolation from the others. For example, in our redemption, we can say that the Father planned it, the Son performed it (by dying on the cross), and the Spirit brought it to perfection by applying Christ's work of redemption in our lives. Because Jesus went to the cross, we tend to say that he was and is our redeemer, but the reality is that Father, Son, and Holy Spirit were all involved in our redemption.

Many through church history have described their perception of the different roles carried out by the respective members of the Trinity.

- An early church father, Irenaeus (125–202) spoke of "the Father planning everything well and giving his commands, the Son carrying these into execution and performing the work of creating, and the Spirit nourishing and increasing [what is made]."
- Puritan minister Thomas Manton (1620–1677) noted, "Our salvation is free in the Father, sure in the Son, ours in the Spirit. The beginning of our salvation is from God the Father, the dispensation is from the Son, and the application from the Holy Ghost."
- J.C. Ryle (1816–1900), an Anglican bishop, said, "In the Divine economy of man's salvation, election is the special work of God the Father; atonement, mediation, and intercession, the special

work of God the Son, and sanctification, the special work of God the Holy Ghost."

- Another evangelical Anglican, J.I. Packer (1926–2020), referred to "the cooperative activity of the Three in saving us—the Father planning, the Son procuring, and the Spirit applying redemption."

- And finally, respected Bible teacher and pastor Jack Hayford (1934–2023) wrote that "The Father may be seen as the Source, the Life Giver and the Creator. The Son may be seen as the Substance, the Transmitter, the Communicator, the Messenger and the Word. The Spirit may be seen as the Stream, the Life Breath, the Revealer, the Power and the Love of the Father. Yet in all this, let us humbly remember that whatever the distinct role, action or function we perceive any member of the Godhead to exercise, the Three-in-One are always coequal, coeternal and coexistent in being, power and holiness."[96]

I especially appreciate Hayford's recommendation to maintain humility. An infinite God is beyond our finite comprehension. Thomas à Kempis (1380–1471) wisely asked, "What good is it for you to be able to discuss the Trinity with great profundity, if you lack humility, and thereby offend the Trinity?"

CAN WE ILLUSTRATE THE TRINITY?

There is an element of mystery to the Trinity that transcends the comprehension of our finite minds. It seems we strive in vain to find words, metaphors, or analogies to help convey the amazing truth of the Trinity. It is inevitable that our feeble attempts will fall short of completely describing the majesty and fullness of an infinite, eternal God.

I'm not trying to be negative in making that assessment, but I'm acknowledging what Scripture says:

To whom then will you liken God? Or what likeness will you compare to Him?

(Isaiah 40:18 NKJV)

To whom will you compare me? Who is my equal?

(Isaiah 46:5)

In spite of the fact that God has no equal or parallel in all of creation, people have tried to explain and illustrate what defies complete understanding. Of the metaphors that have been used to try to illustrate the Trinity, some are more helpful than others, but none are perfect. Some of these metaphors include:

- The three-leafed clover, as explained by St. Patrick
- Water: It takes on three forms—liquid, vapor, and solid.
- A triangle: It is one object with three sides.
- An egg: It is one object, but it's comprised of yolk, white, and shell.
- Space, which can be spoken of in terms of length, width, and depth.
- An apple: This is one fruit, but it has a peel, meat, and core.
- Sun, heat, and light
- Multiplication (1 x 1 x 1 = 1)
- Music (a three-note chord)

Some of these are limitedly beneficial—they get us thinking about the concept of unity and plurality. However, no analogy can fully capture or convey the greatness and grandeur of God. Pressed too far, an illustration can give the false idea that there are three gods (tri-theism) instead of One God who exists in three persons, or at the other erroneous extreme, that the Godhead involves just one person who takes on three roles (modalism).

We are wise not to put too much emphasis on natural illustrations (since Scripture says God is incomparable) and look more to the vast number of biblical examples that show the Father, Son, and Holy Spirit in glorious operation. We will always do better if our focus is on worshiping and marveling at God rather than attempting to define him.

GREAT STATEMENTS ABOUT THE TRINITY

"Have we not one God and one Christ and one Spirit of grace shed upon us?"

—Clement of Rome (35–99)

"As stones of the Father's temple, you have been prepared to be God the Father's building, lifted up to the heights through the crane of Jesus Christ, which is the cross, as you use the Holy Spirit for a rope."

—Ignatius of Antioch (?–117)

"It is the Father who anoints, and it is the Son who is anointed by the Spirit. The Spirit is the unction."

—Irenaeus of Lyon (125–202)

"We believe in one God the Father Almighty, 'who made heaven and earth and the sea and all that is in them' (Exodus 20:11); and in one Christ Jesus, the Son of God who became incarnate for our salvation; and in the Holy Spirit, who through the prophets predicted the plan of God."

—Irenaeus of Lyon (125–202)

"It is protected by the power of God the Father, and the blood of God the Son, and the dew of the Holy Spirit."

—Clement of Alexandria (150–215)

"We pray at a minimum not less than three times in the day. For we are debtors to Three: Father, Son, and Holy Spirit… For the very church itself is—properly and principally—the Spirit Himself, in whom is the Trinity of the One Divinity: Father, Son, and Holy Spirit."

—Tertullian (160–220)

"We accordingly see the incarnate Word. And we know the Father through Him. We also believe in the Son, and we worship the Holy Spirit."

—Hippolytus (170–235)

"For to us there is but one God, the Father, of whom are all things; and one Lord Jesus Christ, by whom are all things; and one Holy Ghost, in whom are all things."

—Gregory of Nazianzus (329–390)

"The Trinity is the one and only and true God, and also how the Father, the Son, and the Holy Spirit are rightly said, believed, understood, to be of one and the same substance or essence."

—Augustine (354–430)

"If there be one God subsisting in three persons, then let us give equal reverence to all the persons in the Trinity. There is not more or less in the Trinity; the Father is not more God than the Son and Holy Ghost. There is an order in the Godhead, but no degrees; one person has not a majority or super eminence above another, therefore we must give equal worship to all the persons."

—Thomas Watson (1620–1686)

"It was in the coming of the Son of God in the likeness of sinful flesh to offer Himself a sacrifice for sin; and in the coming of the Holy Spirit to convict the world of sin, of righteousness and of judgment, that the Trinity of Persons in the Unity of the Godhead was once for all revealed to men."

—B.B. Warfield (1851–1921)

"When we have said these three things, then—that there is but one God, that the Father and the Son and the Spirit is each God, that the Father and the Son and the Spirit is each a distinct person—we have enunciated the doctrine of the Trinity in its completeness."

—B.B. Warfield (1851–1921)

"No one can have faith in Christ without having faith in God the Father and in the Holy Spirit."

—J. Gresham Machen (1881–1937)

"The unity of the Godhead was unmarred by discord. Father, Son, and Holy Spirit delight to honor one another. 'I and my

Father are one' (John 10:30), Jesus claimed, implying they were one not only in essence, but also in attitude and purpose. The Persons of the Trinity cooperated for our redemption in perfect harmony and reciprocity. The Father planned. The Son made the plan possible of realization by yielding up His life to death on the cross. The Spirit bent His fiery energies to the implementation of the plan. It was His appreciation of this harmony that inspired our Lord to pray for His followers: 'That they may be one, as we are' (John 17:11)."[97]

—Oswald Sanders (1902–1992)

"Within the Holy Trinity we see that in principle the notion of subordination does not carry with it the notion of inferiority.... Christ willingly submitted to the Father, without a word of protest. It is precisely that willingness that we are called to imitate in submitting ourselves to authority."[98]

—R.C. Sproul (1939–2017)

"Throughout the ages, the church has said that God is one in essence, being, or nature, and three in person. It has said just the opposite with respect to the person of Christ, who is said to be one person with two natures—one human and one divine."[99]

—R.C. Sproul (1939–2017)

"It is also true that the reality of the Father, the Son, and the Holy Spirit working together as a team for the full salvation of sinners pervades the entire New Testament."[100]

—J.I. Packer (1926–2020)

"God created us so that the joy He has in Himself might be ours. God doesn't simply think about Himself or talk to Himself. He enjoys Himself! He celebrates with infinite and eternal intensity the beauty of who He is as Father, Son, and Holy Spirit. And we've been created to join the party!"[101]

—Sam Storms (1951–)

"And so we see that the Father, Son and Spirit, while distinct persons, are absolutely inseparable from each other. Not confused, but undividable. They are who they are together. They always are together, and thus they always work together."[102]

—Michael Reeves

"The doctrine of the Trinity affirms that the one true God eternally exists as three persons: Father, Son, and Holy Spirit. Each of these three persons is fully God: The Father is fully God. The Son is fully God. The Holy Spirit is fully God. The three persons are equal in nature, glory, and power, sharing in the one Godhead. None of the three persons is dependent on the other for his deity. Rather, each is God of himself: The Father is God of himself. The Son is God of himself. The Holy Spirit is God of himself. Yet there are not three gods, but one God in three persons."[103]

—Gregg R. Allison

QUESTIONS FOR REFLECTION AND DISCUSSION

1. Did you learn something new about Jesus in this chapter? Describe what you learned.

2. Did something you already knew about Jesus become strengthened or reinforced? Describe it.

3. It was stated in this chapter that while the *word* "Trinity" never appears in Scripture, the *concept* of the Trinity is pervasive. After reviewing the Scriptures presented where Father, Son, and Holy Spirit are referenced, are you convinced of their reality and their work?

4. Do you accept the idea of mystery relative to the Trinity? In other words, are you at peace in your heart accepting and believing in something you can't fully comprehend or explain?

5. How did you personally process the idea that, generally speaking, the Father plans, the Son performs, and the Spirit perfects?

6. What is the challenge of trying to use a natural illustration to depict the Trinity when God said that he is incomparable?

7. Did anything you read in this chapter change the way you will relate to Jesus? If so, how?

Chapter Fourteen

CHRIST IN THE HYMNS: ADORATION THROUGH SONG

"I did think I did see all Heaven before me, and the great God Himself seated on His throne, with His great company of angels."
—George Frideric Handel (1685–1759)

Among people of faith, songs are frequently an expression of God's nature and work. When Israel had passed through the Red Sea, Moses and the people of Israel sang a celebratory song and praised God for his saving power (see Exodus 15:1). One of the final admonitions given by Moses took place when he *"recited this entire song publicly to the assembly of Israel"* (Deuteronomy 31:30). David was referred to as the *"sweet psalmist of Israel"* (2 Samuel 23:1) and he first came into Saul's service because he was a *"talented harp player"* (1 Samuel 16:18). When Jesus and his disciples left the upper room and headed to the Garden of Gethsemane, they first sang a hymn (see Matthew 26:30).

The apostle Paul also encouraged expressing praise to God and instructing each other through song. He instructed one congregation to *"Sing psalms and hymns and spiritual songs to God with thankful hearts"* (Colossians 3:16). While beautiful musical expressions can come acapella (without instrumental accompaniment), the word "psalms" that Paul uses (*psalmos* in the Greek) specifically includes the idea of "playing an instrument." One Greek resource notes that "The verb meant primarily the plucking of the strings, and the noun was used of sacred songs chanted to the accompaniment of instrumental music."[104]

Throughout the writings of Paul, there are verses we often read that are believed to be portions of early hymns, known to the believers he was addressing. Even today, it is not uncommon for a preacher, during a sermon, to quote the words of well-known songs to reinforce certain points of the message. It is not unlikely that Paul would have done the same in his epistles. Here are a few of his statements that are commonly believed to be excerpts of early hymns.

Though he was God, he did not think of equality with God as something to cling to. Instead, he gave up his divine privileges; he took the humble position of a slave and was born as a human being. When he appeared in human form, He humbled himself in obedience to God and died a criminal's death on a cross.

Therefore, God elevated him to the place of highest honor and gave him the name above all other names, that at the name of Jesus every knee should bow, in heaven and on earth and under the earth, and every tongue declare that Jesus Christ is Lord, to the glory of God the Father (Philippians 2:6-11).

Christ is the visible image of the invisible God. He existed before anything was created and is supreme over all creation, for through him God created everything in the heavenly realms and on earth. He made the things we can see and the things we can't see—such as thrones, kingdoms, rulers, and authorities in the unseen world. Everything was created through him and for him. He existed before anything else, and he holds all creation together. Christ is also the head of the church, which is his body. He is the beginning, supreme over all who rise from the dead. So he is first in everything. For God in all his fullness was pleased to live in Christ, and through him God reconciled everything himself. He made peace with everything in heaven and on earth by means of Christ's blood on the cross

(Colossians 1:15-20).

Christ was revealed in a human body and vindicated by the Spirit. He was seen by angels and announced to the nations. He was believed in throughout the world and taken to heaven in glory

(1 Timothy 3:16).

Those words are beautiful and powerful simply to read aloud or to meditate upon silently, but can you imagine gathering with believers in the early church and singing those corporately? We can only speculate as to what kind of melody might have been used with these songs, but the early believers were no doubt honoring Christ and encouraging each other in their faith.

AFTER THE EARLIEST DAYS OF THE CHURCH

In the early second century, a Roman governor in Bithynia (modern Turkey) named Pliny was unsure how to deal with the Christians in his province. He wrote Trajan, the Roman emperor, and explained how he had been dealing with them. He sought further guidance on what kind punishment should be administered to the Christians and on what grounds. As a pagan, Pliny described Christianity as a "depraved, excessive superstition" and said that faith in Jesus had "spread not only to the cities but also to the villages and farms."

Through inquiry, Pliny had learned that one of the practices of Christians was that "on a fixed day they used to meet before dawn and recite a hymn among themselves to Christ, as though he were a god." There were other elements, but I emphasize this part to demonstrate that singing hymns—praising and worshiping God through song—was a vital part of the early church.

Around one hundred years after the death of the apostle John, Clement of Alexandria wrote a hymn entitled "Shepherd of Tender Youth." Though the musical notations have been lost, two of the verses are as follows:

> You are our holy Lord,
> The all-subduing Word,
> Healer of strife.
> Yourself You did abase
> That from sin's deep disgrace
> You so might save our race
> And give us life.
>
> Forever be our guide,
> Our shepherd and our pride,
> Our staff and song.
> Jesus, O Christ of God,

By Your enduring Word,

Lead us where You have trod;

Make our faith strong.[105]

The most ancient Greek hymn that has been discovered, with both lyrics and music, is called the "Oxyrhynchus Hymn." It is believed to have been written at the end of the third century, and one translation of its words is as follows:

Let the world be silent

Let not the stars shine their lights

Calm the winds, silence the rivers

Let all praise the Father, the Son and the Holy Spirit

Let all sing together Amen, Amen.

Let kings bow, and God receive the glory!

The sole giver of good things, Amen, Amen.[106]

Below are excerpts from various Christ-exalting hymns through the ages. In many cases, I am simply including a small portion of the respective songs.

OF THE FATHER'S LOVE BEGOTTEN

Aurelius Clemens Prudentius (348–413)

Of the Father's love begotten,

Ere the worlds began to be,

He is Alpha and Omega,

He the source, the ending he

Of the things that are, that have been

And that future years shall see,

Evermore and evermore.

O SPLENDOR OF GOD'S GLORY BRIGHT

Ambrose (339–397)

All praise to God the Father be,

All praise, eternal Son, to Thee,

Whom with the Spirit we adore

Forever and forevermore.

THE DAY OF RESURRECTION

John of Damascus (early 8th century)

The day of resurrection! Earth, tell it out abroad.

The Passover of gladness, the Passover of God!

From death to life eternal, from this world to the sky,

Our Christ hath brought us over, with hymns of victory!

O COME, O COME, EMMANUEL

Author Unknown (9th century Latin hymn)

O come, O come, Emmanuel,

And ransom captive Israel,

That mourns in lonely exile here,

Until the Son of God appear.

Rejoice! Rejoice! Emmanuel

Shall come to thee, O Israel.

O come, Thou Rod of Jesse, free

Thine own from Satan's tyranny;

From depths of hell Thy people save,

And give them victory o'er the grave.

Rejoice! Rejoice! Emmanuel

Shall come to thee, O Israel.

This classic Christmas hymn reflects the heart cry of Israel as God's people longingly waited for Christ's coming. He is implored to come and "ransom captive Israel" and to "free Thine own from Satan's tyranny." In this Christologically rich hymn, Jesus is not only called Emmanuel, but he is referred to as the Son of God, the Rod of Jesse, the Dayspring from on high, the Key of David, and Adonai, Lord of Might.

JESUS, THE VERY THOUGHT OF THEE

Bernard of Clairvaux (1091–1153)

Jesus, the very thought of Thee

With sweetness fills my breast;

But sweeter far Thy face to see

And in Thy presence rest.

Jesus, our only joy be Thou,

As Thou our prize will be;

Jesus, be Thou our glory now

And through eternity.

O SACRED HEAD NOW WOUNDED

Bernard of Clairvaux (1091–1153)

O sacred head now wounded,

With grief and shame weighed down,

Now scornfully surrounded

With thorns thine only crown,

How art Thou pale with anguish,

With sore abuse and scorn.

How does that visage languish,

Which once was bright as morn.

What thou, my Lord, hast suffered,

Was all for sinners' gain,

Mine, mine was the transgression,

But Thine the deadly pain.

Lo, here I fall, my Savior,

'Tis I deserve thy place.

Look on me with thy favor,

Vouchsafe to me thy grace.

FAIREST LORD JESUS

Unknown (1662?)

Fairest Lord Jesus, ruler of all nature,

O thou of God and man the Son,

Thee will I cherish,

Thee will I honor,

Thou, my soul's glory, joy, and crown.

Beautiful Savior! Lord of all the nations!

Son of God and Son of Man!

Glory and honor,

Praise, adoration,

Now and forevermore be thine.

WHEN I SURVEY THE WONDROUS CROSS

Isaac Watts (1674–1748)

When I survey the wondrous cross
on which the Prince of glory died,
my richest gain I count but loss,
and pour contempt on all my pride.
See, from his head, his hands, his feet,
sorrow and love flow mingled down.
Did e'er such love and sorrow meet,
or thorns compose so rich a crown?

MESSIAH

George Frideric Handel (1685–1759)

Messiah is not a single song, but an elaborate oratorio written in three sections with fifty-three movements. This masterpiece panoramically communicates the story of Christ's redemptive work and eternal reign. When performed, it takes approximately two hours and twenty minutes. Handel was so deeply immersed in the writing process that he infrequently ate and seldom left his room during the twenty-four days of intense focus. While composing the 260 pages of music, he remarked, "I did think I did see all Heaven before me, and the great God Himself seated on His throne, with His great company of angels."

The most famous part of *Messiah* is "The Hallelujah Chorus." So powerful and moving is this portion ("and He shall reign forever and ever!") that King George II is said to have stood to his feet as Jesus' majesty was being proclaimed. Of course, the rest of the congregation stood when he did. The audience standing in honor of Christ has become a tradition ever since when that number is performed.

The earlier sections of *Messiah* present Christ's nativity and the prophecies leading up to it ("Behold, a virgin shall conceive and bear a Son, and shall call his name Emmanuel, God with us") as well as his redemptive suffering by which God brought us back into union with himself ("All we like sheep have gone astray; we have turned every one to his own way. And the Lord hath laid on Him the iniquity of us all"). To this day, *Messiah* remains the most frequently performed and highly respected oratorio that has ever been produced.

HARK! THE HERALD ANGELS SING

Charles Wesley (1707–1788)

> Hark! The herald angels sing,
> "Glory to the new-born king;
> Peace on earth and mercy mild
> God and sinners reconciled."
>
> Joyful all ye nations rise,
> Join the triumph of the skies;
> With angelic host proclaim,
> "Christ is born in Bethlehem."
>
> Christ, by highest heaven adored,
> Christ, the everlasting Lord;
> Late in time behold him come,
> Offspring of the Virgin's womb.
>
> Veiled in flesh the Godhead see,
> Hail the incarnate Deity.
> Pleased as man with men to dwell,
> Jesus, our Immanuel.
>
> Hail the heav'n born Prince of Peace!
> Hail the Sun of Righteousness!

Light and life to all He brings,

Risen with healing in His wings.

Mild He lays His glory by,

Born that man no more may die;

Born to raise the sons of earth,

Born to give them second birth.

O COME ALL YE FAITHFUL

John Francis Wade (1711–1786)

O come, all ye faithful,

Joyful and triumphant!

O come ye, O come ye to Bethlehem!

Come and behold him,

Born the King of angels.

God from true God, and

Light from Light eternal,

born of a virgin, to earth he comes!

Only-begotten Son of God the Father.

ALL HAIL THE POWER

Edward Perronet (1726–1792)

All hail the power of Jesus' name!

Let angels prostrate fall;

Bring forth the royal diadem,

And crown Him Lord of all.

Let every kindred, every tribe,

On this terrestrial ball,

To Him all majesty ascribe,
And crown Him Lord of all.

THERE IS A FOUNTAIN

William Cowper (1731–1800)

There is a fountain filled with blood
Drawn from Immanuel's veins,
And sinners plunged beneath that flood
Lose all their guilty stains.

Dear dying Lamb, Thy precious blood
Shall never lose its power,
Till all the ransomed Church of God
Be saved to sin no more.

ROCK OF AGES

Augustus M. Toplady (1740–1778)

Rock of ages, cleft for me,
Let me hide myself in Thee;
Let the water and the blood,
From Thy wounded side which flowed,
Be of sin the double cure,
Save from wrath and make me pure.
Nothing in my hand I bring,
simply to the cross I cling;
naked, come to thee for dress;
helpless, look to thee for grace;
foul, I to the fountain fly;
wash me, Savior, or I die.

THE SOLID ROCK

Edward Mote (1797–1894)

> My hope is built on nothing less
> Than Jesus blood and righteousness;
> I dare not trust the sweetest frame,
> But wholly lean on Jesus' name.
> On Christ the solid rock I stand,
> All other ground is sinking sand,
> All other ground is sinking sand.

CROWN HIM WITH MANY CROWNS

Matthew Bridges (1800–1894)

> Crown him with many crowns,
> the Lamb upon his throne…
> Awake, my soul, and sing
> of him who died for thee,
> and hail him as thy matchless king
> through all eternity.

JESUS PAID IT ALL

Elvina M. Hall (1820–1889)

> I hear the Savior say,
> "Thy strength indeed is small.
> Child of weakness, watch and pray,
> Find in me thine all in all."
> Jesus paid it all,
> All to Him I owe;

Sin had left a crimson stain—

He washed it white as snow.

O WORD OF GOD INCARNATE

William W. How (1823–1897)

O Word of God Incarnate,

O wisdom from on high,

O truth unchanged, unchanging,

O light of our dark sky,

We praise thee for the radiance,

that from the hallowed page,

A lantern to our footsteps,

shines on from age to age.

IN JESUS

James Procter (1826–1860)

He died, He lives, He reigns, He pleads;

There's love in all his words and deeds;

There's all a guilty sinner needs

Forever more in Jesus.

ONCE AND FOR ALL

Philip P. Bliss (1838–1876)

Free from the law—O happy condition!

Jesus hath bled and there is remission;

Cursed by the law and bruised by the fall,

Grace hath redeemed us once and for all.

Now we are free—there's no condemnation!

Jesus provides a perfect salvation;
"Come unto Me"—O hear His sweet call.
Blessed salvation once for all.

I WILL SING THE WONDROUS STORY

Francis H. Rowley (1854–1952)

I will sing the wondrous story
Of the Christ who died for me,
How He left His home in glory
For the cross of Calvary.
I was lost but Jesus found me,
Found the sheep that went astray,
Threw His loving arms around me,
Drew me back into His way.

IN LOVING-KINDNESS JESUS CAME

Charles H. Gabriel (1856–1932)

In loving-kindness Jesus came
My soul in mercy to reclaim,
And from the depths of sin and shame
Through grace He lifted me.

His brow was pierced with many a thorn,
His hands by cruel nails were torn,
When from my guilt and grief, forlorn,
In love He lifted me.

From sinking sand He lifted me,
With tender hand He lifted me,

From shades of night to plains of light,

Oh, praise His name, He lifted me!

AT CALVARY

William R. Newell (1868–1956)

O the love that drew salvation's plan!

O the grace that brought it down to man!

O the mighty gulf that God did span at Calvary!

Mercy there was great, and grace was free,

Pardon there was multiplied to me,

There my burdened soul found liberty at Calvary.

THERE'S SOMETHING ABOUT THAT NAME

Bill (1936–) and Gloria (1942–) Gaither

Jesus, Jesus, Jesus; there's just something about that name.

Master, Savior, Jesus, like the fragrance after the rain;

Jesus, Jesus, Jesus, let all Heaven and earth proclaim;

Kings and kingdoms will all pass away,

But there's something about that name.[107]

MAJESTY

Jack Hayford (1934–2023)

Majesty, worship His Majesty!

Unto Jesus be all glory, honor and praise.

Majesty, Kingdom authority,

Flows from His throne, unto His own,

His anthem raise.

So exalt, lift up on high the name of Jesus.

Magnify, come glorify, Christ Jesus the King.

Majesty, worship His Majesty,

Jesus who died, now glorified,

King of all kings.[108]

HE IS

Jeoffrey Benward (1952–) and Aaron Benward (1973–)

In Genesis, He's the breath of life

In Exodus, the Passover Lamb

In Leviticus, He's our High Priest

Numbers, the fire by night

Deuteronomy, He's Moses' voice

In Joshua, He is salvation's choice

Judges, law giver

In Ruth, the kinsmen-redeemer

First and Second Samuel, our trusted prophet

In Kings and Chronicles, He's sovereign

Ezra, true and faithful scribe

Nehemiah, He's the rebuilder of broken walls and lives

In Esther, He's Mordecai's courage

In Job, the timeless redeemer

In Psalms, He is our morning song

In Proverbs, wisdom's cry

Ecclesiastes, the time and season

In the Song of Solomon, He is the lover's dream

In Isaiah, He's Prince of Peace

Jeremiah, the weeping prophet

In Lamentations, the cry for Israel
Ezekiel, He's the call from sin
In Daniel, the stranger in the fire

In Hosea, He is forever faithful
In Joel, He's the Spirit's power
In Amos, the arms that carry us
In Obadiah, He's the Lord our Savior
In Jonah, He's the great missionary

In Micah, the promise of peace
In Nahum, He is our strength and our shield
In Habakkuk and Zephaniah, He's pleading for revival
In Haggai, He restores a lost heritage
In Zechariah, our fountain

In Malachi, He is the son of righteousness rising with
healing in His wings

In Matthew, Mark, Luke and John, He is God, Man, Messiah
In the book of Acts, He is fire from heaven
In Romans, He's the grace of God
In Corinthians, the power of love
In Galatians, He is freedom from the curse of sin

Ephesians, our glorious treasure
Philippians, the servant's heart
In Colossians, He's the Godhead Trinity
Thessalonians, our coming King
In Timothy, Titus, Philemon, He's our mediator and our
faithful Pastor

In Hebrews, the everlasting covenant

In James, the one who heals the sick.

In First and Second Peter, He is our Shepherd

In John and in Jude, He is the lover coming for His bride

In the Revelation, He is King of Kings and Lord of Lords[109]

BEAUTIFUL CHRIST

Lisa Cooke (1958–)

Beautiful, Beautiful Christ,

None can compare to Your glory.

Beautiful, Beautiful Christ,

All who draw near You cry holy.

Who can resist the splendor of grace,

Seen in Your beautiful, beautiful face.

Who will not bow at the sound of Your name,

Here in this beautiful, beautiful place.

Beautiful, Beautiful Christ,

Your blood for the world on the altar.

Beautiful, Beautiful Christ,

Seated in triumph forever.

WHAT ABOUT DIFFERENT STYLES OF WORSHIP MUSIC?

At the time of this writing, I have been privileged to preach the gospel in more than thirty nations. Many times, I don't understand the words that are being sung, but I always cherish the presence of God's Spirit and the devotion and adoration that is coming from the hearts of the people as they exalt Jesus, both his Person and his work. We tend to think about differences in music styles based on geography, but what about music styles that were generations or even centuries apart?

Rick Renner addressed this issue with great insight:

> The worship of the New Testament Church most likely included musical elements from the Hebrew, Greek, and Roman cultures, depending on where the worship took place. People were being added to the Kingdom of God in various regions throughout the Roman world, such as Asia Minor (modern-day Turkey), Greece, North Africa, and the Middle East. Hundreds and even thousands of miles separated these places, and because each was culturally different, it is likely that the actual styles, music, and expressions of worship varied from region to region and from culture to culture.
>
> The worship of Jewish Christians would have had one particular style, the Greeks another style, and the believers in North Africa a completely different style. The point is that there is room for variation in styles of music when it comes to worshiping God. However, what is most important is not that worship conforms to a certain style—only that *it comes from the heart.*
>
> The sounds and styles of worship may vary from group to group or from generation to generation. The worship I experienced and still love is different from what younger people enter into today, and that's fine. One is not right and the other wrong—they're just different. The styles and

sounds may change, but what cannot change is the one essential ingredient—a humble heart focused in adoration and worship of the King of Kings.[110]

There is a human tendency to think that "my" preferred style of music, perhaps what "I" grew up with, is somehow godlier and more anointed than another style of music that is not to my taste or with which I am not familiar. You and I may have our personal likes and dislikes when it comes to certain musical styles, and that's normal. However, I believe God loves it whenever he is worshiped *"in spirit and in truth"* (John 4:23).

WORSHIP IN HEAVEN

It is not just here on earth that Christ has been and continues to be honored through song; he is glorified in Heaven as well. It is tragic that some people think the book of Revelation is primarily about suffering, the antichrist, the false prophet, etc. Its main theme is Jesus, and he is worshiped without reservation in Heaven; much of this adoration is expressed through song.

In the following section of Scripture, this type of worship begins with the elders, then comes from thousands of millions of angels, and concludes with every creature throughout all creation.

And they sang a new song with these words: "You are worthy to take the scroll and break its seals and open it. For you were slaughtered, and your blood has ransomed people for God from every tribe and language and people and nation. And you have caused them to become a Kingdom of priests for our God. And they will reign on the earth." Then I looked again, and I heard the voices of thousands and millions of *angels around the throne and of the living beings and the elders. **And** **they sang in a mighty chorus**: "Worthy is the Lamb who was slaugh-tered—to receive power and riches and wisdom and strength and honor and glory and blessing." And then I heard every creature in heaven and on earth and under the earth and in the sea. **They sang**: "Blessing and honor and glory and power belong to the one sitting on the throne and to the Lamb forever and ever." And the four living beings said, "Amen!" And the twenty-four elders fell down and worshiped the Lamb*

(Revelation 5:9-14).

It should come as no surprise that Jesus is honored and exalted extravagantly in Heaven. To borrow a statement used in Chapter Four of this book, "in the Revelation all the purposes of God in and through Christ are consummated."[111]

Pastor, Bible teacher, and author Jack Hayford pointed out:

Revelation begins and ends with worship. It is neither for-mulated by liturgical requirements nor manipulated by reli-gious mandates. It is spontaneous, dynamic, explosive, and glorious. It bursts forth from created beings who have never fallen and from redeemed people who have been rescued from their fall. And it is centered on Jesus the Savior and glorifying to God the Father.[112]

CONCLUDING THOUGHTS

If you read this chapter simply with a view toward the historicity of hymns and songs about Christ, you may have missed one of the most important elements. While this theme running through the ages is important, it is vital that we realize the miraculous nature of one man—the Lord Jesus Christ—continuing to exert such dynamic influence in the hearts of people century after century.

Can you think of any person who lived hundreds, even thousands of years ago, who continues to inspire such intense levels of adoration and worship? Generation after generation, worshipers have been moved to effusively praise the Son of God. When men die, they generally have diminishing influence, but Jesus continues to touch millions of lives through the power of the Eternal Spirit of God. You may want to go back and re-read the words of the hymns cited in this chapter, and reflect upon the fact that men and women have been and continue to be profoundly touched by the living Savior.

They weren't writing songs just to be writing songs. Rather, they were in awe at the glorious realization of just how great Jesus was, they were marveling at the magnitude of his work, and they were overwhelmed with the presence of him who is *"the same yesterday, today, and forever"* (Hebrews 13:8).

QUESTIONS FOR REFLECTION AND DISCUSSION

1. Did you learn something new about Jesus in this chapter? Describe it.

2. Did something you already knew about Jesus become strengthened or reinforced? Describe it.

3. What do you make of the fact that the Lord Jesus Christ has inspired songs and music for two millennia?

4. Because of its popularity during the Christmas season, many are familiar with the 9th century Latin hymn, "O Come, O Come Emmanuel." Take a moment and review the words of the portion

shared in this chapter. Can you paraphrase the message using your own words?

5. Review the lyrics of Charles Wesley's great hymn: "Late in time behold him come, offspring of the Virgin's womb. Veiled in flesh the Godhead see, hail the incarnate Deity. Pleased as man with men to dwell, Jesus, our Immanuel." How many major themes about Jesus' identity do you see contained in those words? Describe them.

6. Rick Renner made the following statement: "The sounds and styles of worship may vary from group to group or from generation to generation." How respectful are you of musical styles that may be different from what you are used to depending on your own culture?

7. Did anything you read in this chapter change the way you will relate to Jesus? If so, how?

Chapter Fifteen

TRIBUTES TO THE MASTER: MARVELING AT THE SAVIOR

"Apart from Him, let nothing dazzle you."

—Ignatius of Antioch (?–117)

Throughout the ages, Jesus has profoundly touched the hearts of men and women. Some have conveyed their deep adoration in timeless, devotional expressions. Can you feel the awe and amazement in the following?

> The name of Jesus can still remove distractions from the minds of men, expel demons, and also take away diseases. Furthermore, it produces a marvelous meekness of spirit and a complete change of character.
>
> —Origen of Alexandria (184–253)

A second or third century letter to a recipient named Diognetus contains the line: "God's Son becomes to all those who turn to him their nurse, teacher, brother, counsellor, physician, and Savior, giving them strength, wisdom, comfort, power and glory."

Ambrose (340–397) was the Bishop of Milan, Italy.

> Lord Jesus Christ, you are for me medicine when I am sick;
> You are my strength when I need help;
> You are life itself when I fear death;
> You are the way when I long for heaven;
> You are light when all is dark;
> You are my food when I need nourishment.

Baptized and trained by Ambrose, Augustine (353–430) later became the Bishop of Hippo in Northern Africa. He followed his mentor's example beholding the Savior with awe, and wrote, "In my deepest woundedness I saw your glory, and it dazzled me."

Patrick (390–460), former slave and missionary to Ireland, is credited as the author of a prayer for protection called "St. Patrick's Breastplate." It includes the following words:

> Christ with me,
> Christ before me,
> Christ behind me,
> Christ in me,
> Christ beneath me,
> Christ above me,
> Christ on my right,

Christ on my left,
Christ when I lie down,
Christ when I sit down,
Christ when I arise…

Jesus, the very thought of Thee with sweetness fills my breast;
But sweeter far Thy face to see, and in Thy presence rest.
—Bernard of Clairvaux (1090–1153)

Thomas Brooks (1608–1680) was an English Puritan pastor who vividly saw Jesus as his all in all, as his all-sufficient Savior:

He is a portion that exactly, and directly suits—
The condition of the soul,
The desires of the soul,
The necessities of the soul,
The wants of the soul,
The longings of the soul,
And the prayers of the soul.
The soul can crave nothing,
Nor wish for nothing,
But what is found in Christ.
He is light to enlighten the soul,
Wisdom to counsel the soul,
Power to support the soul,
Goodness to supply the soul,
Mercy to pardon the soul,
Beauty to delight the soul,
Glory to ravish the soul,
And fulness to fill the soul.

Christ is the desire of nations, the joy of angels, the delight of the Father. What solace then must that soul be filled with, that has the possession of Him to all eternity!

—John Bunyan (1628–1688)

John Flavel (1627–1691) said of Jesus, "He is bread to the hungry, water to the thirsty, a garment to the naked, healing to the wounded; and whatever a soul can desire is found in him."

Queen Victoria of England (1819–1901) said of Jesus, "I wish he would come in my lifetime so that I could take my crown and lay it at his feet."

Woe to the man who makes anything else the main subject of his ministry. "God forbid that I should glory save in the cross of our Lord Jesus Christ, by whom the world is crucified unto me, and I unto the world." Preach Christ; lift him up high on the pole of the gospel, as Moses lifted up the serpent in the wilderness, and you will accomplish your life's end, but… if you have left out Christ, there is no manna from heaven, no water from the rock, no refuge from the storm, no healing for the sick, no life for the dead. If you leave out Christ, you have left the sun out of the day, and the moon out of the night, you have left the waters out of the sea, and the floods out of the river, you have left the harvest out of the year, the soul out of the body, you have left joy out of heaven, yea, you have robbed all of its all. There is no gospel worth thinking of, much less worth proclaiming in Jehovah's name, if Jesus be forgotten. We must have Jesus, then, as Alpha and Omega in all our ministrations among the sons of men.[113]

—Charles H. Spurgeon (1834–1892)

The effects, then, of the work of Christ are even to the unbeliever indisputable and historical. It expelled cruelty; it curbed passion; it branded suicide; it punished and repressed infanticide....There was hardly a class whose wrongs it did not remedy. It rescued the gladiator; it freed the slave; it protected the captive; it nursed the sick; it sheltered the orphan; it elevated the woman; it shrouded as with a halo of sacred innocence the tender years of the child. In every region of life its ameliorating influence was felt... It created the very conception of charity and broadened the limits of its obligation from the narrow circle of a neighborhood to the widest horizons of the human race.[114]

—F.W. Farrar (1831–1903)

He was born in an obscure village, the child of a peasant woman. He grew up in still another village, where he worked in a carpenter shop until he was thirty. Then for three years he was an itinerant preacher.

He never wrote a book.

He never held an office.

He never had a family or owned a house.

He didn't go to college.

He never traveled 200 miles from the place where he was born.

He did none of these things one usually associates with greatness.

He had no credentials but himself.

He was only 33 when public opinion turned against him. His friends ran away. He was turned over to his enemies and went through the mockery of a trial. He was nailed to a cross between two thieves.

When he was dying, his executioners gambled for his clothing, the only property he had on earth. When he was dead, he was laid in a borrowed grave through the pity of a friend.

Nineteen centuries have come and gone, and today he is the central figure of the human race, the leader of mankind's progress.

All the armies that ever marched, all the navies that ever sailed, all the parliaments that ever sat, all the kings that ever reigned, put together, have not affected the life of man on earth as much as that One Solitary Life.

—James Allan Francis (1864-1928)

From the heart and pen of an anonymous writer:

To the Artist, He is the One Altogether Lovely
—Song of Solomon 5:15
To the Architect, He is the Chief Cornerstone
—1 Peter 2:6
To the Astronomer, He is the Sun of Righteousness
—Malachi 4:2
To the Baker, He is the Bread of Life—John 6:35
To the Banker, He is the Hidden Treasure
—Matthew 13:44
To the Builder, He is the Sure Foundation—Isaiah 28:16
To the Carpenter, He is the Door—John 10:7
To the Doctor, He is the Great Physician—Jeremiah 8:22
To the Educator, He is the Great Teacher—John 3:2

To the Engineer, He is the New and Living Way
—Hebrews 10:20

To the Farmer, He is the Sower and Lord of Harvest
—Luke 10:2

To the Florist, He is the Rose of Sharon
—Song of Solomon 2:1

To the Geologist, He is the Rock of Ages
—1 Corinthians 10:4

To the Horticulturist, He is the True Vine—John 15:1

To the Judge, He is the Only Righteous Judge of Man
—2 Timothy 4:8

To the Juror, He is the Faithful and True Witness
—Revelation 3:14

To the Jeweler, He is the Pearl of Great Price
—Matthew 13:46

To the Lawyer, He is Counselor, Lawgiver, and True Advocate
—Isaiah 9:6

To the Newspaper man, He is Good News of Great Joy
—Luke 2:10

To the Oculist, He is the Light of the Eyes
—Proverbs 29:13

To the Philanthropist, He is the Unspeakable Gift
—2 Corinthians 9:15

To the Philosopher, He is the Wisdom of God
—1 Corinthians 1:24

To the Preacher, He is the Word of God
—Revelation 19:13

To the Sculptor, He is the Living Stone—1 Peter 2:4

MAGNIFICENT JESUS

To the Servant, He is the Good Master—Matthew 23:8-10

To the Statesman, He is the Desire of All Nations
—Haggai 2:7

To the Student, He is the Incarnate Truth—1 John 5:6

To the Theologian, He is the Author and Finisher of our
Faith—Hebrews 12:2

To the Toiler, He is the Giver of Rest—Matthew 11:28

To the Sinner, He is the Lamb of God Who Takes the Sin
Away—John 1:29

To the Christian, He is the Son of the Living God, the
Savior, the Redeemer, and the Loving Lord.

Henry G. Bosch (1914–1995) wrote:

Socrates taught for 40 years, Plato for 50, Aristotle for 40,
and Jesus for only 3. Yet the influence of Christ's 3-year ministry infinitely transcends the impact left by the combined
130 years of teaching from these men who were among the
greatest philosophers of all antiquity. Jesus painted no pictures; yet, some of the finest paintings of Raphael, Michel-
angelo, and Leonardo da Vinci received their inspiration
from Him.

Jesus wrote no poetry; but Dante, Milton, and scores of
the world's greatest poets were inspired by Him. Jesus composed no music; still Haydn, Handel, Beethoven, Bach, and
Mendelssohn reached their highest perfection of melody in
the hymns, symphonies, and oratories they composed in His
praise. Every sphere of human greatness has been enriched
by this humble Carpenter of Nazareth.

His unique contribution to the race of men is the salvation of the soul! Philosophy could not accomplish that. Nor art. Nor literature. Nor music. Only Jesus Christ can break the enslaving chains of sin and Satan. He alone can speak peace to the human heart, strengthen the weak, and give life to those who are spiritually dead.[115]

THE INDESCRIBABLE CHRIST

Dr. S.M. Lockridge was the pastor of Calvary Baptist Church, San Diego, California, from 1953 to 1993. He entered Heaven in 2000. He is well-known for a passage out of his sermon titled "He's My King":

> The Bible says He's the King of the Jews. He's the King of Israel. He's the King of Righteousness. He's the King of the Ages. He's the King of Heaven. He's the King of Glory. He's the King of Kings, and He is the Lord of Lords. Now that's my King! Do you know Him?
>
> No means of measure can define his limitless love. Well, well, He's enduringly strong. He's entirely sincere. He's eternally steadfast. He's immortally graceful. He's imperially powerful, and He's impartially merciful. Do you know Him?
>
> He's God's Son. He's a sinner's savior. He's the centerpiece of civilization. He's unparalleled. He's unprecedented. Well, He's the loftiest idea in literature. He's the highest personality in philosophy. He's the fundamental doctrine of true theology. Do you know Him?
>
> He supplies strength for the weak. He's available for the tempted and the tried. He sympathizes and He saves. He

heals the sick. He cleansed the lepers. He forgives sinners. He discharges debtors. He delivers the captives. He defends the feeble. He blesses the young. He serves the unfortunate. He regards the aged. He rewards the diligent, and He beautifies the meek. Do you know Him?

My King is the King of knowledge. He's the well-spring of wisdom. He's the doorway of deliverance. He's the pathway of peace. He's the roadway of righteousness. He's the highway of holiness. He's the gateway of glory. Do you know Him?

His life is matchless. His goodness is limitless. His mercy is everlasting. His love never changes. His word is enough. His grace is sufficient. His reign is righteous. His yoke is easy, and His burden is light.

Well... I wish I could describe Him to you, but He's indescribable. He's indescribable. Yeah, He's incomprehensible. He's invincible. He's irresistible. You can't get Him out of your mind. You can't get Him off of your hands. You can't outlive Him, and you can't live without Him.

Well... The Pharisees couldn't stand Him, but they found out they couldn't stop Him. Pilate couldn't find any fault in Him. Mm, Herod couldn't kill Him. Death couldn't handle Him, and the grave couldn't hold Him. That's my King! Yeah!

He always has been, and He always will be. I'm talking about He had no predecessor, and He'll have no successor. You can't impeach Him, and He's not gonna resign. That's my King![116]

Elmer Towns (1932–), a Bible teacher, educator, and author, wrote this of Jesus:

An honest person cannot study the life and ministry of Jesus Christ as taught in the Bible and not be impressed with his influence. The years Jesus traveled throughout Galilee and Judea have had a greater impact upon civilization than any other thirty-year period in the history of the world. Jesus taught a limited group for a limited time, yet his teachings have outlived those who taught a lifetime. Though Jesus Christ was not personally engaged in the arts, he has furnished the theme for more poems and songs, paintings and sculptures than any artist in history. None of the original projects that were built by this Carpenter remain in our museums, yet in almost every city around the world exist buildings and structures erected in his honor. The earthly life of Jesus Christ cannot be denied by an honest student of history.[117]

We read in *The Knowing Jesus Study Bible:*

No one has made a more dramatic impact on this world than Jesus. No one else has inspired such devotion, such compassion for those in need, such moral integrity, such self-sacrificing love for others. No one else has been the topic of more books, the inspiration for more music and art, the focus of more worship than Jesus. Almost 2,000 years after his death, his words still bring hope and renewal to millions of people around the world.[118]

OTHER GREAT STATEMENTS ABOUT JESUS

"Christ was either liar, lunatic, or Lord!"

—Thomas Aquinas (1225–1274)

"In his life, Christ is an example, showing us how to live; in his death, he is a sacrifice, satisfying our sins; in his resurrection, a conqueror; in his ascension, a king; in his intercession, a high priest."

—Martin Luther (1483–1546)

"Christ is full of grace, life, and salvation. The human soul is full of sin, death, and damnation. Now let faith come between them. Sin, death, and damnation will then be Christ's; and grace, life, and salvation will then be the believer's."

—Martin Luther (1483–1546)

"Christ is much more powerful to save, than Adam was to destroy."

—John Calvin (1509–1564)

"No one else holds or has held the place in the heart of the world which Jesus holds. Other gods have been as devoutly worshiped; no other man has been so devoutly loved.

—John Knox (1514–1572)

"Christ is a jewel worth more than a thousand worlds, as all know who have him. Get him, and get all; miss him, and miss all."

—Thomas Brooks (1608–1680)

"They lose nothing who gain Christ."

—Samuel Rutherford (1600–1661)

"Christ and his benefits go inseparably and undividedly… Many would willingly receive his privileges, who will not receive his person; but it cannot be; if we will have one, we must take the other too: Yea, we must accept his person first, and then his benefits: as it is in the marriage covenant, so it is here."

—John Flavel (1627–1691)

"Christ is like a river. A river is continually flowing, there are fresh supplies of water coming from the fountain head continually, so that a man may live by it, and be supplied with water all his life. So Christ is an ever-flowing fountain; he is continually supplying his people, and the fountain is not spent. They who live upon Christ, may have fresh supplies from him to all eternity; they may have an increase of blessedness that is new, and new still, and which will never come to an end."

—Jonathan Edwards (1703–1758)

"How unspeakably wonderful to know that all our concerns are held in hands that bled for us."

—John Newton (1725–1807)

"You will never know the fullness of Christ until you know the emptiness of everything but Christ."

—Charles H. Spurgeon (1834–1892)

"It seems to me that if we get one look at Christ in His love and beauty, this world and its pleasures will look very small to us."

—D.L. Moody (1837–1899)

"Above all, let us never forget the advice which Whitefield gave in one of his letters, let us 'make much of our Lord Jesus Christ.' There are many things of which we may easily make too much in our ministry, give them too much attention, think about them too much. But we can never make too much of Christ."[119]

—J.C. Ryle (1816–1900)

"Today Jesus Christ is being dispatched as the Figurehead of a Religion, a mere example. He is that, but he is infinitely more; He is salvation itself, He is the Gospel of God."

—Oswald Chambers (1874–1917)

"Christ is not a reservoir but a spring. His life is continual, active and ever passing on with an outflow as necessary as its inflow. If we do not perpetually draw the fresh supply from the living Fountain, we shall either grow stagnant or empty. It is, therefore, not so much a perpetual fullness as a perpetual filling."

—A.B. Simpson (1843–1919)

"Jesus combined…tender love to the sinner with uncompromising severity against sin, commanding dignity with winning humility, fearless courage with wise caution, unyielding firmness with sweet gentleness."

—F.F. Bruce (1910–1990)

"Make Jesus Christ your theme! I have seen preachers espouse causes and champion movements, and when the cause died and the movement collapsed, the preacher vanished too. But the man who glories in Christ never grows stale."[120]

—Vance Havner (1901–1986)

"God has and always will have only one man of the hour—our Lord Jesus Christ ."[121]

—Gordon Lindsay (1906–1973)

"Brilliant, untamed, tender, creative, slippery, merciful, clever, loving, irreducible, paradoxically humble—Jesus stands up to scrutiny. He is who I want my God to be… Above all, Jesus reveals a God who is love. On our own, would any of us come up with the notion of a God who loves and yearns to be loved?"[122]

—Philip Yancey (1949–)

QUESTIONS FOR REFLECTION AND DISCUSSION

1. Did you learn something new about Jesus in this chapter? Describe it.

2. Did something you already knew about Jesus become strengthened or reinforced? Describe it.

3. Consider Augustine's statement: "In my deepest woundedness I saw your glory, and it dazzled me." Can you relate to that in your own personal life? If so, how? Can you think of someone you know who could relate to that statement?

4. Do you agree with the assessment made by James Allan Francis in the following? Why or why not? "All the armies that ever marched, all the navies that ever sailed, all the parliaments that ever sat, all the kings that ever reigned, put together, have not affected the life of man on earth as much as that One Solitary Life."

5. What was your reaction when you read the following statement from Gordon Lindsay? "God has only one 'man of the hour' and that is our Lord Jesus Christ."

6. If you were to write out your own tribute to Jesus—even if you don't think you're as eloquent as the people quoted in this chapter—what would you want to make sure you said about Jesus?

7. Did anything you read in this chapter change the way you will relate to Jesus? If so, how?

SAY "YES" TO JESUS!

God loves you—no matter who you are, no matter what is in your past. God loves you so much that he gave his one and only begotten Son for you. Even though all of us have sinned (see Romans 3:23), the Bible tells us that *"everyone who believes in him will not perish but have eternal life"* (John 3:16).

Jesus laid down his life and rose again so that we could not only spend eternity with him in Heaven, but so that we could also have a vibrant relationship with him in the here and now. If you would like to make Jesus the Lord of your life, say the following prayer out loud and mean it from your heart.

> *Dear Heavenly Father,*
>
> *I thank you that Jesus died for my sins on the cross, that he shed his blood for my forgiveness, and that he was raised from the dead so that I could come into right relationship with you.*
>
> *Your word says that if I come to you, you will never cast me out (John 6:37), so I know you won't reject me, but you receive and accept me, and I thank you for it.*
>
> *You said in your word that if I call upon the name of the Lord, I will be saved (Romans 10:13). I am calling on your name right now, so I thank you for saving me.*

You also said that if I will confess with my mouth that Jesus is
Lord and believe with my heart that God raised him from the
dead, I will be saved (Romans 10:9). Jesus, I confess you right
now as my Lord. I turn away from my old life, and I surrender all
that I am to you.
You are alive, and I accept the forgiveness, the mercy, and the new
life that you are offering me now. Thank you for helping me to
live for you all the days of my life. Amen.

NOW WHAT?

Praying as you just prayed is a lot like an introduction at the beginning of a relationship. God doesn't intend for you to greet and accept him through such a prayer and then go on with the rest of your life as though you'd never met him. He desires a growing relationship with you in which you come to know him more and more and grow in your faith and fellowship with him. In other words, what you did in praying that prayer was not a last step, but a first step.

Below are some important steps to move forward in your relationship with God:

GET A BIBLE AND BEGIN READING IT.

I suggest you begin by reading the Gospel of John followed by the Book of Romans. There are many good translations of the Bible; I suggest you use one that is easy for you to understand. The New Living Translation is a good choice.

FIND A GOOD CHURCH AND ATTEND REGULARLY.

It is important to become a part of a church that believes in the lordship of Jesus, the authority of the Bible, and the power of the Holy

Spirit. Your spiritual walk and your spiritual growth will be greatly helped by your involvement in a good church and your fellowship with other believers.

GET BAPTIZED.

Water baptism (see Matthew 28:19) is your public declaration that you have left your old life behind and have begun a new life in Christ. In addition to being baptized in water, ask God to fill you with the Holy Spirit. The Holy Spirit already lives in you if you have accepted Jesus as your Savior, but there is an additional experience by which he fills you with power. In the Bible, you can read all about the outstanding works of the Holy Spirit throughout the Book of Acts.

PRAY.

Prayer involves both listening to and talking with God. You don't have to use fancy or religious-sounding words when you talk to God. As you learn more and more about the Bible, you'll know better how to speak God's "language," but you can always talk to God from your heart and ask him to help you in everything.

TELL OTHERS.

What has happened in your life is a great thing! You have passed from spiritual death to spiritual life. Pray about who God might have you share your good news with. The world is full of hurting people who need to know about God's love and what Jesus can do for them.

Appendix A

CHRIST IN THE CREEDS

Exploring ancient creeds of the church can instruct and remind us of Christian thought regarding the person and work of the Lord Jesus Christ in the early centuries after the completion of the New Testament canon. Scripture alone is inspired, infallible, and completely authoritative, but early expressions of faith can help reveal how early believers diligently sought to articulate their understanding of the Bible's essential teachings. Such concise summaries of essential beliefs served not only to affirm and reinforce Christians' positive convictions, but also helped build a defense against heretical views that sought to infiltrate congregations in the centuries following Jesus' resurrection.

The apostle Paul dealt with various errors such as that propagated by Hymenaeus and Philetus, who claimed the resurrection of believers had already occurred (see 2 Timothy 2:17-18). In Chapter Nine of this book, we explored the false beliefs of Cerinthus, with whose heresies the apostle John contended. Further studies in church history lead us to such figures as Marcion (?–160), who believed the God of the Old Testament was different than the God of the New

Testament and that Jesus was not fully human. We later encounter Arius (?–336), the highly influential Alexandrian church leader who taught that Jesus was a created being, was not God, and did not share in God's eternality.

It is not in the scope of this work to give a complete overview of the aberrant beliefs and heresies with which the early church contended. However, it is helpful to at least have an overview of erroneous teachings that Christians encountered in those days. Some of these include:

- The false belief that Jesus was not God—that he was inferior to and had even been created by God (Arianism)
- The false belief that Jesus did not share in the same essence or substance of God (Arianism)
- The false belief that Jesus was not human, or that he merely appeared to be human (Gnosticism, Docetism)
- The false belief that Jesus was born human and only later became the Son of God when God adopted him (Adoptionism)
- The false belief that Christ had a human body but not a human soul. Rather, the Logos or Word took the place of his mind and spirit. Thus, Christ was not fully human. (Apollinarianism)
- The false belief that that there were two separate natures in Christ, human and divine, but they were not united (Nestorianism)
- The false belief that Christ had only a divine nature. Essentially, his human nature was absorbed into the divine so that they became one nature. (Monophysitism)
- The false belief that the Holy Spirit was not God (Macedonianism)
- The false belief that the Father, Son, and Holy Spirit are three separate gods (Tritheism)

- The false belief that Father, Son, and Holy Spirit were simply different titles for the same person—that God simply appeared at different times in different modes (Modalism)
- The false belief that the God of the Old Testament was totally different than the God of the New Testament (Gnosticism)
- The false belief that matter is evil, and the universe was created by an inferior god, not by the Almighty God (Gnosticism)

Many of the councils and creeds of the early church were written not only to communicate and clarify truth about the Trinity, the Lord Jesus, and the Holy Spirit, but also to counter false teachings that were circulating in that day.

THE APOSTLES' CREED

During my upbringing in church, we recited the Apostles' Creed every Sunday. While Jesus' original band of apostles did not actually write this ancient text, its concise and powerful language expresses the chief elements of their teaching as it was handed down to and understood by successive generations of believers.

Though I did not fully appreciate the gravity or the significance of these statements early in my life, I am glad that I repeated them over and over again as a young person. When I came to a personal, quickened faith in Jesus, I was already familiar with these monumental concepts and they served as significant reference points as I studied Scripture and grew in the Lord.

The word *creed* comes from the Latin word *credo*, which simply means "I believe." Noted church historian Philip Schaff wrote that "As the Lord's Prayer is the Prayer of prayers, the Decalogue[123] the Law of laws, so the Apostles' Creed is the Creed of Creeds."[124] Here are the words that are to this day cherished by countless believers around the world.

> I believe in God the Father Almighty, Maker of heaven and
> earth;
> And in Jesus Christ, his only Son, our Lord;
> Who was conceived by the Holy Ghost, born of the Virgin
> Mary,
> Suffered under Pontius Pilate, was crucified, dead, and
> buried;
> He descended into hell; the third day he rose again from
> the dead;
> He ascended into heaven, and sits at the right hand of God
> the Father Almighty;
> From thence he shall come to judge the quick and the
> dead.
> I believe in the Holy Ghost; the holy catholic church;[125]
> the communion of saints;
> The forgiveness of sins; the resurrection of the body; and
> the life everlasting. Amen.

Prior to the Apostles' Creed, there was an older Roman creed that was somewhat similar. Before that, Ignatius of Antioch (?–117), a disciple of the apostle John, wrote a letter to believers in Tralles in Asia Minor. Though it is not a creed, per se, its language conveys credal types of thought:

> Turn a deaf ear to any speaker who avoids mention of Jesus
> Christ who was of David's line, born of Mary, who was truly

born, ate and drank; was truly persecuted under Pontius Pilate, truly crucified and died while those in heaven, on earth,
and under the earth beheld it; who also was truly raised
from the dead, the Father having raised him, who in like
manner will raise us also who believe in him—his Father, I
say, will raise us in Christ Jesus, apart from whom we have
not true life.[126]

It almost appears that Ignatius is "checking off the boxes," or communicating the key beliefs that are essential for believers to embrace.

THE NICENE CREED (325)

In the fourth century, as debates continued raging over the identity
of Christ and his nature, approximately 300 bishops and deacons from
the eastern end of the Mediterranean gathered in Nicaea, a city a
little more than 40 miles south and east from the capital, Constantinople. After lengthy discussion and debate, church leaders articulated
their beliefs in a formal statement known as the Nicene Creed. Below
is the content of that particular creed as it was affirmed and expanded
upon in a later council in Constantinople in 381.

We believe in one God, the Father Almighty, Maker of
heaven and earth, of all things visible and invisible;

We believe in one Lord, Jesus Christ, the only begotten
Son of God, eternally begotten of the Father; God from
God, Light from Light, true God from true God, begotten, not made, of one substance with the Father. Through
him all things were made. For us and for our salvation he
came down from heaven: by the power of the Holy Spirit he

became incarnate from the Virgin Mary, and was made man. For our sake he was crucified under Pontius Pilate; he suffered death and was buried. On the third day he rose again according to the Scriptures; he ascended into heaven and is seated at the right hand of the Father. He will come again in glory to judge the living and the dead, and his kingdom will have no end.

We believe in the Holy Spirit, the Lord, the giver of life, who proceeds from the Father. With the Father and the Son he is worshiped and glorified. He has spoken through the Prophets. We believe in one holy catholic[127] and apostolic Church. We acknowledge one baptism for the forgiveness of sins. We look for the resurrection of the dead, and the life of the world to come. Amen.

THE CHALCEDONIAN DEFINITION (451)

Another gathering of around 520 bishops, mostly from eastern end of the Mediterranean, gathered in Chalcedon, across the Bosporus from Constantinople. What resulted from their intense deliberations was a "tying up of loose ends." They gave greater clarification and more precise wording to the understanding of Christ's very nature. Their formulation read:

> We, then, following the holy Fathers, all with one consent, teach people to confess one and the same Son, our Lord Jesus Christ, the same perfect in Godhead and also perfect in manhood; truly God and truly man, of a reasonable soul and body; consubstantial with the Father according to the Godhead, and consubstantial with us according to the man-

hood; in all things like unto us, without sin; begotten before all ages of the Father according to the Godhead, and in these latter days, for us and for our salvation, born of the Virgin Mary, the Mother of God, according to the manhood; one and the same Christ, Son, Lord, only begotten, to be acknowledged in two natures which undergo no confusion, no change, no division, no separation; at no point was the difference between the natures taken away by the union, but rather the property of each nature being preserved, and concurring in one Person and one Subsistence, not parted or divided into two persons, but one and the same Son, and only begotten, God the Word, the Lord Jesus Christ; as the prophets from the beginning declared concerning him, and the Lord Jesus Christ himself has taught us, and the creed of the holy Fathers handed it down to us.

If all that leaves your head spinning a bit, please don't worry about it. They were dealing with controversies and issues you and I may not relate to as much, and certainly not in the practicalities of our daily lives. I always think about people who know nothing of the intricacies and subtleties of theological nuance, but have believed the simple truth of the gospel—that God loved us while we were yet sinners, sent his Son, the Lord Jesus Christ, to die as our substitute, to be raised from the dead, and to offer us forgiveness and the opportunity, through faith in him, to become the sons and daughters of God.

Every element of Jesus' nature and works is important, but don't get hung up on it if parts of it seem difficult to understand. Sometimes, for simplicity's sake, we say with David, *"I don't concern myself with matters too great or too awesome for me to grasp. Instead, I have calmed* and quieted myself, like a weaned child who no longer cries for its mother's milk. Yes, like a weaned child is my soul within me" (Psalm 131:1-2). In other words, I trust in Jesus even if his marvelousness exceeds my mental grasp of him.

Many other councils have been held throughout history, and many other creeds, confessions, and catechisms have been written, but we always keep the teaching of the Bible supreme. Let's never get away from having childlike faith (see Matthew 18:2-5), and never lose our "pure and undivided devotion to Christ" (2 Corinthians 11:3). May we all be able to say, with the theologian cited in Chapter One of this book, that our most profound insight is summed up in the words, "Jesus loves me, this I know, for the Bible tells me so."

NOTES

1. Library of Congress, https://www.loc.gov/books/?all=true&q=Jesus+christ# (accessed January 17, 2024).
2. "Status of Global Christianity 2023," The Center for the Study of Global Christianity, https://www.gordonconwell.edu/wp-content/uploads/sites/13/2023/01/Status-of-Global-Christianity-2023.pdf (accessed January 17, 2024).
3. Todd M. Johnson and Gina A. Zurlo, *World Christian Encyclopedia, Third Edition* (Edinburgh, Scotland: Edinburgh University Press, 2020), 6.
4. Billy Graham, *Storm Warning* (Nashville: Thomas Nelson, 2010), 121.
5. C. S. Lewis, *Mere Christianity*, Kindle edition (New York: Harper-Collins, 2021), 52.
6. Adrian Dieleman, *Leadership*, Vol. XV, No. 1 (Winter 1994), 47.
7. Max Lucado, *The Gift for All People,* Kindle edition (Colorado Springs: Multnomah Publishers, 1999), 45.
8. Warren W. Wiersbe, *Be Authentic,* "Be" Commentary Series (Colorado Springs, CO: Chariot Victor Pub., 1997), 148.
9. Henry Gariepy, *100 Portraits of Christ* (Wheaton, IL: Victor Books, 1987), 23.

10. William Barclay, ed., *The Revelation of John, vol. 1, The Daily Study Bible Series* (Philadelphia: The Westminster John Knox Press, 1976), 140.
11. Kenneth S. Wuest, *Wuest's Word Studies from the Greek New Testament: For the English Reader*, vol. 10 (Grand Rapids: Eerdmans, 1997), 37.
12. John D. Barry, et al., *Faithlife Study Bible* (Bellingham, WA: Lexham Press, 2012, 2016), Heb 7:22.
13. Keith Trump, www.gettinggreek.org.
14. Wuest, *Wuest's Word Studies,* 183.
15. C.I. Scofield, ed., *The Scofield Reference Bible: The Holy Bible Containing the Old and New Testaments* (New York; London; Toronto; Melbourne; Bombay: Oxford University Press, 1917), v.
16. For further study, read Hebrews 7:1-10. There we learn that Melchizedek (who was a type of Christ), was recognized by Abraham as being greater than himself.
17. Matthew 5:21-22; 27-28, 33-34, 38-39, 43-44.
18. Leonard Sweet and Frank Viola, *Jesus: A Theography*, Kindle edition (Nashville: Thomas Nelson, 2012), 1.
19. In the New King James version: Matthew 1:22; 2:15; 2:23; 4:14; 8:17; 12:17; 13:35; 21:14; 27:35.
20. Doug Powell, *Holman Quick Source Guide to Christian Apologetics* (Nashville, Holman Reference, 2006), Kindle loc. 249.
21. Millard J. Erickson, *The Concise Dictionary of Christian Theology* (Wheaton, IL: Crossway Books, 2001), Kindle loc. 4663.
22. Arthur T. Pierson, *In Christ* (Los Angeles: T. C. Horton, 1898), vi-viii.
23. C. H. Spurgeon, "The Dew of Christ's Youth," in *The Metropolitan Tabernacle Pulpit Sermons*, vol. 47 (London: Passmore & Alabaster, 1901), 197-198.

24. Sean McDowell, ed. *The Apologetics Study Bible for Students* (Nashville: Holman Bible Publishers, 2009), Kindle loc. 40695.

25. Excerpts from *The Incomparable Christ: The Person and Work of Jesus Christ*, copyright © 1971, by J. Oswald Sanders are used with permission from the publisher. The foregoing book was first published in the United States by Moody Publishers.

26. Robert Jamieson, A. R. Fausset, and David Brown, *Commentary Critical and Explanatory on the Whole Bible*, vol. 1 (Oak Harbor, WA: Logos Research Systems, Inc., 1997), 692.

27. Elmer L. Towns, *What the Faith Is All About: Basic Doctrines of Christianity* (Orlando: Harcourt Brace & Company, 1998), 143.

28. Stanley M. Horton and William W. Menzies, *Bible Doctrines: A Pentecostal Perspective* (Springfield, MO: Gospel Publishing House, 1993), Kindle loc. 1026.

29. Mark Sheridan, *Genesis 12-50, Ancient Christian Commentary on Scripture OT 2* (Downers Grove, IL: InterVarsity Press, 2002), 223.

30. Carl Friedrich Keil and Franz Delitzsch, *Commentary on the Old Testament*, vol. 2 (Peabody, MA: Hendrickson, 1996), 294.

31. Stephen R. Miller, Daniel, vol. 18, *The New American Commentary* (Nashville: Broadman & Holman Publishers, 1994), 123-124.

32. Excerpts from *The Incomparable Christ,* Sanders.

33. Millard J. Erickson, *Christian Theology* (Grand Rapids: Baker Book House, 1985), 753.

34. Hebrews 1:10, which applies to Jesus, is being quoted from Psalm 102:25. Jehovah (YHWH) is used eight times in this particular psalm.

35. R. A. Torrey, *The Fundamental Doctrines of the Christian Faith* (New York, NY: George H. Doran Company, 1918), 73-75.

36. Max Lucado, *Because of Bethlehem: Love Is Born, Hope Is Here* (Nashville: Thomas Nelson, 2016), 27.

37. Excerpts from *The Incomparable Christ,* Sanders.

38. Ibid.

39. Towns, *What the Faith Is All About,* 154.

40. William Barclay, ed., *The Gospel of John, Volume 2, The Daily Study Bible Series* (Philadelphia, PA: Westminster John Knox Press, 1975), 28.

41. Excerpts from *The Incomparable Christ,* Sanders.

42. Excerpts from *Jesus: the Life and Ministry of the Son of God,* copyright © 2017, by A. W. Tozer are used with permission from the publisher. The foregoing book was first published in the United States by Moody Publishers.

43. Excerpts from *The Incomparable Christ,* Sanders.

44. Warren W. Wiersbe, *Be Comforted,* "Be" Commentary Series (Wheaton, IL: Victor Books, 1996), 33.

45. Charles Swindoll, *The Finishing Touch* (Dallas: Word Incorporated, 1994), 575.

46. Excerpts from *Who Is This King of Glory? Experiencing the Fulness of Christ's Work in Our Lives,* copyright © 1996, by Tony Evans are used with permission from the publisher. The foregoing book was first published in the United States by Moody Publishers.

47. Sam Storms, "The Virgin Birth and the Tooth Fairy (3)." Enjoying God Ministries. https://www.samstorms.org/all-articles/post/the-virgin-birth-and-the-tooth-fairy--3- (accessed January 17, 2024).

48. Max Lucado, *God Came Near* (Nashville: Thomas Nelson, 2004), 25.

49. Irenaeus, *Against Heresies,* Alexander Roberts and James Donaldson eds. (Jackson, MI: Ex Fontibus Co., 2015), 110.

50. Irenaeus, *Against Heresies,* 258.

51. Excerpts from *Who Is This King of Glory? Experiencing the Fulness of Christ's Work in Our Lives*, Evans.

52. The soul is often referred to as being comprised of the intellect, will, and emotions.

53. Excerpts from *The Glory of Christ*, copyright © 1997, by Peter Lewis are used with permission from the publisher. The foregoing book was first published in the United States by Moody Publishers.

54. Excerpts from *Jesus: the Life and Ministry of the Son of God*, Tozer.

55. Wihla Hutson and Alfred S. Burt, "Some Children See Him," Copyright 1954, 1957 Hollis Music, Inc., New York, NY.

56. Excerpts from *The Glory of Christ*, Peter Lewis.

57. A. W. Tozer, *No Greater Love: Experiencing the Heart of Jesus Through the Gospel of John* (Minneapolis: Bethany House, 2020), 83.

58. John Stott, *The Authentic Jesus* (Downers Grove, IL: InterVarsity Press, 1985), 81.

59. Andrew David Naselli, *How to Understand and Apply the New Testament: Twelve Steps from Exegesis to Theology* (Phillipsburg, NJ: P&R Publishing, 2017), 21.

60. John Calvin and Henry Beveridge, *Institutes of the Christian Religion*, vol. 3 (Edinburgh: The Calvin Translation Society, 1845), 390–391.

61. Horatius Bonar, *God's Way of Peace: A Book for the Anxious* (Philadelphia: Presbyterian Publication Committee, 1862).

62. William Barclay, ed., *The Gospel of Matthew, vol. 2, The Daily Study Bible* (Philadelphia, PA: The Westminster John Knox Press, 1976), 363.

63. John Peter Lange and Philip Schaff, *A Commentary on the Holy Scriptures: Matthew* (Bellingham, WA: Logos Bible Software, 2008), 512-513.

64. C. Truman Davis, "The Crucifixion of Jesus: The Passion of Christ from a Medical Point of View," *Journal of Arizona Medical Association* Volume 22, No 3 (March 1965), 183-187.

65. John Calvin, John T. McNeil, ed., *Institutes of the Christian Religion* Book II (Philadelphia: The Westminster Press, 1960), 518.

66. Jonathan Edwards, *The Works of Jonathon Edwards* Volume I (Edinburgh UK: Banner of Truth Trust, 1974), 579.

67. Joseph W. Bergeron, M.D., *The Crucifixion of Jesus: A Medical Doctor Examines the Death and Resurrection of Christ* (City: St. Polycarp Publishing House, 2018), 78.

68. William D. Edwards, MD; Wesley J. Gabel, MDiv; Floyd E Hosmer, MS, AMI, "On the Physical Death of Christ," *The Journal of the American Medical Association,* Volume 256 (March 21, 1986).

69. Calvin, McNeil, ed., *Institutes of the Christian Religion* Book II, 519-20.

70. John Maclaurin, "On Glorying in the Cross of Christ" (Philadelphia: Presbyterian Board of Publication).

71. Charles H. Spurgeon, "Christ Made a Curse for Us," in *The Metropolitan Tabernacle Pulpit Sermons*, vol. 15 (London: Passmore & Alabaster, 1869), 308.

72. C. H. Spurgeon, "The Saddest Cry from the Cross," in *The Metropolitan Tabernacle Pulpit Sermons*, vol. 48 (London: Passmore & Alabaster, 1902), 517-518.

73. B. H. Carroll, *An Interpretation of the English Bible: The Four Gospels* (Grand Rapids: Baker Book House, 1948), 393.

74. Excerpt from *Basic Christian Doctrines* by Carl F. H. Henry, copyright © 1975. Used by permission of Baker Books, a division of Baker Publishing Group.

75. Taken from *Peace with God* by Billy Graham. Copyright © 1991 by Billy Graham. Used by permission of HarperCollins Christian Publishing.

76. Eugene Peterson, *Traveling Light: Reflections on the Free Life* (Downers Grove, IL: InterVarsity Press, 1982), 86.

77. Excerpts from *Who Is This King of Glory? Experiencing the Fulness of Christ's Work in Our Lives*, Evans.

78. Craig S. Keener, *The IVP Bible Commentary Background: New Testament* (Downers Grove, IL: IVP Academic, 2014), 544.

79. See also Luke 22:69; Acts 5:31; Hebrews 1:13; 8:1; 10:12-13; 12:2.

80. Excerpts from *Worship: The Reason We Were Created*, copyright © 2017, by A. W. Tozer are used with permission from the publisher. The foregoing book was first published in the United States by Moody Publishers.

81. C. S. Lewis, *Miracles* (New York: Harper Collins, 1996), 179.

82. J. I. Packer, *Concise Theology: A Guide to Historic Christian Beliefs* (Carol Stream, IL: Tyndale House Publishers, 2001), 127.

83. Erwin Lutzer, *Christ Among Other Gods* (Chicago: Moody Publishers, 2016), 151.

84. Max Anders, *What You Need to Know About Jesus in 12 Lessons* (Nashville, Thomas Nelson Publishers, 1995), 155.

85. There is an alternative view of the nature of Jesus' intercession offered by J. Oswald Sanders that is worth mentioning. Sanders writes, "His intercession is not vocal. It is not an audible saying of prayers. In his great annual act of intercession, Aaron uttered not one word…On the day of atonement it was the blood that spoke, not Aaron. It is the presence of our Intercessor, bearing in His body the evidence of His victory, that speaks for us." This is from his book, *Spiritual Maturity* (Moody Publishers, Chicago,

Illinois, 1962), 110. Whatever Jesus' intercession entails, whether it involves spoken words or merely His Presence, we can be certain that it is sufficient.

86. Charles Swindoll, *Growing Deep in the Christian Life: Essential Truths for Becoming Strong in the Faith* (Grand Rapids: Zondervan, 1993), 268.

87. Peter Enns, *The Moody Handbook of Theology* (Chicago: Moody Publishers, 2014), 205.

88. Jack Hayford, *Explaining the Trinity,* Kindle edition (Lancaster, UK: Sovereign Word, 2012), loc. 52.

89. Gregory of Nazianzus, *Orations 40.41.*

90. R.C.H. Lenski, *The Interpretation of St. John's Gospel* (Minneapolis, MN: Augsburg Publishing House, 1961), 1021.

91. Barclay Moon Newman and Eugene Albert Nida, *A Handbook on the Gospel of John, UBS Handbook Series* (New York: United Bible Societies, 1993), 475.

92. Benjamin Breckenridge Warfield, "The Biblical Doctrine of the Trinity" in *Biblical Doctrines.*

93. William Evans, *Great Doctrines of the Bible* (Chicago: Moody Publishers, 1949), 26-27.

94. Andrew Louth and Marco Conti, *Genesis 1–11, Ancient Christian Commentary on Scripture OT 1* (Downers Grove, IL: InterVarsity Press, 2001), 28.

95. John Calvin and John King, *Commentary on the First Book of Moses Called Genesis*, vol. 1 (Bellingham, WA: Logos Bible Software, 2010), 92–93.

96. Hayford, *Explaining the Trinity,* 255.

97. Excerpts from *The Incomparable Christ,* Sanders.

98. R. C. Sproul, *The Intimate Marriage* (Phillipsburg, NJ: P&R Publishing, 1975), 45.

99. R. C. Sproul, *What Is the Trinity*, Kindle edition (Sanford, FL: Reformation Trust Publishing, 2011), 32.

100. J. I. Packer, *Affirming the Apostles' Creed,* Kindle edition (Wheaton, IL: Crossway Books, 2008), 19.

101. Sam Storms, "Does Life have a Meaning?" Enjoying God Ministries. https://www.samstorms.org/enjoying-god-blog/post/does-life-have-a-meaning (accessed January 17, 2024).

102. Michael Reeves, *Delighting in the Trinity: An Introduction to the Christian Faith* (Downers Grove, IL: Intervarsity Press, 2012), Kindle loc. 34.

103. Gregg R. Allison, *50 Core Truths of the Christian Faith: A Guide to Understanding and Teaching Theology* (Grand Rapids, MI: Baker Books, 2018), Kindle loc. 90.

104. Cleon L. Rogers Jr. and Cleon Rogers III, *The New Linguistic and Exegetical Key to the Greek New Testament* (Grand Rapids, MI: Zondervan Publishing House, 1998), 444.

105. Titus Flavius Clemens, "Shepherd of Tender Youth," Henry M. Dexter, trans. 1846, https://library.timelesstruths.org/music/Shepherd_of_Tender_Youth.

106. Garrett Dunahugh, trans., http://chantblog.blogspot.com/2011/03/oxyrhynchus-hymn.html.

107. Copyright © 1970 Hanna Street Music (BMI) (adm. at CapitolCMGPublishing.com) All rights reserved. Used by permission.

108. Copyright © 1984 New Spring Publishing Inc. (ASCAP) (adm. at CapitolCMGPublishing.com) All rights reserved. Used by permission.

109. Copyright © 1994 Birdwing Music (ASCAP) Shepherd's Fold Music (BMI) (adm. at CapitolCMGPublishing.com) All rights reserved. Used by permission.

110. Rick Renner, *A Life Ablaze: Ten Simple Keys to Living on Fire for God* (Shippensburg, PA: Harrison House, 2020), 187-88.

111. C. I. Scofield, ed., *The Scofield Reference Bible*, v.

112. Jack Hayford, *E Quake: A New Approach to Understanding the End Time Mysteries in the Book of Revelation* (Nashville, TN: Thomas Nelson Publishers, 1999), 24.

113. Charles H. Spurgeon, *Metropolitan Tabernacles Pulpit*, Volume 9, "Alpha and Omega," December 27, 1863.

114. F. W. Farrar, *The Life of Christ*, Kindle edition. Chapter LXI. 1874.

115. Henry G. Bosch, quoted in *Encyclopedia of 7700 Illustrations*, compiled by Paul Lee Tan (Chicago: Assurance Publishers, 1979), 647.

116. Selections taken from S. M. Lockridge, sermon, Calvary Baptist Church, https://www.youtube.com/watch?v=4BhI4JKACUs.

117. Towns, *What the Faith Is All About*, 139.

118. Edward Hindson and Edward Dobson, eds. *The Knowing Jesus Study Bible* (Grand Rapids: Zondervan Publishing House, 1999), front and back flap.

119. J.C. Ryle, *Home Truths, Seventh Series*, "What Is Our Position?" (Ipswich, Steam Press, 1859), 268.

120. Vance Havner, *The Vance Havner Quote Book* (Grand Rapids: Baker Book House, 1986), 171.

121. Gordon Lindsay, *The Charismatic Ministry* (Dallas: Christ for the Nations, 2013), 169.

122. Philip Yancey, *The Jesus I Never Knew* (Grand Rapids: Zonder-van, 1995), Kindle loc. 265-67.

123. The Decalogue is another term for the Ten Commandments.

124. Philip Schaff, *The Creeds of Christendom*, 6th ed., vol. 1 (New York: Harper and Brothers, 1919), 14.

125. The word *catholic* does not refer to the Roman Catholic Church, but rather, the universal Church—the entire Body of Christ as a whole, comprised of every born-again person.

126. Ignatius of Antioch, "Letter to the Traillians," in *The Early Christian Fathers*, ed. Henry Bettenson (London: Oxford University Press, 1956), 60-61.

127. The word *catholic* does not refer to the Roman Catholic Church, but rather, the universal Church—the entire Body of Christ as a whole, comprised of every born-again person.

ABOUT THE AUTHOR

Bible teacher Tony Cooke graduated from RHEMA Bible Training Center in 1980, studied religion at Butler University, received a bachelor's in church ministries from North Central University, and a master's in theological studies/church history from Liberty University. Tony has traveled to more than thirty nations and nearly all fifty states teaching the Bible. He is the author of sixteen books, of which various titles have been translated and published in more than a dozen other languages. Tony and his wife, Lisa, reside in Broken Arrow, Oklahoma.

www.tonycooke.org